BETTER
LIBRARY
DESIGN

BETTER
LIBRARY
DESIGN

IDEAS FROM LIBRARYJOURNAL

EDITED BY *LIBRARY JOURNAL*'S
REBECCA T. MILLER AND **BARBARA A. GENCO**

ROWMAN & LITTLEFIELD
Lanham • Boulder • New York • London

Published by Rowman & Littlefield
A wholly owned subsidary of The Rowman & Littlefield Publishing Group, Inc.
4501 Forbes Boulevard, Suite 1200, Lanham, Maryland 20706
www.rowman.com

Unit A, Whitacre Mews, 26034 Stannary Street, London SE11 4 AB

Cover design and interior design/layout by Kevin Henegan

Front cover photo credits: top left photo ©Timothy Hursley, top right photo by
Chuck Choi; bottom left photo by Drake Busch, bottom center photo by Mark Boisclair,
bottom right photo ©Brad Feinknoff

Back cover photo credits: top left photo ©Jeff Goldberg/Esto; bottom left photo
by Ema Peter, courtesy of Bing Thom Architects; right photo by Paul Brokering

British Library Cataloguing in Publication Information Available

Library of Congress Cataloguing-in-Publication Data

Library of Congress Control Number: 2015952824

The paper used in this publication meets the minimum requirements of American
National Standard for Information Sciences—Permanence of Paper for Printed Library
Materials, ANSI/NISO Z39.48-1992

Printed in the United States of America

dedication

*For John and Harper and all their peers lucky enough to grow up with
these excellent, inspiring libraries. And for the librarians and their community members
who continue to make them ever better.—R.T.M.*

*For my Pratt SILS students and all librarians who strive to create
the best, most welcoming spaces for their communities. Thank you, Kevin Henegan,
for making this book so beautiful and so useful.—B.A.G.*

contents

introduction

AN ERA OF INNOVATION

Just as library services are experiencing rapid evolution, so are library spaces. The result is an exciting array of solutions that we at *Library Journal* have been following avidly for more than a decade. As we learned about great design in the field, we have shared those stories in the magazine and in our biannual supplement *Library by Design* (*LBD*). Over the years we have seen library space design become increasingly dynamic, anticipating and responding to patron needs in light of the digital revolution, the changing demand for an otherwise disappearing "third place" for community of many forms, and the growing urgency to be not just well built but sustainable.

Here we gather some of that compelling coverage, reaching back to 2009 to surface design challenges and savvy approaches to solving them. Since the articles are published here as they were originally, some of the projects are now completed or no longer in use (as with temporary facilities), but the lessons from them and the trends thus illustrated continue to resonate. Stories from *LJ*, *LBD*, and our sister publication *School Library Journal* reflect the exciting world of library design today. They demonstrate how smart and easy it is to go green (LEED or no). They celebrate partnerships that enable buildings to deliver more. They highlight a surprising range of design strategies, temporary and permanent, that allow for stronger and more flexible libraries built for people first and collections second. They show off beautiful environments that reflect the vibrant services offered within. It is our hope that this book will motivate even richer library design in projects large and small.

An endeavor like this is even more complicated than it looks. I want to thank first my coeditor, Barbara A. Genco, for braving an initial sweeping pass of the pages and pages of design coverage done since 2009 by *LJ*, *LBD*, and *SLJ*. Her enthusiasm and knowledge matched the goals of the early vision and enabled the project to get off the ground. Special kudos to Kevin Henegan, *LJ*'s design director, who tackled a daunting design challenge of his own with steady calm and delivered a vibrant presentation to explore. I'd also like to thank *LJ* executive editor Meredith Schwartz, *LJ* managing editor Bette-Lee Fox, and *SLJ* art production designer Josephine Marc-Anthony for the heavy lifting on this project; and Francine Fialkoff, former editor in chief of *LJ* and the ongoing project lead on our Design Institute events, for her foresight to dive deeper into design coverage and her continued insight into the trends in the field.

Last but not least, I'd like to thank the many librarians, trustees, community members, and architects and designers who work together to make our library buildings centerpieces in our towns and cities and on our campuses. Your work is inspiring, and we look forward to watching—and sharing more—as the world of library design continues to evolve and enrich all of our lives.

Rebecca T. Miller, Editorial Director

1
flexible strategies

POP-UP LIBRARIES, INTERIM SPACES, AND MORE

Libraries have always been nimble, but the creativity keeps on coming, as the seven strategies shown here make temporary spaces exciting to serve the library mission and engagement, reinvigorate once prime real estate, and find unique ways to bring the library into the community, by car or dumpster. Some of these projects, here shared from *LJ*'s design coverage since 2009 as originally published, are now complete, but the lessons are as vital as ever.

In the Interims

DC's approach to short-term spaces connects the library to the community and moves the library forward By Ginnie Cooper

DCPL's Washington Highlands Interim Library

way to introduce library service into a neighborhood, test a new service model, or, if you're fortunate to have resources for a new library, provide temporary service while replacement libraries are under way.

Service at a reasonable price

The four interim libraries DCPL opened in 2007 addressed a gaping need in the communities they served, as those neighborhoods had seen their branches closed in 2004 and watched hope for the promised new buildings dwindle as plans were abandoned. The libraries, as originally designed, did not meet the needs of the community, and the library board was concerned that it would spend nearly $30 million on four libraries that would be outdated by the time they were opened. Residents lost confidence that their new libraries would ever be built. So, when I joined DCPL in 2006, the library board's directive was to get those replacement libraries up and running. In addition to moving rapidly to raise the new structures, we decided to bridge the gap immediately with temporary service.

These temporary libraries provided much needed service to neighborhoods without libraries, but, equally as important, the strategy offered an opportunity to try new and different ways of presenting library service. We introduced a new service model with the interim libraries.

The interim libraries were designed with an open floor plan. A service desk was placed toward the entrance so that users could be greeted upon entry. On the other side was space for teens and public computing. The areas were separated by 48" bookshelves so that the entire library could be monitored from the service desk. There were also two six-person tables for reading behind the service desk. Books, DVDs, periodicals, and nonprint items were placed on 84" bookshelves that lined the walls. On one side were areas for children and magazines. In the center of the rear of the building were four 84" double-faced bookshelves. The design scheme was used at all the temporary libraries to ensure that each community was served equally.

We leased storefronts or trailers, renovated them, and outfitted them with furniture and computers for about $1.5 million. Creating a tempo-

Residents had seen temporary libraries before. In the 1970s in the District of Columbia, 1000 square foot portastructures were built to serve as libraries for seven years. They were closed in 2009, long after their life expectancy, despite being much too small to provide adequate library service.

So you can imagine that 30 years later, with those initial portastructures still limping along, patrons of the District of Columbia Public Library (DCPL) were prepared for the worst when we opened several 4200 square foot libraries in storefronts and in trailers as temporary replacements for four full-service facilities that had already been closed for two years.

They were pleasantly surprised. Today, as we phase out four of the interim libraries and open four new full-service branches, we are reflecting on the value of those spaces. We hear from residents and library staff that they love the interim libraries. Within two years of their opening, the interim libraries circulated more than twice as many books as the much larger buildings they replaced.

In these tough economic times, constructing new libraries may be too expensive for many library systems across the country. But the need to provide service is not going away. Interim libraries will continue to be part of the DCPL service strategy, as they can be a cost-effective

Thinking About an Interim Library?

In DC, we opened temporary libraries to provide service to neighborhoods without libraries. An interim library can also meet a specific need. For instance, a neighborhood may have such a large number of teens that you may want to consider opening a teen library center. Or a community may have limited access to computers, making a computer center the most meaningful offering. In designing your interim library:

CONSIDER THE PURPOSE Will it be in service for a defined or indeterminate length of time? Are you introducing a new service

model, or temporarily replacing library service until new libraries are built? Regardless, it's valuable to identify how long the interim library will be open to help you choose whether to lease or buy. We knew the interim libraries would be open for no more than three years, so it was cost effective to lease storefront space or trailers.

CHECK THE TRENDS This is particularly useful if your temporary library addresses a specific need. Your city's planning office and census data can help you understand the demographics and changes under way in the neighborhood. If an area has a

high school, a teen library center might make sense. But if the school is closing in the six months, reconsider.

DO THE MATH How much will it cost? How long will the temporary library operate? Will utilities be included in the lease? How much will it cost to keep the library clean?

STREAMLINE SERVICE Emphasize the services that are most important to your audience. Are there more young children in the area? If so, you may want to merchandise more children's books and nonprint media as well as host more children's programs.

PLAY WITH THE LAYOUT Examine how your layout supports your audience's use of the library and its services and explore if changing

the floor plan would make sense.

CONCENTRATE THE COLLECTION Your interim library may provide a specialty service such as computer use–only or teen centers. Regardless of the purpose, the collection at that location should showcase the books, DVDs, and other nonprint media the library system offers. Users may find a concentration of anime, manga, urban fiction, and *Twilight* and Percy Jackson movies at the teen library center. Or they may find books like *Excel for Dummies* and *Absolute Beginner's Guide to Computer Basics* and computer classes at the computer use–only center.

MEASURE IMPACT Count the various services provided, and tweak the plan accordingly.

rary library may be less expensive in a different region or with different resources. Library systems may have access to storefronts that don't require renovation; cheaper leases based on the real estate market and an inventory of suitable furniture, computers, and bookshelves could be used to create a successful temporary location. In addition, estimate the cost for staffing and books at a temporary site. In these tough economic times, it may be particularly important that the interim library be cost effective.

A new service model A key component of the interim library was design flexibility. Instead of walls, bookshelves and furniture would be used to separate the areas for teens, children, and adults. As the demographics of a neighborhood shifts and, say, you have fewer children than expected and an increase in adult users, you can adjust the space to ensure that it reflects the library services needed most.

The open layout of the interim libraries meant that programs like children's story times impact the entire space—those kids are seen or heard throughout the building. This library service model was new for the public, and it changed how library staff worked and interacted with users.

It was new to DCPL to put a team of staffers in one room with one desk. Story times, community meetings, author talks, and musical performances took place among the books and computers. Staff who conducted programs also checked out books and assisted on the computers.

Generally, six people—two librarians, two library associates, and two library technicians—worked at a temporary library at any given time. Some checked out books and answered questions. Other staff shelved books, planned projects in the staff work room, helped library users with a computer question, or ran a program.

The one-room, one-desk layout in the interim libraries gives us the ability to make adjustments as we learn about our users and their needs. When we first opened the interim libraries, we had teen

corners that featured popular YA books, comfortable chairs, and tables. When our teens visited, they would use books, computers, tables, and chairs throughout the building. Instead of corralling the teens into the corner we designated, we adjusted our floor plan to remove the teen corner.

A changed experience for staff and patrons With the introduction of the new service model, we knew that we wanted to change the way people experience libraries. Our ultimate goal was to debut the service model at the interim libraries and replicate it as much as possible in the new libraries when they opened.

The interim library's one-room service model supported the idea that programs, events, or meetings—even operas—can happen anytime, anywhere in the library.

Staff at the interim libraries, regardless of title or areas of responsibility, help run different areas of the library. This means that everyone troubleshoots basic computer issues, is familiar with the collection, and keeps up-to-date on programs.

In DC, our goal was to use only current employees who volunteered to work at the interim libraries, supplemented with new hires. By volunteering to work in the new spaces, the staffers demonstrated a

ONE DESIGN Interim libraries not only provide needed service to communities, but they can also introduce elements of what is to come with the completion of the permanent libraries, if those are in the works. The design for DCPL's interims, including Mt. Pleasant Interim Library the (left), located in a storefront, and the Petworth Interim Library (right), set in the parking lot of the original 1939 building, are replicable. Similar lighting, 48" shelves to maximize sight lines, and double-faced shelving to create separation, topped up the usability and flexibility of the 4200 square foot spaces

DC's 21st-Century Branches

By Rebecca Miller

Flexibility is the key concept in the design of new branches at the District of Columbia Public Library (DCPL). What that means generally is anyone's guess, but a tour of two new buildings in DC's historically burdened library system proves it doesn't denote an empty box with movable walls. Instead, it translates to sleek modern design, green features throughout, and plenty of technology for patrons, all of which and more, as Director Ginnie Cooper says, look to the future instead of the past.

Two busloads of librarians glimpsed that future on June 26, 2010, breaking away from the Urban Libraries Council membership meeting during the American Library Association annual conference. They traveled with Cooper to the

Anacostia Neighborhood Library, which opened on April 26, and the Benning Neighborhood Library, opened April 5. These branches, and a handful of other completed projects, are part of an aggressive reinvigoration of the library that includes an innovative interim library strategy and plans for three new permanent branches and three major renovations in the next year.

Spaces without walls The promised flexibility is created by playing with walls, or rather having very few of them. Space is defined in the high-raftered public spaces, instead, with partial walls to divide big service areas, or with shelving to shelter readers from the hubbub of the library. Important exceptions include small group study spaces and small program rooms. Each

building also has a multipurpose meeting room on the lower level that holds at least 100.

Underfoot, a raised floor houses the electrical and mechanical systems in an accessible space, also anticipating the changes to come as service needs shift and technology develops.

The high ceilings and the sight lines created by the open design

commitment to the new direction and a willingness to learn new things and enhance existing skills. Most important, they had to embrace a team approach to providing service.

To support the staff, we held workshops led by trainers who had implemented similar changes and offered one-on-one coaching. We also regularly acknowledged creative and innovative programs developed by the staff. Some great programming came about as a result, including a weekly sing-a-long story time at one interim and a staff-hosted jazz concert at another.

This has been good for staff and for users. We regularly hear feedback from patrons about the excellent customer service they receive, or how easy it is to find what they need. As we transition to the new, multifloor facilities, some staff say they'll miss working with their colleagues in one room.

A look and feel forward We created a brand for all the interim libraries using the same color scheme, similar signage, and similar layout. The temporary library interiors were designed like a retail brand to connect with users and show how the new libraries would look. We wanted the public to think of libraries as bright, airy, and welcoming places. We wanted the books and other items to pop out from the shelves and be a focal point. To make the collection stand out, we used off-white steel bookshelves and matte orange signage with white lettering. The furniture was more modern, featuring chairs made from polyurethane foam and steel.

We also improved how we merchandized and shelved books and DVDs and other nonprint media. At the time the interim libraries opened, DCPL was overhauling its collection systemwide, including at the interim spaces. Introducing more nonprint media like CDs and DVD

was a big part of the change. More current and relevant books were available, and staff were trained to merchandize the collection so that new books and media were quickly and easily visible. Picture book bins were introduced. Because programming at the interim libraries took place in the same room as the collections, the staff were encouraged to merchandize books complementing their programs.

We developed a 3000–5000 square foot space that incorporated public computers, spaces for teens and children, an area for magazines, and a small reading area. Since the new libraries would feature a lot of natural light and comfortable furniture, the temporary libraries were outfitted similarly to give the public a window into the look and feel of the libraries under construction.

Location, location, location Because the community had been without service for a few years, we worked hard to open the temporary libraries as soon as possible. Thus, we picked locations for the interim libraries that weren't far from the closed libraries in order to attract the

OPEN SPACES The one-room layout of the interim libraries was a test case for buildingwide programming in the permanent libraries; it was a huge success, with more intimate interaction among users of all ages and library staff. Clockwise from top, story time at Georgetown Interim Library; a jazz concert at Francis Gregory Interim Library; and a reptile demonstration

FUTURE FOCUS The sleek, spacious, sunny reading area of the Anacostia Neighborhood Library (far left) and the modern, colorful exterior of the Benning Neighborhood Library (right) are both representative of DCPL's systemwide "reinvigoration," which includes the implementation of interim libraries to ensure continued service. Bottom row, librarians tour DCPL's newest branches last June: left to right, the group pours into Anacostia; DCPL director Ginnie Cooper (in multicolored sweater) addresses librarians inside; separate return bins for popular materials help to streamline processing. At Benning, *LJ* Librarian of the Year 2006 Rivkah Sass (center) speaks with fellow tour participants; Benning's extensively daylit, multilevel interior; Columbus Metropolitan Library, OH, director Pat Losinski (right) speaks with tour group members in Benning's reading area, where public art enlivens the stacks

invite visitors deep into the space. Vast glass exterior walls enable daylighting and convey transparency in a larger sense, encouraging views both in to what the library holds and out toward the neighborhoods.

Setting a bar These branches, like all new projects in the DCPL lineup, are informed by a design program created to set a standard for all buildings in the system. A template or a springboard, depending on your perspective and how well the library pulls off local community input for extras, the document details the mission and identifies "the key components of a new 21st century neighborhood library" (it can be found at bit.ly/dhMIHM).

The language is grand (under Building: "a destination, an anchor, a place for learning and meeting that is welcoming and comfortable for the whole community") and nitty-gritty (under Community Meeting Spaces: "study rooms [six, each for one or two people] with Wi-Fi"). In between it touches on everything from the building's look and feel to LEED certification and accessibility goals to required public service areas and the collection gathered in them to seating needs and basic technology to deliver to patrons.

At Anacostia, a glowing modern cube in the middle of a neighborhood full of red brick duplexes and houses, a tour participant asked about the obvious contrast with the surroundings. No aesthetic clash, according to Cooper. Rather, the building reflects the neighborhood's forward gaze. "The community recognized that what had been torn down was of the past 50 years," she said, and they saw this as the future.

Rebecca Miller is Executive Editor, Features, LJ

same users. But we also wanted to attract those who had never used the library. Could we do both? In most cases we could. Each new space had large, colorful banners placed in front that listed the name of the library. Librarians visited schools and day-care centers, manned tables at community events, and invited community organizations into the new library. As construction began, family-friendly employment information fairs were held near the interims so that residents could learn about the library and potential employment. Word of mouth did its work, too.

We first looked for storefronts that were near the closed libraries. If storefront locations were unavailable, we used trailers either on the same plot of land as the closed libraries or within a few blocks. Our first group of temporary libraries included one storefront and three trailers. Now we have three storefront and two trailer facilities.

A success by any measure You don't know if something is working unless you measure its success. We tracked the effectiveness of the interim libraries through traditional measures like circulation, and we

tracked the number of people and how long they were on the computers. Public computers were used throughout the day by adults looking or jobs and children connecting with classmates or doing homework.

There are other less scientific ways to measure success as well, such as referrals to the library by other users, comments on blogs and online discussion lists, and feedback directly to staff. We are also capturing this feedback. As we've transitioned from interim to permanent buildings, we've seen comments on neighborhood blogs about how wonderful and helpful the staff are at the interim locales.

Our experience with interim libraries has informed a great deal of what we do in the new libraries. The one-room, one-desk model allowed us to serve customers better and to take a team approach to staffing. We are replicating this in the new multifloor structures. We are also designing buildingwide programming, so story times are held in the children's room but also in the meeting room, for instance, and a musical performance can happen in an open space near the DVDs and CDs, not just in the community meeting room.

When we opened the first interim libraries in 2007, we restored library service for hundreds of residents. We weren't certain how the community would react. We had to build trust with residents who had lost service or felt it was inadequate. We accomplished this with the interim library model. Based on that success, the library board has made a commitment always to provide interim facilities while new libraries are under construction.

We have opened four more interim libraries and three permanent one-room, one-desk libraries since 2007. It's a model that works and continues to help us transform the library system in the District of Columbia.

Ginnie Cooper joined the District of Columbia Public Library as Chief Librarian and Executive Director in July 2006. A librarian since 1970, she has also led the Brooklyn Public Library, NY; Multnomah County Library, Portland, OR; and Alameda County Library, CA

DATE JUNE 15, 2012

Meet the Bookless Mobile

By Meredith Schwartz

When Smitty Miller was hired at Canada's Fraser Valley Regional Library last November for the newly created position of community development librarian, she had just one assignment: build a mobile initiative. "I, of course, said, 'duh, build a book mobile,'" Miller told *LJ*.

She began researching the project, visiting King County to see their Library to Go, costing out Sprinter vans at dealerships, etc. There was only one problem: "you don't have enough money or enough time," the head of the Association of Bookmobile and Outreach Services bottom-lined it for Miller at the end of a long conversation. Fraser Valley's libraries and literacy grant from British Columbia would not even come close to covering the approximately $200,000 it would have cost to start a bookmobile.

Miller had no choice but to go back to the drawing board. "After I was done crying, I said, 'what if we went all the way to the other end? What can the library offer on roller-skates, on a bicycle?' So I decided to take the books out of the equation." She settled on a small car, which, despite its size, she wanted to make a big, flashy impact. They chose a Nissan Cube because "It's very unexpected, since part of what we wanted to do is break stereotypes."

"I went into a local car audio shop and asked them about speakers with suction cups," for the roof of the car to broadcast in parades, Miller said. "After they were done laughing" they told Miller what was really involved in fitting out a car for audio broadcasting, which was also out of her budget.

However, as Miller described what the project was about,

with what she calls "the quieter heart": delivering library services to marginalized populations at food banks, soup kitchens, transition houses, etc. She registers people for library cards, forgives fines ($1000 so far), teaches senior citizens how to use technology, and so on. The key, she says, is to have a conversation rather than delivering a dissertation, and to meet people where they are – literally as well as figuratively. "I've issued kids' first library cards while their mothers are in line at the food bank," she says.

Miller rarely sees her own office. She's always on the road between Fraser Valley's 15 municipalities. When she gets there, she doesn't go in cold. Instead, she meets with each area's manager and asks, "If you had a librarian one day a week who could do anything you wanted to do not in the library, what would it be?" Local librarians have had her focus on seniors, on the homeless, even on making an inventory of community partners. She also invites local staff, board members, and Friends of the Library to ride along.

To judge LiLi's success, the library partnered with the Social Planning and Research Council of British Columbia to conduct a formal evaluation process which captures qualitative as well as quantitative measures; the final report will be issued in November.

LiLi's gadget bar (top); Smitty Miller and LiLi (left); LiLi gets here makeover (right)

Though the grant which funds Library Live is annual, the Fraser Valley CEO has committed to at least two years of

the salesman got interested despite her empty wallet. "He talked to the owner [Rick Francoeur] and within 24 hours" the company, 360 Fabrication, had decided to help pro bono. 360 ended up donating over $35000 worth of labor, time, and equipment, as well as facilitating donations from speaker and tire vendors.

After a month of taking the car apart, rewiring it, and putting it back together, LiLi (short for Library Live) was tricked out with an embedded, articulated 37 inch LCD TV; an Xbox, computer monitor, gadget bar, two 3G Internet-connected laptops; and, yes, external speakers. "They're not held on with suction cups," Miller laughed. She even has a few books on board, donated by First Book Canada, but they're not for loaning, they're for giving away.

LiLi and Miller started Library Live and On Tour! On April 25, and already they're booked solid. Their dual mission combines traditional PR venues (parades, festivals, etc.), where Miller preaches the message that today's library is anything but stodgy,

the project, and the hope is win more grants sufficient not only to persist, but expand. "We are talking about a second car within two years, and our dream is a fleet of cars, going into communities, being loud, and delivering services that only libraries can provide," said Miller.

Miller's getting good at loud. "This is the best thing that has happened to me as a librarian," she said. "I was playing Lady Gaga at top volume at a barbeque at a women's homeless transition house. This guy came to the fence and said, 'could you turn it down?' and I was like, YES! It shows I'm not stuffy; it makes it accessible to people who didn't think the library was for them."

Miller and LiLi are making some noise beyond Fraser Valley, too, with press coverage everywhere from Boing Boing to Hot Rod magazine to the Seattle Post Intelligencer. "We're pretty excited when we get in Hot Rod magazine; it gets us to audiences we wouldn't normally get to," said Miller.

Repurposing Retail

From big-box store to strip mall outlet locations, libraries are finding success in a storefront world By Louise Schaper

The trend toward putting public libraries in retail spaces such as big-box stores, malls, strip centers, and main street buildings shows no sign of slowing. The McAllen Public Library, TX, main library, which opened in late 2011 in a former Walmart, garnered many awards, including the coveted American Institute of Architects (AIA) Honor Award for Interior Architecture. McAllen residents got a lot of library compared with what they would have gotten building new, reduced their impact on the environment, and turned a blight into a flourishing center of community life.

Retail locations work, according to Leanne Larson, MS&R's lead interior designer on the McAllen project, because they are likely to offer "a desirable location, easy access, ample parking, clear vision of the front door, and... [a] floor plate [that is] wide open, which makes it easier to reconfigure into the library program."

David Schnee, AIA, principal, Group 4 Architecture and architect for the Otay Ranch Branch, CA (see next page), notes, "The decision to go retail is often made because a community can't afford a stand-alone library." If viewed as a "starter" library, retail locations are sometimes looked down upon. But Schnee thinks the idea of an "express library" is an important offering within a community's portfolio of library services. Located in high-traffic areas, they operate with few staff and a focused set of services.

Alan Barocas, senior vice president of mall leasing, General Growth Properties, says libraries can help retail centers become more effective one-stop shopping experiences. They attract customers who make repeat visits, promote how we educate our kids, and further the concept of family shopping where there's something for everyone. Plus, he adds, the library benefits from a venue with instant traffic.

The projects below show how retail locations can make the most of these retail-space benefits:
1. They stretch tight budgets through repurposing existing spaces
2. They invigorate retail environments in a quadruple win for customers, communities, retailers, and libraries
3. They take advantage of the steady stream of traffic to expose many people to the library experience.

MESA COUNTY LIBRARIES COLORADO
Palisade Branch

When the ten-year, $1 per year lease on the library's city-owned space expired, the future of Mesa County Libraries' (MCL) Palisade Branch (right) was most uncertain. Renting wasn't attractive. "Even if we got a screaming deal," comments the library's director, Eve Tallman, "you're looking at ten years of rent when we could have purchased a building for the same price."

Word spread quickly that MCL was looking to purchase a property. One owner offered his main street building housing an art gallery, jewelry shop, and architect's office. About 70 years old, it featured wood floors, big windows, and a patio. The library district, which has plenty of experience locating libraries in retail spaces, deemed this one a perfect site, and a deal was struck to purchase the building for $395,000. That was mid-2011, and by the fall the new branch was open for business.

Alchemy of an old retail space Despite the charm and location of this older building, some basic renovations were required. Not only did the building's mysterious wiring present challenges, Americans with Disabilities Act (ADA)–compliant restrooms had to be created, automatic doors installed, new carpet and linoleum laid, furnishings procured, and some walls removed and others painted—all on a very modest budget of $45,000.

Professional design services and engineering were used only for the most basic requirements, e.g., ADA restroom design. There was, says Tallman, "very little creative architecture."

The 4,100 square foot Palisade Branch encompasses one big room, two meeting rooms, a library auxiliary bookstore, and a shaded outdoor space.

Prescription for main street ills The entities displaced by the library relocated into three vacant downtown Palisade spaces to create what Tallman calls "our own little urban renewal project."

The art gallery–turned–library is now the town hot spot. The covered patio and picnic table are a gathering space for caffeine lovers. Library walls exhibit works by local artists purchased by the library's auxiliary. Even the Lions Club meets at the library.

One year later, the win-win is apparent. The library reported increases in checkouts, visits, and new library cards, while Palisade's businesses reported increased sales in the year following the library opening.

Many ways to score a retail space It wasn't the first time MCL created a library in a retail space. Its Orchard Mesa Branch was sited in a new, empty strip mall. As the anchor "store," it received a free rent period before paying $4,000 a month. Following a $150,000 build out, circulation rose 1,000 percent from its previous location in a middle school. The downside? "We don't own it," says Tallman, "and you never know whom your neighbors will be."

Tallman is presently immersed in a double dose of retail therapy. MCL's headquarters library, a 1950s Grand Junction downtown grocery store that was turned into a library in 1973, is being given new life as a 21st-century library by Barker Rinker Seacat Architecture. By not scrapping the building, savings are estimated at between $10 million and $15 million, according to Tallman.

Meanwhile, patrons aren't complaining about the headquarter's temporary digs—a former furniture store—owing to ample reading nooks and plenty of display space.

Tallman says it's easier to create a library from an empty box store than an old building like Palisade's. "Libraries can form up spaces using ceiling clouds, carpet treatment, lighting, stack arrangements, or ceiling treatments." Palisade, she adds, has too many exterior doors and unattractive exposed conduit necessitated by concrete block walls. "New retail spaces, assuming they are rectangles, are much easier."

CHULA VISTA PUBLIC LIBRARY **CALIFORNIA**
Otay Ranch Branch

Just before the library put shovels in the dirt, plans fell apart for Chula Vista's new 30,000 square foot library to serve the city's rapidly growing east side. That was in 2007. Since then the library has walked what its director, Betty Wasniz, calls "a long and winding road" to its new, rescaled, but decidedly upscale digs in the Otay Ranch Town Center.

Picture this: a rapidly growing city of a quarter of a million people meets the economic crash head on. The library is forced to reduce its staff from 70 to 21 FTE, and plans for the new library are put on hold. Over 100,000 residents in the newest area of town are left with partial library services, located deep within a high school and accessible only after 3:30 p.m.

Community members formed a library foundation and began fundraising. Library leaders pursued endless ideas for providing adequate services. As businesses failed and the amount of empty retail space increased, that plan for the big new library, with its large debt service, began to recede. A new idea, sparked by the retail decline, took hold.

Doing business with a corporation Unfortunately, that new idea received a cool reception when library officials first approached the

Otay Ranch Town Center to inquire about a space. Owned by a REIT (real estate investment trust), this high-end lifestyle shopping center was the nicest in the area, with many amenities. Built in a growth area that stopped growing, it had many empty storefronts. Shopping center officials generously offered a low-cost space but in an undesirable location. Library officials turned it down.

Six months later, Wasniz got a call to meet the mall manager in the open-air food court. This time, the manager offered a vacant pizza parlor and two other adjacent spaces for the library's use.

After months of negotiation, working through the complexities of corporate and city processes, a lease was crafted. The terms—$1 a year plus utilities for three years, with a two-year extension—required the library to be open at least five days a week.

Make the most of retail opportunities By redirecting $200,000 from RFID conversion and $50,000 from the foundation, the library hired Group 4 Architecture, Research + Planning, to design a library that would be flexible, welcoming to library neophytes, comfortable, and matched to the high-end feel of the shopping complex.

The library opened in spring 2012. Its high-impact location, coupled with vibrant interiors that spill out onto the food court, garners heavy foot traffic. Parents and kids stop by for a program or materials after shopping. Tagalong spouses make a beeline for the library while their mates shop. Shoppers check their email or download a book while relaxing in the food court. No one goes home empty-handed.

Wheeled stacks, pegboard walls, and excellent sight lines provide flexibility. By matching the mall aesthetics, placing plenty of furniture outside, and offering Wi-Fi to the food court area and beyond, the space draws people in who might not otherwise visit a stand-alone library.

Benefits of the mall location are numerous. Custodial, security, and public relations services are provided by the mall. Partnerships with other tenants, i.e., the Apple Store and Barnes & Noble, provide help with ebook downloading to visitors.

Plan B presents possibilities Though Otay Ranch's 3,412 square foot space is small, its constant foot traffic, frequent school district trips, and a story time that takes over the whole library creates a lively atmosphere. And while it's Plan B, Otay Ranch Branch offers a world of possibilities.

"So many people walk in and see the library who might not come into a library," Wasniz comments. And while there isn't the permanence of an owned building, she's already acting like a retailer—lobbying for a toy store to locate next door.

CEDAR RAPIDS PUBLIC LIBRARY IOWA

Ladd Library

No one believed it could be done. After losing its Central Library to the 2009 flood, the Cedar Rapids Public Library (CRPL) sought not only to rebuild it but also to add a substantial branch to the rapidly growing west side of the city. Federal Emergency Management Agency (FEMA) funds were barely enough to rebuild Central, but the library doggedly persisted with its vision for the branch.

The library opted for the lower up-front cost of retail space and leased 21,000 square feet of a largely empty 120,000 square foot retail box. Formerly a Target, it was bought by the owner to flip, but it sat unsold. The lease costs the library $90,000 annually, much less than the going rate. The five-year lease can be renewed at the same rate and permits the library to walk away if funding is cut.

The turnkey cost of renovation was $2.1 million. To save money and ensure brand continuity, the library piggybacked on the furniture, flooring, and lighting packages for the new Central Library that's set to open in August. Private funds, including a surprise legacy gift, paid the tab.

Anchoring for the future OPN Architects, hired for both the Ladd Library and the new Central Library, rethought the space to bring in natural light and emphasize the dramatic ceiling heights. Windows cut into the concrete block walls capture large expanses of natural light. Columns every 30 feet offer opportunity for data and power. Excellent sight lines mean the space can be operated with just 5.5 customer service staff members. A drive-up lane and window, along with a materials handling system, are welcome additions and relatively easy to achieve.

Ladd Library features a popular collection, plain-language stack signage, lots of media, and retail-like face-out displays. New ideas introduced at Ladd, like a media dispenser in a 24-7 vestibule, iPad catalog stations, and curvilinear shelving, serve as a test bed for the opening of the Central Library.

With the library having opened in February, it's too soon for Bob Pasicznyuk, library director since 2009, to tell the story of what works and what doesn't, but patrons immediately voted with their feet. With about 5,000 people at the opening and a continual stampede of new traffic, the library is overrun with requests for new library cards. And while some parents would rather see a separate children's area, it hasn't stopped swarms of youth and adults, with friends in tow, from flocking to the branch, with visits that sometimes last all day.

Now that the library is in and drawing foot traffic, a pizza chain has opened up, and several major prospective tenants are rumored to be interested. Doing double duty, Ladd Library has become an anchor to the Cedar Rapids' west side community and to a retail complex that has a better future ahead.

Louise Schaper, retired Executive Director Fayetteville Public Library, AR, is a Library Consultant and Freelance Writer

---

DATE JUNE 15, 2012

Inflato Dumpsters Provide Mobile Lab Space

By Dodie Ownes

You may be familiar with John Locke's Department of Urban Betterment (DUB) for being behind the 2012 installation of mini-libraries in New York City telephone booths. Now DUB is at it again with the concept and design of the Inflato Dumpster, giving the phrase "dumpster diving" a whole new meaning.

The Inflato Dumpster is a blow-up structure fit inside of, well, a 11613inflato Inflato Dumpsters Provide Mobile Lab Space I Design Innovationdumpster. The portable structure takes up about two parking spaces, and can serve as a mobile learning laboratory, or even as a temporary branch library. DUB's vision is to make it

possible for a learning space to be available in any neighborhood, to serve any demographic, at a low cost. Lightweight materials make transport easy, and the dome material allows natural light to enter the space. One interior wall can be used as a projection screen. This temporary classroom could be used for anything from providing computer training to job seekers to a meeting place for book clubs, community workshops, or as a hackerspace.

Looking Through the Labrary Lens

Lessons from the Harvard Labrary inform how we see transformative library spaces By Jennifer Koerber

Makers seek to design at the Bubbler program at Madison Public Library

In fall 2012, the Harvard Labrary—a temporary "pop-up" space in an empty storefront in Harvard Square, Cambridge, MA—was opened as a public gallery for design student projects from the semester-long Library Test Kitchen (LTK) seminar at Harvard's Graduate School of Design.

Describing the Labrary, LTK instructor Jeff Goldenson said that it's "a place where libraries can outsource risk and innovation," a "pop-up R&D department" that explores ideas too disruptive for a traditional library location. By bringing student projects to the public and inviting interaction and response, the Labrary became an exploration of what it means to be a library space. Though it was only open briefly, the Labrary suggested new ways of looking at nontraditional library space design.

Unfinished or use raw space To
create the Labrary, seminar students and instructors painted walls, built a rough-hewn ergonomic stage in one corner, and added track lights. This blank canvas allowed students to adapt their work to the space and vice versa.

If your library is undergoing a renovation or building a new space, don't plan every square foot right away. With an unstructured area to grow into, you can take advantage of new trends. Or plan to leave the space raw, with the expectation that its use will change over time.

For instance, the unfinished basement of the new Fountaindale Public Library, IL, was reserved for future, unspecified use. After two years of surveys and analysis, the library built Studio 300, a digital media creation space for the general public. Six audio recording studios, two video recording studios, and three group collaboration rooms take advantage of the lightless, temperature controlled, and sound-isolated basement space. Studio 300 opened on March 16.

Before the Madison Public Library, WI, shut down the main library to move to a new building, it held a one-day, one-night art show and fundraiser called BOOKLESS in the empty structure. More than 5,000 artists and visitors graffitied the walls, danced and played music, and otherwise tore the place apart. The vibrant event inspired library planners to rethink the new media

center as the touchstone of a creative and collaborative series of systemwide programs: the Bubbler.

It's not just about the gadgets At the
Labrary, Harvard students and members of the public alike came to work on projects. One class meeting was even held in the cozy inflatable reading room—a ten-foot-tall inflatable Mylar room with bean bags and cushions on its carpeted floor.

In public libraries, something like this might be a library-based coworking space. Coworking areas allow for more noise than a traditional library and offer a more work-focused environment than a coffee shop, without the expense of a commercial space. As Emily Badger writes in The Atlantic: Cities, "[Libraries] offer a more familiar entry-point for potential entrepreneurs less likely to walk into a traditional start-up incubator. Public libraries long ago democratized access to knowledge; now they could do the same in a start-up economy."

What that coworking space might look like varies widely. The Orlando Public Library, FL, has a single coworking room that the public can reserve for $10 for two hours, with table, chairs, whiteboard, TV, and phone.

Taking it to the next level, Arizona State University (ASU) and the Phoenix Public Library have partnered to develop the Alexandria Network: "support for the innovation economy through EUREKA spaces, which combine elements of coworking space with expert library fact-finding services and ASU start-up resources."

Let visitors make their own fun As
a student showcase, the Labrary let the public engage with student projects on the theme of the "future of libraries," ranging from Bookface—an installation that photographed visitors lying with their faces obscured by a laptop, then published those images to Tumblr—to tables that emanated ambient noise to keep the space from getting "too" quiet. Ben Brady, a coteacher of the seminar, said that at the beginning, "a lot of people were asking 'What is this place?' and with the student projects in place, people were more engaged with exploring the space themselves."

Engagement with the space can encourage a feeling of temporary ownership, which in turn encourages things like informal class meetings, displays of work by local artists, a wide variety of collaboration, and even dance parties.

One way to encourage informal engagement is through library Maker spaces, from a created space in the middle of the library stacks (Westport PL, CT) to a new dedicated wing (Fayetteville Free Library, NY). Maker spaces can offer both formal programs and unstructured access to the tools of the Maker's arsenal—3-D printers, large-format printers and scanners, small electronics kits, and more.

In addition to more curriculum-oriented tech, the Taylor Family Digital Library at University of Calgary, Alta., has a computer-based DJ station for students to record their own remixed tracks.

Some aren't permanent The Labrary
was a temporary effort from the start, with few of the construction choices of a permanent space. If libraries build with impermanence in mind, they can benefit from the lightweight infrastructure of a mutable space.

When the café in the lobby of the Oak Park Public Library, IL, closed, the library chose to use the room for monthly interactive library-focused installations. The Idea Box is small and fronted with glass. Installations have ranged from a public-created and -curated magnetic poetry "collection" to presentations from live artists and folk musicians and interactive night sky exhibits.

Back at the Madison PL, each Bubbler program may last an hour or two, or be a week- or month-long gallery of work or interactive experience. It can be anywhere, include any topic, and even be brought off-site as needed.

Jennifer Koerber is Web Services Librarian, Boston Public Library, and an independent trainer and speaker in emerging technologies and the social web

Storefront Solution

A grassroots library experiment brought temporary service
back to Boston's Chinatown By Rebecca Miller

For three months last winter, people walking along Washington Street in Boston's dense Chinatown had one fewer vacant storefront glowering at them. In its place glowed a little library project, drawing people in from the sidewalk and engaging them with a packed collection of donated books, computers, inventive programming, and space to study, make art, or hold meetings.

The Chinatown Storefront Library, open from October 14, 2009, through January 17, 2010, was the brainchild of Leslie and Sam Davol of Boston Street Lab, a nonprofit focused on livable cities. Their inspiration was a fruitless wait for Boston Public Library (BPL) to respond to community advocacy for a neighborhood branch—BPL had closed the previous Chinatown branch in 1956.

Experimental attitude Using their experience transforming urban spaces for civic purposes, the Davols, joined by program manager Amy Cheung, ventured right into libraryland to create a demonstration project for the community. They used what they knew from their involvement with the Friends of the Chinatown Library and leaned on knowhow from BPL and Simmons College, then plunged ahead.

Mostly, though, they remained responsive. They made a plan, engaged Harvard students in a furniture design process even before they found the 3000 square foot space, and built grass-roots support—lots of it. Intentionally funded on a shoestring to reinforce its temporary intent and express an alternative to costly planning efforts, the project drew on in-kind services, donations, and vast volunteer time. Over 50 small donations met cash needs, and fellowships supported the furniture design.

Transparent community building Once in the space, the trio shaped the collection and programs to fulfill its potential and innovated as needed. Along the way, they learned more about Chinatown and greater Boston through patron analysis—all blogged in detail.

Perhaps most significant, the project offered real alternative insight into how to give the community a place to land and learn when full library service is out of reach. That insight, especially valuable as BPL contracts in the face of drastic cuts, will be put to use in a second iteration of the Chinatown Storefront Library, currently in the planning stages for a fall 2010 opening, says Leslie Davol, for a tentative two-year run. ▶

Rebecca Miller is Executive Editor, Features, LJ

Storefront Solution
Inside the Library

Where Wishes Just Might Come True

Taking advantage of an existing display kitchen for the circulation area and reference desk was one of many space-based decisions made by the project leads, Boston Street Lab's (at left, r.–l.) Leslie and Sam Davol and Amy Cheung. A Wish Tree by Yoko Ono added cultural flair and a sense of contemplative intent to anchor the deeper desire for the library space to enrich the community.

A Street Life

The donated space on the street level facing the heavily trafficked Washington Street had been most recently used for hiring by W Hotel & Residences. It put the library eye to eye with the community, allowing for serendipitous discovery by passersby and steady outreach with signage in both English and Chinese.

Furniture Made To Move

The project's temporary nature and undetermined home required shelving and furniture that could be used and reused in various settings. It inspired a stimulating set of interconnected units by students at Harvard University's Graduate School of Design. Curves with red accents surprised the eye as they formed distinct spaces for separate activities and united shelving and work surfaces. The remarkable children's space (left) inside the front doors was backed by a YA collection (below) that outgrew expectations and stretched into the highest shelves.

An Invitation To Create

The Drawing Lab, by artist Deb Putnoi, demonstrated the project's hunger to make use of the space provided. It turned one of two existing three-walled rooms into an activity hive with a series of project-driven art experiences inspiring patrons to Touch, Look, Listen, and, ultimately, trust their artistic impulses.

Space Turned Reading Room

A second semi-enclosed area farther back in the library welcomed patrons, who could spread out at a big table to study or hold small meetings. Staff enhanced the room's value with a wall dedicated to local resources (left).

A Sense of Solitude

Two rooms tucked in the back provided critical break space. Library volunteers and organizers could take refuge in either a small kitchen or the printer room–turned–staff workspace (left), with a sliding door and a jury-rigged "alarm" made with a bell on a dolly to protect personal property.

The Value of Flexibility

The shelving units provided a spine down the center of the high-ceilinged space, were flexible enough to encase a standing structural column, and included platforms for standing access to public access computers (right) and more shelving for a well-thumbed collection (below), cataloged via LibraryThing. The units also added significant visual interest with interior views to what was essentially a big white box.

A History Lesson

A neighborhood time line and an exhibit on Chinese restaurants adorned the walls, affixing the space to the past, just as the burgeoning collection required the acquisition of extra shelving from IKEA, anchoring it in the here and now.

Storefront Stats

MONTHS OPEN	3	EVENTS	110
HOURS	427	VOLUNTEERS	39
BOOKS DONATED over 5000		PAID STAFF	2
		BSL PROJECT COST	$12,900
SHELVED	4100	CUSTOM FURNITURE	$24,600 (approx.)
CARDS ISSUED	540		
CIRC	1,374 books, 54% in Chinese	TOTAL IN-KIND	$30,400* (approx.)

*Does not include value of volunteer time, design time, space, books, Boston Street Lab (BSL) staff time, translation services

The Off-Site Librarian

By Meredith Schwartz

When one of the bookmobiles at the Fort Vancouver Regional Library (FVRL), WA, wore out, spending a quarter of a million dollars to buy a new one was not an option. Yet patrons in remote, rural locations in Clark County still needed library service. The innovative solution was the Yacolt Library Express (YLE): a building that is open to the public nearly 70 hours a week, yet staff only spend about ten hours there during the same period.

According to *The Oregonian*, before its cancellation the Clark County bookmobile program had dwindled from a peak of 270 stops in the 1970s to a mere six and from twice to once a week. So while there isn't a Library Express at every location served by the bookmobile, the availability of seven-day-a-week library service nearby is a reasonable trade-off. The 400 square foot YLE is located in a 100-year-old building that was formerly Yacolt City Hall and before that served as a garage for the fire truck and was also the local jail.

The branch opened in September 2012. "All in all, the process went from 'What should we do?' to 'The door's open' in about nine months," Sam Wallin, rural services coordinator at FVRL, told a local newspaper. Wallin presented on the creative concept at this year's Association of Rural and Small Libraries (ARSL) conference, held in September in Tacoma.

Trusting technology

To make the building accessible to patrons without staff yet maintain security, Fort Vancouver turned to Telepen, a UK-based vendor that allowed the system to use existing library cards as keys. Once inside, security cameras keep an eye on things, and door counters let Fort Vancouver know when patrons enter and exit. Standard self-checkout stations have been modified also to allow patrons to check in books. Two computers provide access to the Internet (in addition to a 24-7 Wi-Fi hot spot), and the telephone lets patrons connect in real time to staff at other Fort Vancouver locations.

Staff support

YLE hours of operation are set to match those of the most extensive schedule at other system branches, so that patrons are never in the library without access to real-time, if remote, support. Every weekday, staffers bring holds, tidy up, and reshelve the books that were checked in by patrons.

The plan as originally conceptualized had the building running on only a few weekly hours of staff time, but Fort Vancouver quickly realized that model was unsustainable. Today, the YLE takes about 40 to 50 hours of staff time per week, though not all of them are spent on-site. Wallin estimates start-up costs for the Yacolt branch at $50,000 to $60,000, mostly outlaid for security. Ongoing expenses, including utilities, staff time, travel, and insurance, come to about $50,000 annually.

Expanding service

The YLE dramatically increased usage compared to the bookmobile that it replaced. An average of 80 visitors per day come Monday through Friday, while weekend visits range from five to 50. In comparison, the bookmobile served only about 70 to 80 people per week.

ON THE TOWN A security camera "captures" a young patron at play (l.); the 100-year-old building now stands for library service

With a collection of 2,500 to 3,000 titles on the shelves and an average of 700 holds picked up per month, the YLE circulated 50,000 items in 2013 and is on track to hit the same number this year—almost as many as Fort Vancouver circulates from its smaller, fully staffed locations. (The inspiration for the project, King County Library System's Library Express at Redmond Ridge, which opened in 2009, circulates between 5,000 and 6,000 items per year.)

The YLE even hosts the occasional event, such as poetry night. As well, it boasts its own Friends of the Library, with some 25 volunteers.

One size fits some

The YLE is not without its issues. It doesn't work as well for remote patrons outside of Yacolt as the bookmobile did, though it is still better than the drive to the nearest staffed branch in Battle Ground, WA, which can take nearly half an hour in each direction. The YLE can't accept payments or allow interlibrary loan pickups, so patrons still need to visit Battle Ground to access some services. Technical problems can take a long time to fix—though Wallin tells an ingenious *Mission Impossible*-style story of convincing a patron to pick up the phone via a terminal in order to talk through a remote troubleshooting procedure. Also, it is difficult remotely to police unruly patrons, including the teens who managed to lock one of their number into an old disused jail cell.

In addition, Wallin is clear that a largely unstaffed outpost wouldn't work equally well for every location as it does for Yacolt—a small town with a low crime rate and no homeless population who might seek an overnight stay.

Nonetheless, Wallin feels the model is worth exploring. He shares a variety of other remote service offerings on his Pinterest (ow.ly/DwRRJ) and offers to talk personally with librarians considering implementing a similar outpost. Check him out at swallin@fvrl.org.

Meredith Schwartz is Senior Editor, News & Features, LJ

2
building partnerships

MIXED-USE BUILDINGS

Libraries have always been good at sharing. These projects take it to the next level, with cooperative ventures, here shared from *LJ*'s design coverage since 2009 as originally published, that range from communal civic campuses to buildings including other institutions or even private homes, to fully integrated operations some liken to marriages.

Powerful Partnerships

Libraries built with other organizations can break down barriers and enhance use By Marta Murvosh

Marriage. That's how many librarians describe collaborative efforts with other organizations to fund and construct new library buildings, including joint-use facilities, to serve their communities.

As this whirlwind tour of over a dozen projects across the country illustrates, libraries nationwide have joined forces with private developers; nonprofit housing authorities; colleges and universities; municipal, county and state governments; and others to share land and buildings. At times, construction partnerships have revitalized neighborhoods and led to innovation in service delivery.

"Libraries in general have become much more willing to talk about nontraditional ways of partnership in terms of facilities and shared space, so we are seeing a lot more of it," says Louise Schaper, a library consultant and former executive director of the Fayetteville Public Library, AR, who is the project manager for *LJ*'s New Landmark Libraries.

The projects take all forms, but there are several primary types of partnerships:

- **Shared sites:** The library and at least one other organization build on land owned by at least one partner.
- **Shared buildings:** The partners each set up house in a building that one or all of the partners paid to build. They share ownership, or one partner leases from another. Often, they share parts of the building, such as meeting rooms and common areas.
- **Mixed-use development:** The library and its partners enter a condominium agreement. Often the library owns the site, and each partner owns its own space in the development.
- **Integrated libraries:** Two libraries with combined staff in the same building serve customer groups once served separately.

Benefits abound Sharing a building with another organization can save money because costly necessities, such as elevators, bathrooms, and boiler rooms, need not be duplicated, says Clint Kinney, city manager of Fruita, CO, where the library and recreation center share a building.

A library-developer partnership for a multiuse building may attract grants and tax credits for urban redevelopment or affordable housing, says Paula Kiely, director of the Milwaukee Public Library, which has partnered with two housing developers. Indeed, private developers see the high foot traffic as a plus for retail sites, says Joe Huberty, a partner at Engberg Anderson in Milwaukee.

In the public arena, some government agencies struggling with dwindling sales tax revenue see libraries as partners that bring cash to the table, says Bruce Flynn, a principal at Barker Rinker Seacat Architecture in Denver.

Projects that work can transform a neighborhood, says Mark Schatz, principal at Schwartz/Silver Architects, the Boston firm

South Mountain Community Library, AZ

that designed Boston Public Library's (BPL) Grove Hall branch, which shares a building with Grove Hall Community Center and is also an addition to Jeremiah E. Burke High School in Dorchester, MA. Libraries built with partners in Boston, Milwaukee, and Rifle, CO, have been credited with helping spur economic development and bringing a sense of community to their neighborhoods.

Collaborating with outside organizations on construction can be a new experience for many library directors, and it's not easy, says Dennis Humphries, principal at Humphries Poli Architects in Denver. "Labor is in the center of collaboration. It takes work," Humphries says. "It should push you to a higher level."

Successful partnerships occur when all the organizations involved have a unified vision for the communities they serve, says Patricia Senn Breivik, the former dean at San José State University Library, CA. Breivik, now VP of consulting firm Nehemiah Communications, helped lead the integration of staff at San José Public Library and San José State to build the Dr. Martin Luther King Jr. Library, which set the benchmark for integrated public-academic libraries and was the 2004 *LJ*/Gale Library of the Year.

Such partnership, however, doesn't always come naturally. "Things like that often don't happen unless the key person is retiring or leaving for another job. It's hard to break down barriers," says Bob Fonte, director of the Stark County Park District, Canton, OH, where a library and nature center share a structure.

Library leaders may need to reenvision their roles in their communities. "Librarians have to see themselves as leaders in their cities, not just in the libraries or universities," Breivik says.

Shared sites

Libraries have long shared acreage with other organizations as part of a civic campus, but today's partnerships provide more than a convenient location for government services.

GARFIELD COUNTY PUBLIC
LIBRARY DISTRICT **COLORADO**

Rifle Library

Seeking to develop a walkable, livable downtown on a limited budget, Matt Sturgeon, Rifle assistant city manager, approached the Garfield County Public Library District (GCPLD) about finding a site in the commercial core for the replacement of the tiny Rifle Library.

The library-owned land in downtown was too small, and the city had an adjacent parcel. Together, the two agencies could maximize their land, says Amelia Shelley, GCPLD executive director. As a result, the library, city, and its Downtown Development Authority agreed to a complicated land swap. They closed a road and built a $10 million

North Beach Library

The North Beach Library has long shared a site with the Joe DiMaggio Playground, but the relationship has been less than ideal. A disagreement over land prices in the 1950s resulted in the existing library coming to rest on top of a tennis court, says Julie Christensen, government liaison for the Friends of Joe DiMaggio Playground.

Plans are now under way to replace the aging branch with a $14.5 million building on the triangular parcel bordered by Columbus Avenue and Lombard and Mason Streets—the library's original location planned 60 years ago. "Obviously, we're correcting a wound. It was a mistake to develop a library on a park in the 1950s," Christensen says.

The library will be triangular, and each point will feature two levels of windows, offering three separate reading areas for children, teens, and adults, says architect Marsha Maytum, principal at Leddy Maytum Stacy Architects, San Francisco. Each point will showcase views of a few of San Francisco's iconic sites—Coit Tower, the Transamerica Pyramid, and the spires of Saint Peter and Saint Paul Church—Maytum says.

Solar panels and angled clerestory windows to draw natural light

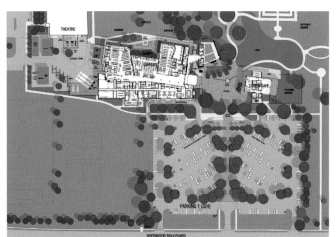

library and a much-needed two-level parking structure, paid for with a $1.7 million state grant, Sturgeon says. Since the library opened in 2010, the downtown has attracted a multiplex theater, and this summer the community will dedicate a ten-mile trail near the library, he says.

"It's not enough to build a library," Sturgeon says. "Everything we do is because dollars are so limited. We just push the envelope as much as we can. Understand that to do that, we have to work with as many people as we can."

Funded mainly by a 2006 bond measure, the library will eventually share an elevator, stairs, restroom, and entryway with a future city hall. The library paid for a larger computer server and boiler rooms in anticipation of that addition, Shelley says.

The library's cozy indoor and outdoor seating near windows and on patios and a second-story terrace offers views of the rugged mountains, red cliffs, and blue skies of this small Western Colorado community, says Bruce Flynn, library design principal at Barker Rinker Seacat, the building's architect. Inside, brightly colored, technology-friendly spaces allow for different types of use and collaboration. A historic stained-glass window commemorates Theodore Roosevelt's visits to Rifle. The library and current city hall share a plant-lined plaza featuring Wi-Fi.

"The library is kind of the last best place where you can accommodate all members of the community across cultures, across socioeconomic boundaries, across the generations," Flynn says. "We are huge believers in the library as the heart of the community.

Clockwise from top left: Rifle Library, CO, Main Library, LA, and North Beach Library, CA

will make the building greener, says Mindy Linetzky, the Department of Public Works City and County of San Francisco administrator who oversaw the $106 million bond measure to construct or renovate 24 libraries. North Beach is the last of these projects.

The city also plans to close the short section of Mason Street between the new library and the playground in hopes of restructuring the playground, which features a pool; basketball, tennis, and bocce ball courts; and two small baseball fields. Changes include relocating the children's play area from near a bus stop to a central spot, making it safer, Christensen says. A retaining wall will be removed and the site graded to improve pedestrian flow, Maytum says. The city and playground Friends group is seeking grants to fund the $5 million needed to update the space.

Improving both the library and the playground will serve the neighborhood's rich blend of ethnicities, generations, and socioeconomic extremes. "This allows the library to step up its programming efforts and cater to those distinct groups," Christensen says. "It is our Lions Club, our bowling club. It's the place where our neighborhood really comes together."

EAST BATON ROUGH PARISH LIBRARY **LOUISIANA**

Main Library

The search for a new site for East Baton Rouge Parish Library's Main Library in Independence Park has deepened an existing partnership with the Recreation and Park Commission for the Parish of East Baton Rouge (BREC), which owns the park.

Construction started this winter on a $43.5 million project, which includes the new library, its outdoor Internet Plaza and gardens, and a cybercafé, which BREC is building. With the library's planned 120 computers, both agencies will serve the needs of Louisianans who lack access to high-speed technology, says Mary Stein, interim codirector and assistant library director over administration and manager of the Main Library. Already librarians are brainstorming how they can "buddy up" with their parks partners to commingle and enhance programs for both park and library users once doors open in early 2014. "If they are here, we want them to use the whole of the park," Stein says. "Ideally, you could spend a whole day here."

Partnering makes sense for the library district. While it is a separate political entity from the park and parish, it is required to have approval of the Baton Rouge mayor and council for grant applications, budgets, and even the payment of authors and performers. "There are a lot of cooks in that kitchen," Stein says. Partnerships with the park, which answers to its board, can mean streamlining some of that approval process.

Determining a location for the library at Independence Park that would not disturb established gardens was difficult. The resulting long, skinny site has southern exposure that offered a challenge to architect Denelle Wrightson, director of library architecture at Dewberry in Dallas. Library users will be bathed in natural light but kept cool when Southern temperatures soar in public areas on the north side. Back-of-shop functions will be on the south side, Stein says. A stained-glass window in the children's area both depicts swarming purple martin swallows and filters the view of the shipping yard. On the roof, a terrace offers a place to read or enjoy the park.

Park staff can open airport-sized bathrooms after hours, and chair storage has inside and outside access so that both agencies can use the furnishings, Stein says. The gardens surrounding the library will be upgraded as well, Wrightson says, and the park district will maintain them. "They are using the library as a catalyst to create these other public spaces for the community, including a courtyard and reading gardens and terraces in the park."

Shared buildings

Libraries sharing buildings with centers of recreation and learning report that their partners bring exposure to new users. Libraries are also forming partnerships to share buildings with other agencies focused on education, such as colleges and historic societies. In the East Bay Area of California, the Lafayette Library and Learning Center building is shared by the library and the Glenn Seaborg Learning Consortium, a partnership of 12 education, science, and arts institutions.

In Central Arizona, the Prescott Valley Public Library's (PVPL) partnership with North Arizona University and Yavapai College offered added classroom space to the institution, and, three years after opening, 50 university students attend class in the library building, says Stuart Mattson, PVPL library director. Still, librarians look to deepen the partnership. "It's really exciting, and there's been a lot of potential and still is a lot of potential for development as far as interaction between students and library staff," says Kathy Hellman, PVPL manager. "We're still getting a handle on what we as librarians can offer to students and faculty."

MESA COUNTY PUBLIC LIBRARY DISTRICT **COLORADO**

Fruita Branch

Hundreds of new library users discovered the Fruita branch of the Mesa County Public Library District (MCPLD) as a result of sharing a building with the city's senior and recreation centers. The $10.2 million, 7000 square foot branch opened in February 2011 on city-owned land. Annual circulation skyrocketed by 57 percent, from 86,549 items in 2010 to 136,239 in 2011, says Bob Kretschman, library district public information manager.

"It gets a lot of business that we didn't have in our old branch," says Eve Tallman, MCPLD director. "It's a natural combination where people can feed their mind and exercise their bodies."

The partnership was born when the library had passed a bond referendum and was looking for land at the same time the city had been unsuccessful at getting voters to raise taxes to build a recreation center, Tallman says. Fruita city manager Clint Kinney offered the library free land, if the new branch joined the planned recreation/senior center complex. Voters approved, boosting the city's sales tax by 1¢. The library district put in $2.4 million, and the city raised $2 million in grants and donations.

The city's architect Sink Combs Dethlefs subcontracted with Humphries Poli Architects to design the library. Humphries Poli principal

Dennis Humphries says the combination intrigued him. "There's a significant sharing of resources," Humphries says. This allowed the library to concentrate on features that would enhance services.

Tallman worked with Humphries to ensure that the sound of basketballs would not impact readers. The library also sacrificed its dream of drive-up service, offering a walk-up window instead. "That way moms don't have to unload all the kids from the car seats," Tallman says.

The library district has a 99-year lease with a buyout clause, and so far the city is pleased with the partnerships. "They bring a lot of people to the community center that wouldn't normally come," says Kinney. "It's an incredibly symbiotic relationship."

BOSTON PUBLIC LIBRARY
DORCHESTER, MASSACHUSETTS

Grove Hall Branch

A challenged neighborhood got a "shot in the arm" when Boston Public Library's (BPL) Grove Hall Branch was collocated with the expansion of Jeremiah E. Burke High School and the Grove Hall Community Center, says Mark Schatz, principal at Schwartz/Silver Architects, the Boston firm that designed the colorful building.

Librarians, who worked to tailor the collection to the neighborhood's diverse needs, have heard from library users that the library promotes feelings of safety and community, says Christine Schonhart, BPL's director of branch libraries.

The combination of the school, library, and community center in one of Boston's largest and most diverse neighborhoods was part of Mayor Thomas Menino's Community Learning Initiative. The first two stories are open to the public as the library and community center, Schatz says. The school library occupies the third floor. The gymnasium is on the fourth. After school, the gym and the school library are open to the public. Gym noise is masked by special materials, Schatz says.

To bring in natural light and attract passersby into the branch library, Schatz created a two-story brightly multicolored glass façade that sets it apart from the school and community center, which has red brick façade similar to the brick art deco school. A "funky" bright red stairwell connects the different levels of the library, school, and gym, striking the balance between keeping the school sections secure during the day and inviting the public in at night. "We wanted a lot of glass," Shatz says. "We didn't want it to look corporate. We wanted it to be playful and a lot of fun."

One form of fun: the library brings in performers and musicians to make the most of a jazz lounge for quiet contemplation. Also, on the second floor, teens have their own area, including a quiet space. The library added a YA librarian to the tutors offered by the Boston Centers for Youth and Family, Schonhart says. "It changes a library especially when a teenager can recognize a space just for them," she says. Something's working: in the first year, branch circulation rose almost 40 percent and an impressive 1200 new library cardholders signed up.

"The beauty of it is you sit out on the deck of the library and look out on the lake and in the winter by fireplace and look out window." Fonte says. "It's a psychological respite."

HOWARD COUNTY LIBRARY SYSTEM
ELLICOTT CITY, MARYLAND

Charles E. Miller Branch & Historical Center

The Howard County Historical Society has enjoyed increased visibility over the handful of months since it moved this past winter into the Howard County Library (HCL) System Charles E. Miller Branch & Historical Center. "The rewards have been incredible," says Lisa Mason-Chaney, historical society executive director. "Working with the library staff has been a wonderful experience, and being located in the library has given the historical society much greater visibility."

In January, the historical society had an unheard of 223 visitors, signed up 30 new members, and tripled its volunteer hours, says Valerie J. Gross, HCL president and CEO.

When the library system decided to replace its aging, cramped Miller branch with a two-story 63,000 square foot building, inviting the historical society to join them seemed to be a smart move, Gross says. The library's mission of education and bringing history to life would be bolstered by joining forces with the historical society. The society's extensive archival collection features Babe Ruth's marriage license, for instance. In turn, the society's experts would add to the library's historical expertise, and the thousands of library users would be exposed to the historical society, Gross says.

The Miller branch embraces both the past and future with historic displays and solar panels and a vegetative roof. The library worked with the society to design

STARK COUNTY LIBRARY DISTRICT
CANTON, OHIO

Perry-Sippo Branch

To play up the partnership between Perry-Sippo Branch and the Exploration Gateway of Stark County Park District (SCPD) in Canton, OH, architect Dan Meehan drew inspiration from bodies of water and trails.

Geometric designs resembling waves, fins, and tree rings adorn bookshelves and other fixtures. The shelves are positioned like schools of fish, says Meehan, a principal at Holzheimer Bolek + Meehan Architects, LLC, in Cleveland. Information trees are constructed of material that changes color as library users walk around them. Kids can walk under an aquarium to enter the children's area. An open deck offers views of Sippo Lake. Hiking trails start at the library building. "You sense it's more than a library," says Meehan of the branch, which replaced a building destroyed by fire in another location. "It's a real special space."

Behind the scenes, the staffs of the Exploration Gateway and the library share locker and break rooms, aiding cross-pollination, Meehan says. The library leases from the nature center, and the organizations share an entry/exhibit hall.

The combination has resulted in the nature center and the library door counts hitting 200,000 and 140,000 each year, respectively, says Bob Fonte, director of SCPD. He says he expected between 25,000 and 50,000 people in the first year.

Clockwise from far left: Fruita Branch, CO, Grove Hall Branch, MA, Perry-Sippo Branch, OH, and Charles E. Miller Branch and Historical Center, MD

a 1000 square foot reading and research room that's shared with the branch. The historic collection is kept in a secure climate-controlled, windowless room with restricted access. The shared room acts as an archives reading room when the historical society is open, restricting what users can bring in when rare documents are being examined, Gross says. When the archive is closed, library users can bring drinks and backpacks into the space. The society pays a portion of the utilities in lieu of rent.

"We worked with them to design the Historical Center, a vision that brings history to life in unprecedented ways," Gross says.

Mixed-use development

A branch library in Portland, OR, is considered to be part of the first public-private housing partnership. Since it opened, other libraries nationwide have entered into similar arrangements, with lessons learned for libraries.

This partnership between a library and a developer resulted in the Hollywood Library, a small retail space occupied by a coffee shop, and the medium- and low-income Bookmark Apartments in Portland on land owned by Multnomah County Library (MCL), says Michael T. Harrington, library facilities and operations manager. Starting in 1999, the library system studied the feasibility of mixing library, retail, and housing environments. The building opened in 2002.

MCL then worked with a development consultant to issue a Request for Proposals for the building. Sockeye Development, LLC, a subsidiary of developer Shiels Obletz Johnsen, received the contract and manages the apartments and the coffee shop lease. The library system then embarked on other mixed-use partnerships, including Sellwood Library. "It's one of our busiest branches," says Harrington of Hollywood. "It would have been nice to have more space."

Cities with redevelopment agencies and strong nonprofit housing authorities tend to be where many of these partnerships occur.

opment of condos and commercial building on KCLS-owned land stalled, victim of the developer's inability to get financing during the recession, KCLS decided to construct a stand-alone library, expected to open this summer, Smith says. The process involved revisiting the agreement with the developer, which has a two-year deadline to obtain financing that expires this year, allowing KCLS to look for another partner, if necessary. "We spent quite a bit of money on attorney fees," Smith says. "It was the lengthy process to get the library built, and it had to be redesigned."

Lesson learned, KCLS changed its approach with another library-housing partnership for its proposed Renton Highlands branch, Smith says. This project is proceeding. "We're kind of waiting to see how that plays out," Smith says. "We're designing the building so that if we need to we can pull out and build it by itself."

MILWAUKEE PUBLIC LIBRARY
Villard Square Branch

Milwaukee Public Library (MPL) owns land in prime locations, lending bargaining power when it came to finding a partner for a building that combines housing with a replacement for the Villard Square Branch. It also opened the door to innovative pro-

SAN FRANCISCO PUBLIC LIBRARY
Mission Bay Branch

Another example of a library in a mixed-use development is Mission Bay, Honorable Mention for *LJ*'s 2011 New Landmark Libraries, and its partner Mission Creek Senior Housing in San Francisco. Architect Bruce Prescott helped ensure the library and the nonprofit housing developer shared "real partnership and not just a land exchange" by designing a space that would be welcoming to all ages, especially seniors, says Mindy Linetzky, who oversaw the library's $106 million bond measure to construct or renovate 24 libraries for the Department of Public Works City and County of San Francisco.

KING COUNTY LIBRARY SYSTEM
WASHINGTON
Burien Library

King County Library System (KCLS), *LJ*'s 2011 Library of the Year, has extensive experience with partnering with different organizations and guiding other libraries. KCLS has partnered with developers, nonprofits, and municipal governments to build or lease libraries, including mixed-use facilities. KCLS partnered with Burien City to build a combined city hall and library on municipal land. The building opened in 2009, but construction required compromise. The municipal government wanted the library to occupy two floors of a three-story civic building with the "presence" of a "dominant agency," says Greg Smith, KCLS director of facilities management services. The library prefers single-story structures because they cost less to staff; however, the joint venture saved both partners money. The partnership brought the city a state grant to pay for a parking garage, Smith says.

The library's legal agreement came in handy when a change in city leadership led to a request to pay a smaller share of the maintenance costs, says Kay Johnson, KCLS director of facilities development. Since opening, the library has attracted people to downtown Burien, where they can enjoy a park and other amenities. "We have a good building, and it's a good way to spend public funds," Smith says. "It's a gathering place."

When plans to build the Newcastle Library as part of a mixed-use devel-

Clockwise from left: Mission Bay Branch, CA, Burien Library, WA, and Villard Square Branch, WI

grams such as laptop checkout and roving reference.

"They were astute enough to recognize that their libraries were on pretty valuable land," says Joe Huberty, a partner at Engberg Anderson, an architectural, planning, and design firm with offices in Milwaukee. Additionally, Director Paula Kiely had positioned MPL as an innovative player in the community that actively helps people enrich their daily lives, Huberty adds.

The library and apartments geared toward grandparents raising their grandchildren opened last October. The project reduced costs for both the library and developer, which received tax credits, Kiely says.

At 12,770 square feet, the new library is smaller than the 15,000 square foot building the project replaced, but it feels larger, in part because of huge windows and the flexibility built into the design, Kiely says. The meeting room, for example, is divided by sliding glass panels so it never feels cut off from the rest of the library. The room doubles as a reading area or a teen study space.

The exterior windows entice community members to visit as they walk or drive past, Kiely says. Moving to a new building offered the opportunity to install radio-frequency identification (RFID) technology and self-check, pilot roving reference for the entire library system, and 40 laptops for in-library checkout. "People want to use computers where they are comfortable, not necessarily next to someone," she says. Year-to-date figures for this February indicate that library visits were up 126 percent, and circulation rose by 108 percent.

Integrated service

A handful of library building partnerships have resulted in libraries integrating operations with their partners. Librarians working in these environments joke that they are married to their building partners.

In Australia, integrated-service libraries are commonplace, generally a combination of public libraries and schools, serving students and the community at large. In the United States, joint libraries and integrated service are unusual, and when they occur, they tend to be between public and academic libraries. At least one joint academic-public library has broken up when the Irving City Council and the North Lake Community Library ended its two-year partnership in 2004 with North Lake College in Texas after a new college president started, says Dewberry's Denelle Wrightson.

The Martin Luther King Jr. Library in San José, CA, has set the standard for these partnerships. The eight-story King library was the brainchild of then–San José mayor Susan Hammer and then–San José State University president Robert Caret. The pair wanted to forge deeper connections between the community and the university, says Jane Light, San José Public Library director.

Hammer and Caret immediately encountered opposition in part because they didn't go through the city council and other political and bureaucratic channels, Light says. Different stakeholders feared that their interests would suffer under an integrated library, she says.

They also needed to find money for construction and move other university offices from the old Clark Library to elsewhere on campus, says consultant Patricia Senn Breivik, who worked with Light to bring the partnership to fruition. She was then San José State University Library dean. "You don't announce a major thing like this without having 60 percent of the funding in hand, and they didn't have it," says Breivik, adding that fundraising was easier with such an inspiring project.

Breivik and Light were challenged by merging two different organizations with different cultures, structures, labor groups, and pay scales. Public and academic librarians shadowed one another on the job. Each institution brought strengths that enhance the other, such as the public library's strong collection of language materials and the academic library's history collection. The two library leaders set up committees on every possible issue, and the committees worked through policies and procedures and made recommendations; library staff gave input at open hearings.

"We really believed it had to be truly integrated. There were no models at that level," Breivik says. "The library is still the crown jewel for the downtown area."

Notable to the project are the library's two main entrances, connecting it to the campus and to the community. Those told the community that the university was opening up its doors to the city, Breivik says. Today, the King Library sees up to 12,000 people each day. It was *LJ*'s 2004 Library of the Year (www.libraryjournal.com/article/CA423793.html).

"The message to a lot of families where no one had ever gone to college or dreamed about goingto college was: 'You can do it,'" says Breivik. "It's only one step beyond your public library."

VIRGINIA

Virginia Beach/Tidewater Community College Joint Library

The King Library in San José inspired librarians at Virginia Beach Public Library (VBPL) and Tidewater Community College (TCC) to strive to combine TCC's library with a new public branch, says Marcy Sims, director of VBPL.

The city and college even hired the same architects, Anderson Brulé of San José and Carrier Johnson of San Diego, to work with RRMM Architects of Norfolk to design a 120,000 square foot facility that will open in 2013 with the goal of providing seamless service to students and the general public. Construction began in February.

The college and city decided to partner in 2004 when former TCC president Deborah DiCroce and Virginia Beach city manager Jim Spore realized that each institution planned to build libraries across the street from each other, Sims says. "We're really creating new territory for the both of us," Sims says. "We realized that we aren't that different. Our end goal is quality service to our customers."

The floor plan was driven by anticipating users' experiences and the California architects' desire to build as green as possible. The building, shaped like a crescent bisected by four glass rectangles, includes a clerestory designed at an angle to act as a "light machine," capturing sunlight in the arched section of the building. Inside, users will have comfortable seating. "We looked at creating spaces that people would want to gravitate to for either study or leisure reading," Sims says.

Like the King Library, Virginia Beach's first floor will be for people on the go. It will have a "marketplace" layout featuring popular fiction and nonfiction, CDs, and DVDs, Sims says. Many of the library's 380 computers will be on the first floor, including individual and collaborative workstations and spots for quick printing.

A 35'-wide, 400'-long walkway called "Main Street" follows the arced wall, connecting the different sections of the branch and four open stairwells. Main Street ends in the "Living Room," with newspaper and magazine racks and fireplace seating.

The upper story will be quieter and filled

Virginia Beach/ Tidewater Community College Joint Library

with more scholarly resources, carrels for library users to settle in with a laptop or a book, and collaborative study rooms. "We'll have a lot of small group study rooms to address how students do their work today in a team environment," Sims says.

PHOENIX

South Mountain Community Library

The spacious South Mountain Community Library's open floor plan, flowing from one area into another, inspires users to look outside of themselves and imagine possibilities, says division chair for the Library and Teaching & Learning Center Amy MacPherson. "When you walk into the building, the vista, the horizon is so far in front of you that it allows for expansiveness of thought and creative thinking."

The 51,600 square foot, two-story library opened in August 2011 with an integration of library staff from Phoenix Public Library (PPL) and South Mountain Community College.

The building's exterior features a stratified copper rain screen that protects the building from heat and weather. Its texture calls to mind library card barcodes, says James Richärd, principal and architect at richärd + bauer, which designed the library. Many of the interior walls are constructed of glass etched with designs and textures inspired by the community's agricultural heritage, including asters, citrus groves, and sorghum and cotton fields.

The college paid for almost two-thirds of the building. The city library system provides the bulk of the collection. The cultural shift that the staff from the public and academic libraries underwent and continue to experience during the merger of operations was reflected in integrating the reference and circulation desks. Different cultures can have different priorities, says Annette Vigil, one of two South Mountain comanagers. (Vigil works for PPL and comanager Lydia Johnson, a college faculty librarian, reports to MacPherson.)

"We are married in this building," Vigil says. "This is a great experience. We are figuring it out as we go along."

Like the King Library, South Mountain offers grab-and-go items, such as DVDs and new releases, on the ground floor, where the children and teen areas also are located. That energy combined with people heading to and from community meeting rooms can generate noise that is dampened by variegated cedar slats backed with acoustical material lining the ceiling and some walls.

The collection on each floor is laid out similarly; for example, nonfiction about children is found on the second floor directly in the same area that children's picture books are located on the floor below, Richärd

says. The upper floor is designated a quieter area; frosted glass encloses study and activity rooms. In the study areas, whiteboards called "wall talkers" stretch from floor to ceiling. "You can write from the baseboard to as far as you can reach; you can have big ideas," MacPherson says. "We have 44" screens in the study rooms so you can project huge and not have everyone huddled around a laptop."

Both MacPherson and Vigil emphasize that the operation does not save money; instead, it offers the college and community at large access to a greater number of resources. Like the King Library, South Mountain has opened its doors to everyone. Tots who first come to the library for baby story time will grow into teens who enroll in college because they have always gone to college, notes MacPherson. "An integrated library allows me to change many more people's lives."

Marta Murvosh, MLS, is a freelance writer/researcher and aspiring librarian living and working in Northwestern Washington. You can follow her via www.facebook.com/MartaMurvosh

DATE LIBRARY BY DESIGN, FALL 2011

Novel Library, Novel Design

Prescott Valley Public Library experiments with a new staffing strategy By Ted Johnson

Inspired by a regional lava dome, the 55,000 square foot Prescott Valley Public Library, AZ, houses a new hybrid university, town council chambers, and public meeting space in addition to the new library. A folded corten skin and glass window wall wrap the outer shell, offering views of the surrounding community and distant mountains. The library and the university wing (a partnership between Northern Arizona University and Yavapai College) envelop the "volcanic cone" as it erupts from the site. Hiking up an extinct volcano, Glassford Hill, the design team examined the local geology and flora so that they could infuse the entire campus with those colors and textures, from the landscaping to the interior furnishings.

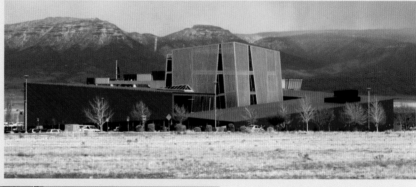

The purpose of the design is to evoke a feeling of adventure and wonder. From the expansive Children's Division with its interactive wall to the Virtual Interactive Room, each space invites individual contemplation and study as well as group interaction. Small group "campsites," a genealogy room, a computer lab, an observation terrace, and patios for adults and teens meet the needs of a diverse and changing community. The interior ceiling is lined with an irregular surface of breathtaking cedar.

Facing an economic downturn, hiring freeze, and a new, larger library building with new technologies, a novel staffing strategy was developed. Of course, we expected the building to attract many new patrons. And as everyone knows, a slow economy means a busier public library. When it was all added up, the town needed to pull more than a "rabbit" out of its administrative hat. Unwilling to back out of a ten-year plan to build a new library, management opted to mobilize available staff from nearly every other town department to operate the new facility temporarily.

It is a complex experiment with early signs of success. The full story of how we pulled it off and what remains to be solved can be found with the web version of this article at www.libraryjournal.com.

Shelving with everyone's boss Thanks to the award-winning design by richärd + bauer Architects, Prescott Valley Public Library, which opened in late 2009, is a stunning gathering place for people from across northern Arizona. It is also the site of a radical staffing experiment.

Ted Johnson is Assistant Library Director, Prescott Valley Public Library, AZ

Capitol Designs

DCPL's ambitious construction project brings a building focus to the urban system By Sarah Bayliss

A renaissance in library architecture is under way in Washington, DC, thanks to the vision of District of Columbia Public Library (DCPL) chief librarian and executive director Ginnie Cooper. Since she arrived at DCPL in 2006, Cooper has overseen the construction and renovation of 14 branch libraries, with eight more renovations and reconstructions to go. Collectively, the upgraded branches and new buildings—the latter conceived by world-class architects, including Adjaye Associates, Davis Brody Bond Aedas, and the Freelon Group—have earned an astonishing 26 awards for their design excellence.

Now, they've earned the plan's ultimate architect an award of her own: the American Institute of Architects (AIA) recently saluted Cooper's accomplishments with a 2013 Thomas Jefferson Award for Public Architecture. As the first librarian to receive the award, which recognizes a commitment to design in public buildings as part of American cultural heritage, "I am thrilled," says Cooper. But, she quickly adds, "I am much more excited that the importance of libraries in urban environments is being recognized."

How did Cooper orchestrate this design revolution? With local support, experience, and the conviction that inspiring design can both produce magnificent library buildings and uplift communities. Cooper was recruited to run DCPL with the mandate to transform the capital city's lackluster library system. Her efforts have had the near-constant backing of the three DC mayors, who have been in office since she arrived, though it dipped during the tenure of Mayor Adrian Fenty (2007–11), she says.

No stranger to a hard hat, Cooper was already seasoned in library renovation when she arrived in DC. As director of the Multnomah County Library, OR, from 1990 to 2003, she garnered support for two capital bonds to improve all 19 branch libraries and renovate the 1912 Central Library. She got married in the Multnomah Central Library while it was under construction. Though the DC branches are her most high-profile accomplishment, "What I did at Multnomah County is also front and center in the AIA award," Cooper says.

"We were really lucky that there were architects who wanted to be a presence in Washington, DC, and eager to work with us," says Cooper. And as with the Multnomah renovations, overseen by architect Thomas Hacker, she says, "We didn't want people to feel like they had cookie-cutter libraries."

When DCPL issues a Request for Information from architectural candidates for each project, Cooper conducts community focus groups to find out what each neighborhood wants and also lays the groundwork via her set of requirements. "Driving forces for design" include a mandate that the buildings must have "a prominent entry with lots of natural light" and be "at least LEED (Leadership in Energy & Environmental Design) Silver certified." With library use and technology changing so rapidly, "flexibility is another hallmark," Cooper says. That means raised floors and as few walls as possible.

From there, architects submit their proposals, which undergo an approval process that includes presenting their ideas to committees

NATURALLY INSPIRED
The Francis A. Gregory Library interior reflects its park setting with organic touches, designed by Adjaye and Wiencek + Associates

made up of library, architecture, and community representatives. Winning architects also work with a local architectural partner.

The results have been a group of buildings as different from one another as they are inspiring. The Freelon Group's new $14.7 million Anacostia Neighborhood Library (dollar figures include fees for design, construction, furnishing, fixtures, and equipment) is angular, streamlined, and sleek. Adjaye and Wiencek + Associates' $18 million Francis A. Gregory Library, in a park setting, is organic-feeling, with diamond-shaped windows overlooking a double-height seating area with hand-painted lamps. Adjaye and Wiencek's more block-like $15.8 million William O. Lockridge/Bellevue Library features raised pavilions surrounding a central nucleus, a primary color palette inside the building, and an outdoor patio. Plentiful natural light and a connection to the outdoors is a hallmark of all the new buildings.

Support from the city and the library board has been key to Cooper's success, but "building trust" with the community has also been a journey. Starting out, "People didn't expect much of us, and the library hadn't delivered much," says Cooper. The renovation and rebuilding plans were initially met with a community attitude of "I'll believe it when I see

PHOTO ARRAY Another award-winning branch is the William O. Lockridge/Bellevue Library (below), also designed by Adjaye and Wiencek + Associates; renderings for the proposed renovation of the Martin Luther King Jr. Memorial Library (above l.–r.), DCPL's main facility; and the Petworth Neighborhood Library (r.)

it," according to DCPL media relations manager George Williams. But over time, this "healthy skepticism" turned around, he says. "Now the conversation is, 'When are you doing my neighborhood?'"

While the diverse library buildings in DC are adding a welcome architectural charge to the city's landscape, Cooper says the "bigger changes" are "what's happening inside the buildings," many of which are in DC's poorer sections. At the new $15.7 million Dorothy I. Height/Benning Neighborhood Library, 5,000 people signed up for library cards within a few months of opening. At the Tenley-Friendship Library, attendance at children's programs tripled. Such increased patronage is happening throughout the system.

Cooper's most ambitious renovation, still in the proposal and planning stage, would transform the main Mies van der Rohe–designed Martin Luther King Jr. Memorial Library, opened in 1972 and designated a landmark in 2007. "I hate it," Cooper says of the flagship library building, an enormous, dark, steel-and-glass rectangle where her office is located. Aside from the uninviting exterior, the structure is "riddled with lead paint," among other problems, according to Cooper. There are no bathrooms on the main floor, and the single-pane windows, which cost $12,000–$16,000 each to replace, make it roasting in the summer and cold in the winter. She just might get her wish: DC mayor Vincent Gray included the main library renovation in his fiscal 2013 budget, to be funded by creating additional space to host private, paying tenants.

After the nonprofit Urban Land Institute produced a report with upgrading recommendations based in part on interviews with 70 local residents, the Freelon Group presented some initial design concepts last fall. They involve creating an enormous lightwell in the middle of the build-

ing, forming more inviting new outdoor spaces, and adding additional floors and an underground parking facility to bring in revenue. Initial estimates for the renovation are between $175 million and $250 million.

Plans are also on the table for a new $16.5 million Woodridge Library, an elegant, all-white structure by Wiencek + Associates and Bing Thom Architects (the award-winning Bing Thom also conceived the $36 million Surrey City Centre Library in British Columbia). In addition, sketches for the new mixed-use West End Library, designed by Enrique Norten of Ten Arquitectos, suggest a building that resembles a collection of loosely stacked glass blocks. The structure would feature a two-level, 21,000 square foot library beneath an eight-story residential apartment building. However, at press time the groundbreaking was on hold, pending litigation brought by the Ralph Nader–founded D.C. Library Renaissance Project. (Ironically, the litigation puts the project at odds with Cooper, despite its taking credit for inspiring the Cooper-led transformation process.)

Among the completed branches, the new $15 million Watha T. Daniel/Shaw Library, conceived by Davis Brody Bond Aedas, is probably the greatest contrast to what it replaced, in Cooper's view. "It used to look like a Soviet bunker," she says. "When the late Max Bond talked to a community group about the building, he said, 'It will be a beacon, a lantern in the district instead of something that says go away.'" The new library, near Howard University, is an inviting, glass-sheathed, triangle-shaped building featuring neon sculptures.

While the new DC buildings have attracted the most attention from the architecture world, Cooper is also proud of DCPL's renovations of older branches, including that of the Georgetown Neighborhood Library, following a fire in 2007, and the $10 million historic renovation of the Northeast Neighborhood Library, now in progress. "There is something very warm about these historic renovations," she says, "They remind me of the libraries I grew up in."

Sarah Bayliss is Features Editor, School Library Journal

Serving Two Masters

Design fosters teamwork at Tidewater Community College/Virginia Beach Joint-Use Library By Ian Chant

Joint-use libraries, especially partnerships between public libraries and colleges, are rare but not unheard of. In an era of belt-tightening, pooling resources with a partner that shares many of your institution's goals can be a tempting proposition for schools and cities alike. It's complex, but as seen at the Tidewater Community College/City of Virginia Beach Joint-Use Library, opened in 2013, it can also be extremely rewarding.

While their missions are broadly the same, academic and public libraries differ in important details of their practices, from collection development to peak hours of operation. Where populations with varying needs collide, tensions can arise between students seeking study time and families coming for story time. Those differences mean that many such operations, says Virginia Beach Public Library (VBPL) director Eva Poole, don't live up to their potential, becoming "roommates rather than partners." That's just what the staffers at the joint-use building are working to avoid, and the building was designed to make that teamwork easier to accomplish.

Throwing in together The idea for a joint-use library came up when Virginia Beach city manager Jim Spore and then–Tidewater Community College (TCC) president Deborah Croce learned at a meeting that both the city and the college had had plans for a new library. The planned facilities were, in fact, just across the street from each other. That initial meeting planted the seed that the two organizations could pool their resources on a library that would serve the needs of the Virginia Beach community as well as TCC students without sacrificing the services needed by either.

"Mutual respect for each community is at the heart of the solution," says Dan Hickok, who led the project for RRMM Architects, the architect of record. (Carrier Johnson + CULTURE [CJ+C] served as the design architect and Anderson Brulé Architects as the interior design/feasibility study architect.) "That the building treats the community and the campus with parity as it goes to site access, entry sequence, and the building's interior organization was critical."

Early planning meetings included a devil's advocate–style roundtable, a meeting moderated by architects and designers, with representatives from VBPL and TCC listing all the reasons they could think of that a joint project wouldn't work. Then, small groups formed to attack sets of concerns that had been raised. By the end of the day, both city and college staffers were in agreement that there wasn't a problem they had thought of that couldn't be addressed.

To design a building that met the demands of this wide variety of uses, CJ+C and RRMM employed a design that ensured parity in access and interior organization. One technique at play is the large, wel-

BRIDGING INSIDE AND OUT (top): The north and east facades are stepped to engage the garden spaces that create outdoor study rooms. The north and east elevations are clad with full-height clear glazing panels, opening the view to passersby. The curved south elevation (bottom) is accentuated by cantilevered spaces that pop out from the exterior. These glass crystals act as picture windows to the functions within, inviting usage

coming, inclusive space. "The long gallery two-story space that unites all spaces was intended to allow the mix of both users in a naturally lit environment while also acting as a clear path to a destination queue," RRMM's Hickok tells *LJ*. "There is no mistaking where to go or how to get there." Gordon Carrier, CJ+C's founder and design principal, explains that the purpose of the main corridor was "to have places that felt more like living rooms, that didn't really have affiliation with a particular user. The main corridor is meant to be a space where the confluence of both users feels very comfortable together. We tried to create a mix…so you didn't feel you've interrupted someone else's space."

The front of the 124,000 square foot building is a glass facade that also acts as a light receiver, bathing the entire building in natural, northern light, which produces little heat or glare. "You have access to the outdoors almost wherever you are in the building," Bill Ramsey, TCC's

director of planning and development, told the *Virginian-Pilot.* "It's designed to be very open and welcoming so that the public and students alike feel like they're free to explore." Meanwhile, the rounded south end, with its few windows, is designed to keep out harsh southern light in summer, as well as to prevent a long wall vista, so that the library offers "an equal presence to the community across the street as it does to the college," Carrier tells *LJ.*

The emphasis on factors such as natural light and openness was important from a design perspective, as they don't just serve one community or another—everyone who uses the library benefits from gentle, pleasant light and a library that feels inviting.

The final price tag for the project was $43 million, 80 percent of which was provided by TCC.

Geographically, the building is situated as a gateway of sorts, welcoming students onto the TCC campus while also creating a bridge between the campus and the community at large. To emphasize that sense of hospitality, the joint building was designed with an eye toward fitting into the environment of Virginia Beach—no small feat for a huge glass and steel structure in an area with a strong tradition of agriculture.

"The architects also wanted to be very true to the history of the agriculture of Virginia Beach, both as farm- and marshland," says Poole. "They kept many of the trees on the site to show the hedgerows that used to be here, and we have lovely marsh ponds that attract wildlife to the grounds." In fact, says Carrier, the shapes defined by the original hedgerows determined the size and shape of the library.

As an added bonus, the water retention properties and wildlife habitat provided by the pools helped the new building land its Leadership in Energy and Environmental Design (LEED) Gold certification. The design also encourages interaction between patrons and local wildlife, says Steven Litherland, TCC associate vice president for libraries—unfortunately, sometimes a little too much of it, to the detriment of an on-site café.

"The historical use of the site is agricultural and wetlands, and this heritage is preserved in the site through tree rows and retention ponds, which attract geese," Litherland explains. "We have a patio right outside the coffee shop, and patrons who dare to sit there are promptly chased away by the very territorial geese."

Balancing priorities

While the design embraces openness, the joint-use library also has practical concerns to consider. The building serves two masters. TCC students need quiet places to read and study, while parents in the community need space where their kids can be kids, and plenty of TCC attendees are both students and parents. Virginia Beach's population of just over 400,000 residents includes many young families who make use of the system's ten branches.

Owing to its size and resources, the joint-use building was initially marketed as a second main library by VBPL, and its popularity with users from both communities has helped it fulfill that promise. The design of the space lets this busy branch strike a balance that works for all constituencies.

Students, for instance, don't naturally head toward the children's area downstairs, while kids do gravitate toward this brightly decorated space. It makes an obvious stopping place prior to the stairs that lead to the more study-focused spaces on the second level. "The design of the building allows us to host children's programming that doesn't disturb the quiet in the rest of the building," says Poole.

The first floor is home to the children's section and general interest public collection. Upstairs on the second floor is the reference collection and academic offerings. Both floors are peppered liberally with study rooms where TCC students can go to concentrate. Meeting rooms are used by both kinds of patrons, for collaborative study, conferences, or community gatherings. Of the four classrooms, one is used for

PART, NOT APART The library's eastern terminus (top) provides panoramic views of the garden and the neighborhood beyond. The arboreal theme of the children's area service desk (inset) brings the green motif indoors

VBPL programming, another serves as a professional development space for TCC faculty, and the remaining two are devoted to TCC's information literacy education efforts. Nonetheless, with enough heads-up, those spaces can also be reallocated as needed for students or community members.

"We do support requests for student orientations, short-term use by regular classes, and similar events that do not interfere with library instruction," says Litherland. "The facility in general is in high demand for various events, and we have to be mindful of balancing everyone's needs."

A hybrid approach

Since it opened its doors in August 2013, the branch has seen significant, steady use from students and community members alike. The branch's 200 public use computers—another 160 are reserved for TCC students—are in constant use, while the numerous study rooms are regularly filled to capacity, says Poole.

"The interior design is focused on unifying available services, making high activity zones conveniently located and creating technology-rich individual and group study destinations," says Hickok, adding that the sense of equity and co-ownership is also reflected in how library staff interact with one another. "All staff, whether college or city, report to one library director and all nonowner-specific spaces… are supervised by both the city and college staff."

In all, VBPL provides 27 employees for the library, while TCC con-

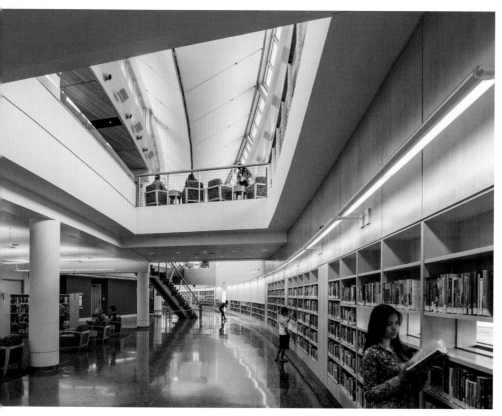

tributes 29, with all staff overseen by Director Sarah Greene. VBPL and TCC staff the circulation desks in equal number; patrons checking out a book or paying a fine could be interacting with folks from either system on any given day. The upstairs reference desk is staffed primarily by TCC employees, while the downstairs children's area is mostly managed by VBPL librarians.

This hybrid situation has made for some unexpected synergies and opportunities for partnerships. One win is around early learning. "Our children's librarian and one of the TCC academic librarians hold sessions for the Early Childhood Development classes on the campus," Neva White, VBPL's community services manager at the library, points out. "The academic librarian can speak to the students about how to find information for assignments and such, but the children's librarian is much more experienced at talking with the students about the practical side of choosing books that are appropriate for differing ages and developmental stages of children."

Serving two distinct communities also means that the library is open different hours than the standard VBPL branches, making it accessible to patrons who aren't as well served by other locations. On weekdays, it opens at 7:30 a.m., a full two and a half hours before any other branch, and doesn't close until 9 p.m.

"Those who want to pick up items before they head into their jobs can do that, and students needing to print that last-minute assignment before class have time to do that," says White. "We get to see working families who can't quite make it to the branches that close at 7 p.m. and people who like to get going early in the morning who can visit us between 7:30 a.m. and 10 a.m."

The dual nature of the library, says Litherland, has strengthened the relationship between TCC and the larger Virginia Beach community. Daily visits run between 1,000 and 1,500, and while the library doesn't distinguish between students and public patrons, both populations get a library that is enhanced with an added element of service for the other.

"The facility, collections, and services are an incredible resource for the community, drawing them onto the college campus and illuminating the benefits of lifelong learning," says Litherland. "TCC students now have convenient access to a great popular collection and outstanding children's library programming."

Both collections are available for all patrons to borrow, though the rules of each differ and govern how a given item will circulate. That means a TCC student who doesn't have a VBPL card can check out anything from the library collection, but if it's VBPL's item, the city library will determine the due date and so forth. The same goes for VBPL members who want to check out items from the TCC collection. A custom connector links the two ILS systems, and patrons can choose to search a combined catalog or browse the two collections separately. Services like subscriptions and interlibrary loan are managed independently by the two library systems, but while they're at the joint library, patrons have access to the full, combined suite.

Early teamwork required To those considering similar collaborative projects, Poole points out that one of the challenges is simply how many moving parts are involved on both sides. Litherland concurs. "Coming from the academic side of librarianship, I'll say I wish I'd known more about public libraries, their priorities, operations, funding issues," he says.

Litherland and Poole both agree that communication from the very first step is key, and that it's never too early to get people on both sides of the table involved in planning and brainstorming. Oh, and expect a big table.

"Make sure you get the frontline staff from both entities working together...from the very beginning," says Poole. "Our opening design sessions involved faculty, staff of both organizations, students, and the community."

That early teamwork served to overcome skepticism about the project and put people in a "we could actually do this" mind-set. Instead of looking for reasons the project couldn't work, the team began seeking opportunities in which they could work together—and finding them.

Still, the work of collaboration is ongoing. "We had to work very hard to learn each other's styles and goals, and we continually do things together like hold staff meetings, management meetings, team building activities, and training," says White. Luckily, though, one design characteristic has helped to foster closeness between the two staffs. "Having one lounge means we have to share a rather small space to house our lunches and microwaves, which means we'd have to interact with each other whether we wanted to or not."

Poole adds another piece of advice: don't expect everything to go smoothly from day one, and make understanding among staff members a priority. "It will be rough in the beginning, because the culture of academic libraries and public libraries is very different," Poole tells *LJ.* "We worked very hard to do joint training, social events, and shadowing with the staff so that we all understood how our jobs fit in with each other."

Beyond having staff comprehend the goals and mission of their colleagues from the other system, White says the crux to working together effectively is getting them to work toward one another's goals.

"At VBPL, we make it very clear to staff that one of our goals is to increase student enrollment at TCC, and the TCC staff understand that one of their goals is to make sure that children have strong literacy skills before they enter school," White tells *LJ.* "For us all, we understand that everyone who walks into the building is a student or a potential student, and they want to make sure they get the best service possible."

Ian Chant is a former editor at LJ *and a freelance journalist whose work has appeared in* Scientific American *and* Popular Mechanics *and on* NPR

3
classic buildings updated

REVITALIZING LOCAL LANDMARKS

They say the greenest buildings are the ones that already exist. While renovating or expanding cultural landmarks can be tricky at best, the projects here—shared from *LJ*'s design coverage since 2009 as originally published—illustrate just how dynamic, uplifting, and anchoring the results can be. Many of these projects are now live and serving their communities with grandeur, but the insights from the process resonate.

Growing Room

St. Louis Public Library completes a major
renovation that respects a 101-year-old design
By Marta Murvosh

There was never a doubt that the St. Louis Central Library building would remain a library and be restored, St. Louis Public Library (SLPL) executive director Waller McGuire tells *LJ*. Patrons love to tell McGuire of their first experience at the library when they were children and a parent or grandparent led them up the granite steps and into the marbled Grand Hall. "The St. Louis community and beyond has a real attachment to the Central Library building," McGuire says. "The St. Louis community loves Central."

However, what was in doubt was the footprint. The original plan called for a proposed expansion outside the building's original granite walls. But a local architectural firm took the risk of trying to convince library leaders that was the wrong way to go.

Two years and $55 million later, the risk appears to have paid off. The restored and renovated 101-year-old Central Library reopened on December 9, 2012. Together, architects and librarians had almost doubled the square footage open to the public without expanding the original walls an inch.

Inside, SLPL patrons are discovering new spaces that serve dedicated readers, serious researchers, teens and children, and people exploring technology or recording their own music.

Underneath marble and wood floors and inside 19th-century ventilation, shafts run the power cords and fiber-optic cables to blend with 21st-century technology services, including expanded Wi-Fi and newly added self-checkout. The past, the present, and the future live side by side on the second floor in the Great Hall, with the original oak reading desks retrofitted to provide power for library users and brighter and energy-efficient lights glowing in century-old bronze fixtures.

In the middle of the first floor, the Center for the Reader offers 5,700 square feet of space dedicated to popular reading. Quotes from books emboss the recessed ceiling, and the furniture invites people to curl up or to gather for impromptu discussions. "We wanted to create that sort of rich, beautiful, convenient environment dedicated to the story," says McGuire. "We placed that in the heart of the building."

"Pretty risky" Initially, SLPL leadership wanted to expand the Central Library to create room for a computer commons and other services, McGuire says. A consultant recommended adding onto the library to meet the needs of 21st-century library users.

The architects at Cannon Design of St. Louis, one of the firms vying to work on the historic Carnegie building, had a different idea. Cannon recommended that we "don't touch the exterior walls," McGuire says.

Cannon's lead architect, George Z. Nikolajevich, says he wanted to respect as much as possible the original design created by Cass Gilbert, the 19th-century architect who also built the U.S. Supreme Court building and New York's Woolworth Building.

Inspired by Renaissance palaces in Italy, Gilbert designed the Central Library to be constructed of Maine granite, white oak, marble, and Carnegie steel. With high ceilings decorated with molded plaster and carved and painted wood, including one inspired by Michelangelo's ceiling in the Laurentian Library, the Beaux Arts–style building is often referred to by St. Louis residents as the people's palace.

Rather than expand the library's footprint, Nikolajevich and the

Cannon team sought ways to preserve Gilbert's original intent while increasing the space available to the public. As a result, a coal bin became a 250-plus-seat auditorium, while bathrooms and staff locker rooms were transformed into centers for discovering popular books and new technology. Where seven stories of book stacks previously created a fire and earthquake hazard, Nikolajevich found room for a computer commons, a café, a staff lounge, special collections storage, and a northern entrance and service point.

Working inside the existing structure would result in a "huge costs savings," and Cannon's ideas found favor with SLPL's Board of Directors, McGuire says. "It's pretty risky for architects not to listen to the owners," McGuire says. "It was really smart of the board. Instead of saying no and getting their back up, they said, 'We agree. We like their proposal.'"

DEFT TOUCHES (clockwise from above left): SLPL's historic facade, both today and yesterday (inset). Engraved with thousands of titles from the library's collection, a stainless steel canopy arises from a pool of water outside the new north entrance. The canopy shelters visitors but doesn't touch the historic facade. SLPL's Great Hall maintained its grandeur even as the rest of the library gained flexibility. The new north atrium offers views of a computer commons and the special collections (the latter is closed to the public). The atrium takes the place of seven stories of closed stacks, with glass floors that were a fire and earthquake hazard and gives the library a north entrance onto Lucas Park

Inspiring history Central Library first opened on January 6, 1912, thanks to Andrew Carnegie's $1 million gift, half of which was to offset a $1.5 million cost for Central. "It was designed to be a place to be inspired and uplifted," McGuire says.

At the core of the Central Library was the delivery room, where the public asked for books that were stored behind the scenes in the "stacks" in the north wing, says Abigail Van Slyck, an art history professor and the associate dean of the faculty at Connecticut College, a private liberal arts college in New London, and an expert on the history of Carnegie libraries. The natural light pouring in from three sides is a metaphor for the enlightenment from the books, says Van Slyck. "One of the things that these buildings like the St. Louis Library show us is that we did lose something there in terms of spiritual uplift," Van Slyck says.

When construction workers removed the main service desk in the delivery room for restoration, they discovered that a century of foot traffic had worn the two-inch-thick marble in front of the desk to a quarter inch. "That's 100 years of patrons asking for service," McGuire says. "That means something to a librarian."

Preparations In order for the Central Library to close its bronze doors temporarily in June 2010, SLPL had to renovate two other buildings. The entire project cost $70 million. The bulk of the funds came from bonds being repaid by taxpayers and the SLPL Foundation's capital campaign that had raised $18 million as of March. The foundation only needs to raise $2 million more to meet its $20 million goal. The foundation has become a powerful asset that the library did not have ten years ago, when planning the restoration began, McGuire says. "They

did it stepping out in one of the worst economic climates. The library wouldn't have been able to take it on."

To free up space for public services, SLPL decided to move all support services from Central across the street to the newly renovated administrative center, which cost $300,000. This opened up space for public use. (SLPL also remodeled 200,000 square feet of the administrative center for a charter high school that pays rent to SLPL, offsetting repayment of the $45 million bond for the Central renovation, according to McGuire.)

Next, SLPL spent more than $2 million to renovate the Compton building, which also acted as a temporary public reference facility for the library's local history, genealogy, and government documents collections while Central was closed, McGuire says. Compton continues to house SLPL's digitization center and much of the historic document and serials collections. Some of Central's collections will remain at Compton. Finally, SLPL staff installed 26 miles of shelving, plus staff, in a former warehouse to store temporarily most of Central's four million items, so that collection could be shipped to SLPL's 16 other branches while Central was closed.

As a result of moving the administrative offices, Central Library opened up 38,800 square feet of public space for a net total of 84,690 square feet, says Lynn S. Grossman of Cannon Design and one of Central Library's project architects (along with Matthew Huff). To meet the demand for increased services at Central, 10.5 full-time equivalent employees (FTE) were added, totaling 94.5 FTE, McGuire says.

Removing the stacks One major challenge the architects and library leaders faced was Central's confined seven stories of bookshelves built like "tinker toys" on top of one another, McGuire says. Glass floors separated each cramped section of the stack tower. "I'm six-four, and I had to duck in some places in the stack tower," he says.

Closed to the public, the stacks floated like a separate structure within the walls of Central's north wing. Yet what made the "stacks" a 19th-century engineering feat also made them a modern fire and earthquake hazard for the staff, say architects and library leaders.

Cannon's Nikolajevich says he was inspired by the idea of a building floating within a building. The architect converted the north wing housing the stacks into an atrium. He then used glass walls for the com-

ENGAGING YOUNGER PATRONS Top: teens are invited to "DREAM" in the new 2,200 square foot teen lounge, with typography and rainbow glass designed by Deanna Kuhlmann, a St. Louis graphic designer. Right: the children's area was also expanded, with an additional 2,500 square feet for story time and crafts, and brightened with quotes from children's books and designs also created by Kuhlmann

puter commons planned for the second floor and new staff rooms and special collections storage on the third floor to create the appearance of floating rooms. "The trick is to find the balance in new and old," Nikolajevich says.

Once the stacks were removed from the north wing, light poured in from the windows that Gilbert designed, flooding the space. Through the glass, the library was now connected to Lucas Park in a way it hadn't been, says Lynn S. Grossman, the Central Library's interior architect. "The first time we saw that space and the windows open to the park, it was just breathtaking," Grossman says.

To give the public a northern entrance, a few lower windows were converted into doorways to the atrium, channeling patrons to an information desk. Outside the entrance, Nikolajevich designed a 15-foot-tall stainless steel canopy that appears to float on a reflecting pool to shelters library patrons from the elements, McGuire says. The canopy does not touch the historic façade.

The public submitted their favorite quotes from works found in the library, and 10,000 phrases were engraved into the steel. "That was George Nikolajevich's baby," McGuire says. "After he designed it, I wanted to scribble all over it."

Auditorium The new auditorium and restored Great Hall have attracted outside groups interested in the library as a venue for special events. The Partnership for Downtown St. Louis held its gala fundraiser in the Great Hall in January, shortly after the library reopened. Acknowledging the interest in the library as a venue, the SLPL Foundation has funded an events coordinator, McGuire says. The library is seeking a partner willing to pay $3 million for naming rights to the auditorium.

Open on Sundays On the first floor, gutting offices, aging bathrooms, and a staff locker room resulted in a gain of 12,260 square feet, bringing the total to 29,710. This space houses the Center for the Reader, the teen and children's areas, and popular nonfiction titles, such as science and technology.

By collocating all the more popular items on one floor for easy access

by library users, Central staff also can open just the first floor, allowing the library to open on Sunday with a skeleton crew. "It hasn't been opened on Sundays before. On Sundays, we only open the first floor and that is manageable and affordable," McGuire says.

The children's library has increased by 2,500 square feet for story time and crafts and been brightened with quotes from children's books and colorful statues.

A glass wall striped in rainbow colors and "DREAM" in huge white letters marks the 2,200 square foot teen lounge and invites teens inside to Central's first dedicated teen space.

Nearby, musically inclined patrons can mix their own CDs in a recording studio, while the Creative Experience offers 1,640 square feet dedicated to showcasing state-of-the-art technology, interactive computing, and collaborative learning and play, McGuire says. "We wanted to create these areas of delight and serendipity and appeal."

Grand stairs and hall The granite staircase to the second floor entrance on Olive Street required $1 million as construction crews numbered each granite slab as it was removed. The structure beneath the steps was repaired, and stoneworkers then reassembled the granite blocks like a giant puzzle, McGuire says.

Once up the stairs, patrons walk through the Olive Street lobby and proceed into what many call the heart of Central Library, the Great Hall

Reading Room, which lovers of the library describe as the spirit of the building and a symbol of the illumination that libraries bring to communities. As part of the restoration, the bronze tubes once used for delivering books were saved and polished. The ornamental ceiling plaster was repaired from damage incurred during the 1950s when fluorescent lights were installed, according to Cannon architects.

On the second and third floors, crews discovered space under the marble floors left by the 19th-century craftsmen where they could now install wires for electricity, cables, and routers for Wi-Fi and other technology, Grossman says. Hidden ventilation shafts designed by Gilbert were now going to accommodate modern wiring, heating, and cooling ducts and fire protection systems. "This was amazing, forward-thinking by Cass Gilbert," Nikolajevich says.

Renovated light fixtures and LED lights in stacks increased illumination. Enclosed on two sides with glass, a computer commons brings in light from the windows in the north wing's atrium.

Another challenge of a historic library was to create an intuitive flow from one section to another and locate resources so users could conveniently find them, McGuire says. The fine arts and architecture rooms are located near the library's literature and performing arts collections. Government documents and resources for business, law, and languages are clustered together. Philosophy, religion, psychology, and social sciences also are located together. "It was another way to make this very remarkable and structured building work for us," McGuire says. "We tried to design connectivity."

CREATING SPACE (Clockwise from top left): Modern lighting, including book shelves illuminated with LED lights, brighten the adult literature room, which will be renamed the Waller F. McGuire Room. The oak tables and the painted ceiling beams were cleaned and restored. Five rooms were added to the library for training or meetings. The Creative Experience features interactive computer screens and space devoted to new technology and collaborative learning and is located on the library's first floor

Away from the bustle By removing the warren of offices from the third floor and returning to Gilbert's original walls, the library's public space increased by almost five times, from 4,020 square feet to 19,360 square feet. Modern compact shelving prevented the rooms from feeling overwhelmed, McGuire says.

Stairwells with stained glass windows were opened to the public, and, in the Carnegie room, a skylight was rediscovered. Historic photos were reproduced, enlarged, and hung.

The third floor now holds genealogy, St. Louis studies and history, plus rare book and special collections, all collocated to make things easier for researchers. The furnishings are configured to serve people who will spend days on projects, but, at the same time, the worktables don't isolate the library users. "The genealogists, for example, are a passionate bunch who like that they can work away from bustle and that they can form connections across the table," McGuire says.

Economic impact Besides having a place in the hearts of St. Louis residents, the restoration of Central Library also put money in the community's pocketbook and helped the decade-long revitalization of the city's downtown core.

Since construction began on Central in 2010, three other downtown buildings have been developed as mixed-use projects, providing housing and commercial sectors and making a "significant impact," says Maggie Campbell, president and CEO of the Partnership for Downtown St. Louis, which manages the 165 square block Downtown St. Louis Community Improvement area. According to Campbell, in recent years, the downtown has been the fastest growing residential neighborhood in the region.

The restoration project was projected to create 431 direct and indirect jobs, according to a 2009 economic impact study commissioned by SLPL. Multiplier effects were expected to pump an additional $120.8 million into the regional economy, according to the study by Development Strategies, a St. Louis-based economic development consulting firm. McGuire says that when construction was under way, an average of 100 people were working on the proj-

ect. Many of the contractors and artisans on the project are based in the city, he says.

The library board hired contractors that employed women and minorities, McGuire says. In St. Louis, minorities make up 56.1 percent of the population, and 26 percent of the city's 318,000 residents live below poverty level, according to the Bureau of the Census's 2012 estimates. The board felt the focus on diversity helped many people during the recession and has since decided that the library should continue this policy. "We're a challenged city—economically challenged and educationally challenged," McGuire says. "Like many cities, you have great wealth and great poverty cheek to jowl."

As for the impact on the library's own economics, though there are a few construction tasks remaining, McGuire says he expects the project will come in two or three percent under budget.

Marta Murvosh, MLS, is a freelance writer/researcher and aspiring librarian living and working in Northwestern Washington. You can follow her via www.facebook.com/MartaMurvosh

History Updated

A green redo reinvigorates a neoclassical gem

By Teresa L. Jacobsen

After completing a complicated four-plus-year construction project, the Golden State is seeking silver this time—a Leadership in Energy & Environmental Design (LEED) Silver certification for its newly renovated Stanley Mosk Library and Courts Building, to be precise. The reopening celebration for the California State Library (CSL) was held in February and capped a remarkable collaborative effort led by California's Department of General Services (DGS), landlords of the property.

The CSL and the Third District Court of Appeals share tenancy in half of a matched set of neoclassic buildings located near California's Capitol building, in downtown Sacramento.

Time had not been kind to this 1920s-era structure, and the DGS knew that meeting its goals—public safety, fire suppression, American with Disabilities Act (ADA) requirements, and the removal of hazardous substances—would be challenging.

Undoing unimprovements Rude surprises awaited the contractors behind every wall. The walls themselves—where one might have hoped to thread cabling and pipe—were solid. Therefore, most of the rework occurred in the ceiling crawl spaces. The plumbing system had dead ends and defied logic, becoming a total redo.

Hi-Fog, a relatively new form of fire suppression designed to use 80 percent less water than a typical water-based system, was installed throughout—with superb camouflaging. Only careful examination can discover the disguised sprinkler heads in the gorgeous painted ceilings.

The core of the five-story edifice houses two light wells and a stack tower, and this area had suffered over the years. HVAC ducting, installed in the 1970s, had closed off the light wells. These wells are now uncovered, bringing in natural light. Where artificial light is necessary, dropped ceilings and fluorescent panels have been replaced with the original chandeliers. Sent out to specialists for restorative work, they now host most compact fluorescent and LED bulbs.

Numerous windows, suffering from dry rot, were repaired and now sport low-e (low-emissivity) coating. Motorized window shades throughout the building replaced mangled venetian blinds and sun-worn draperies.

Emergency exit routes used to be a bit dicey. Now two emergency stairwells are easily accessible and each floor includes an ADA area of refuge. Improvements throughout make it possible for the wheelchair-bound to get into the building and navigate all floors with ease.

For the library visitor, the most striking two rooms are on the third floor. The Circulation Room, with its two bronze statues, leaded windows, and marble tile floor, retains a wall of card catalogs (a nostalgic touch that's popular with the public). A circulation desk and black linoleum had covered the tile floor detailing since 1954.

PERIOD DETAILS (Clockwise, from top): Updates like smoke detectors, fire-suppression heads, and security cameras are unobtrusive against the Frank Van Sloan mural in the memorial vestibule; reference librarian Suzanne Grimshaw helps a customer in the Gillis Reading Room; and the newly uncovered floor tile in the circulation room

Across the hall, two massive leather-covered doors (new cowhides were required!) open to reveal the breathtaking Gillis Reading Room, bathed in natural light and dominated by a stunning Maynard Dixon mural. Dixon, one of the West's most prominent artists, painted the mural in 1928. The room's floors are new cork, designed to mimic the original. Amid the period details, modern scanners and printers are available, and the Wi-Fi is robust.

Working around the work All occupants needed to relocate during the renovation. CSL has a second facility (the Annex) across the street, so some materials and staff could go there. A warehouse seven miles away in West Sacramento became home to the Mosk Building's approximately 35 miles of compact shelving and 15 of its library staffers. David Cismowski, chief, State Library Services Bureau, noted that although budget limitations required that existing compact shelving be reinstalled in the Mosk Building, new shelving has been purchased for the nearby Annex. Staff and materials have been moving back since mid-2013.

In a recent phone conversation, former state librarian Susan Hildreth (now director, U.S. Institute of Museum and Library Services) commented that a massive undertaking such as this gives impetus to "rethinking the service strategy." Early on in the process, she was able to broker a deal with the courts whereby the Annex now totally belongs to the library, while the courts acquired space in the Mosk Building. This agreement helped streamline a previously awkward workflow.

A success—affordably Pella McCormick, project director, is frequently credited with the success of the project. Shelley Whitaker took over from McCormick in late 2012 and closed the work. "The advertisement for services thoughtfully addressed the scope of the project, not the least of which was the preservation of the extensive historic elements of the building," she wrote in an email. "Along with the skilled team that Carey and Company [architects] brought to the project, Pella created a broad outreach with the client end users that kept them not only part of the design and decision-making process but kept them involved and informed along the way."

The project came in under budget, costing roughly $49 million.

For Gary Kurutz, curator emeritus of special collections and the executive director of the CSL Foundation, the final results are dramatic. He told *Library by Design* that the contractors did a "remarkable job of respecting historicity" and that he "could not have been more pleased."

The California Preservation Foundation recognized the renovation as one of 20 "outstanding" projects for 2013.

Teresa (Terry) L. Jacobsen is a retired California librarian. She has served as LJ's Mystery columnist since 2011

A Cutting-Edge Undertaking

Connecting old and new with a Main Street mentality By Ann Kim

Having received the largest grant in the history of the Massachusetts Board of Library Commissioners, $10.7 million, the Cambridge Public Library restored its 27,200 square foot landmark main building and expanded it with a striking 76,700 square foot glass-enclosed addition. A decade-long undertaking, with a total project cost of $90 million, the library opened in October 2009.

Susan Flannery, director of libraries, architects William Rawn Associates and Ann Beha Architects, and the 18-member Design Advisory Committee based their vision on the principles of transparency, inclusiveness, and sustainability.

The transparent library The main feature exemplifying those principles is the 180'-long, 42'-high double-skin curtain wall—the first comprehensive U.S. application of such a system by Gartner Steel and Glass GmbH, based in Würzburg, Germany. It transmits daylight deep into the building, maximizes thermal comfort in reading areas along the glass, provides a connection between patrons and the civic park just outside, and saves energy.

The double-skin system consists of inner and outer glass walls separated by a three-foot-deep multistory flue cavity—a passageway for directing air currents—that works like a chimney. Its movable sunshades (which also act as a light shelf to reflect daylight onto the ceiling and deeper into the space) balances the light levels to avoid glare.

Sustainable strategies That double-skin façade is only the most noticeable sustainable feature of the structure, which has been submitted for Leadership in Energy & Environmental Design (LEED) certification.

Other green strategies include open

space enhancements that increased the park area by half an acre; the 33,000 square foot green roof with four inches of soil to allow tree planting; a 400,000-gallon neighborhoodwide storm-water management facility; a construction waste recycling program that diverted 95 percent of construction waste from landfills; and the use of low-VOC paints, adhesives, carpeting, and other materials.

A makeover, in and out The original building, listed on the National Register of Historic Places, also received a face-lift, care of Ann Beha Architects. The original façade of brownstone and granite was cleaned and restored, the stone porch entrance was transformed to include an outdoor seating area, and major spaces within the library were renovated to include an Information Commons and a YA room and lounge.

During the programming stages, participants searched for a way to connect the new wing with the historic building. The solution was to divide the new wing into four zones that run lengthwise and parallel to the curtain wall. The center zone acts as a Main Street, housing the circulation and service desks and running through the addition and the historic wing, which largely consists of reading and computer areas.

The community's "civic heart" At the library opening, over 1700 residents gathered and checked out 5000 items by the end of the day. The hybrid nature of the facility—with elements of both a bookstore and a library—make it possible for users to find a quiet area to read and study or a social space to talk and eat or drink. Flannery notes that "there is an intuitive quality about these spaces and it has worked amazingly smoothly."

Circulation is up 70 percent over the same period last year, and program attendance for library-sponsored events is up 175 percent. More twentysomethings are taking advantage of the free Wi-Fi, while the teen lounge "has been successful beyond our wildest imaginings," says Flannery. "The most reliable manifestation of success is that the library is filled from opening to closing each day with residents of all ages. All parts of the building are equally used, with individuals finding just the right space."

With the historic wing restored and its interior spaces reconfigured to adapt to modern times, the glass addition welcoming visitors and patrons, open and accessible spaces throughout, and sustainable strategies, Cambridge Public Library has redefined what it means to be the "civic heart" of the community.

Ann Kim is a New York–based freelance writer and editor

Lighting Quality, Not Quantity

A selective lighting approach yields wholesale rewards
for Madison Public Library By Traci Engel Lesneski & Carla Gallin

When it comes to thinking about lighting, two common misconceptions dominate library design. The first is that cutting energy consumption equals sustainability—it doesn't. Then there's the notion that everything in a library space should be equally lit, which in practice just means that lighting fails to draw attention to or emphasize any part of the space. Dashing these notions guided the lighting design during the renovation of Madison Public Library's (MPL) Central Library, WI. The result is an architecturally integrated lighting system that helps to transform a decrepit 1965 building into a state-of-the-art facility, registered for Leadership in Energy & Environmental Design (LEED) Gold certification, with a highly flexible architectural interior and an operational lighting demand almost half of what is allowed by code.

The architectural design of the renovated Central Library addresses sustainability on many levels, most notably through the use of a raised-floor mechanical plenum, ultra-efficient mechanical systems, a photovoltaic (PV) array, and a green roof. Windows were expanded to let in more daylight, simultaneously cutting power consumption and lighting the space in a way that organically connects users to the time of day and the weather. Each lounge chair, study table, computer table, display kiosk, and book range/row of shelving is designed to be moved. Thus the library can be fully reconfigured to address ongoing shifts in library service, collection storage, and spaces for collaboration without undertaking another renovation. Meeting the energy targets and providing a healthy, high-quality library interior required developing a selective lighting system combined with automated lighting controls.

The wrong cuts won't last The health and well-being of building occupants depend on lighting that is visually comfortable for reading and navigating the space, as well as glare-free, color-corrected, visually interesting, and at an appropriate level as advised by organizations including the Illuminating Engineering Society of North America.

Designers and engineers must avoid reducing ambient light levels in an effort to lower energy use at the expense of light quality. Though this strategy may result in the minimum recommended light levels, a focus solely on light reduction will result in interior spaces that appear dark thanks to contrast between reading surfaces such as desks and walls. That perception of darkness can create the need for extra lighting down the road. It will also lead users to override daylight compensation controls, which reduce interior light levels based on the amount of daylight available. Once these changes are made, energy savings will be lost.

The renovated MPL Central Library avoids these problems by using a selective lighting system that addresses visual and psychological health as the primary goal and reduces light intensity where appropriate. The result is a 46 percent reduction in lighting energy demand relative to basic code requirements and an energy use reduction of an estimated 70 percent relative to the lighting originally installed in the 1965 building.

A BRIGHT IDEA Winona floor lamps supplement extensive natural light as needed in the W. Jerome Frautschi Madison Room

Unconventional wisdom We have all benefited from studies, like Cornell's groundbreaking 1988 report (bit.ly/1i8XtJ4), that document the importance of interior daylight in improved productivity and emotional wellness and from surveys illustrating that indirect light improves visual comfort. However, these reports do not address whether uniform lighting throughout a space is healthy, visually interesting, or conducive to energy-reduction strategies. Some other examinations suggest that uniform indirect lighting can affect people adversely and most indirect lighting strategies result in high energy consumption.

In general, buildings in the United States are overilluminated. Libraries, where it is most economical at the time of construction to provide one overall ambient lighting system, are no exception to this rule. Library lighting designs consistently incorporate direct/indirect lighting systems as an accepted method of creating visually comfortable and consistent spaces. Conventional wisdom states that a uniform lighting system will allow for more flexibility in the future because book ranges, study areas, and lounge seating can be moved anywhere anytime the library staff choose to do so. However, a single, consistently uniform, lighting system must provide sufficient illumination for the most intensive task: lighting stacks. That means the same lighting system will make study tables, computer tables, and lounge seating overly bright and users uncomfortable while increasing energy costs.

Light where you need it By contrast, the lighting system in the Central Library is fully integrated into the flexible architectural design and optimizes task and surface lighting, with minimal ambient light. The selective lighting system was designed to craft a relaxed, visually

switched off when not needed. Meanwhile, daylight sensors dim the interior electric lighting when sufficient daylight is available. These reductions in lighting use put the typical operational lighting demand at around 0.70 watts/sf, meaning that the library runs 46 percent below the energy code allowance and fully 70 percent below the installed lighting of the building before the renovation.

Light that moves with you The renovation of the Central Branch prioritized increased flexibility, which created a need for mobile furniture, display kiosks, and stacks. A raised floor allows for an underfloor mechanical and electrical distribution system while also strengthening the selective lighting concept, by allowing lighting to be integrated into the furniture, stacks, and lounge seating layouts. Thus, lighting, cords, and plugs are as easy to move as tables, kiosks, seats, and stacks. Receptacles under the raised floor are color-coded to identify specific plug locations for automated building- controlled lighting and equipment, daylight-controlled lighting, and computers and equipment required to be fully on at all times.

The lighting mounted on the book stacks was specifically designed to break apart at 3', 6', or 12' intervals, depending on the length of the shelving range. Sections can be removed incrementally as the size of print collections decreases over time. Electrical codes required the stack lighting to be hard-wired into the underfloor system, but the underfloor electrical boxes can easily be modified when book stacks are ultimately removed.

Visual variety A hallmark of design excellence is visual variety. Successful lighting strategies respond to interior details. The Central Library's unconventional lighting strategy reflects the atypical character of the library's architecture. Visually interesting spaces include variety in scale, texture, color, and especially lighting. At MPL, the design team wished to play up the texture of the existing building's concrete structure and to provide visual interest by creating a variety of light intensity/color/type conditions customized to each function, for instance, in lighting the local art on display. The Madison community has a rich and deep appreciation for the arts, and the design team honored that tradition through integrating art into the building wherever possible. While incandescent lighting has fallen into disfavor of late, it is still the best option for showcasing art. The lighting in the Central Library is primarily fluorescent, but low-voltage halogen lamps accent a historic restored mural and light the third floor gallery. Color-corrected low-voltage MR16 bulbs were specifically chosen for longevity and intensity and can be easily replaced with LED MR16 bulbs when technological advances make those less energy-intensive lights a satisfactory option.

In addition, the children's area reading caves are illuminated via pressure-sensitive pads that trigger the lighting when a child climbs into the cave. A combination of LED and fluorescent strips is used inside the caves: LED for its very small size and sparkle and fluorescent to provide adequate light for reading.

This approach continues even outside the building: the library responded to public concern about the darkness of the adjacent streets "by opening up windows along the street, adding an LED light wall and lighted Madison Public Library sign," Director Greg Mickells says. These served dual purposes, "providing a more welcoming, safer presence and also bringing more visibility to the activity occurring inside the library building. Combined with our lighted 'Question Mark' sculpture, lighting of the building's exterior serves as an ongoing advertisement for the

interesting, and energy-efficient building that can be fully reconfigured without uniform light levels. Lighting was designed based on the visual requirements of specific functions (e.g., reading, browsing, using a computer), and the ambient light in each function zone was intensified to compensate for visual contrast. Overall ambient light is at an appropriate level of 15 footcandles, whereas walls and ceilings are illuminated to develop an impression of brightness, give form and clarity to very large rooms, and reduce contrast owing to daylight. The result is a system that enhances the spatial qualities of the interior and significantly reduces the lighting energy demand while still providing flexibility in how spaces can be used.

"I was excited by the plan to feature up-lighting on the main levels and have been extremely pleased by the results," says Mark Benno, MPL's administrative services manager. "Not only does it soften the glare of traditional fluorescent lighting, but it accents one of the building's strengths: the original waffle slab ceiling. The geometric pattern of the ceiling, combined with light reflecting off of its surface, produces a well-lit environment without harsh, direct light."

Energy codes require lighting systems' electrical demand to be calculated based on the worst-case condition, in which every luminaire that is hard-wired into the building is operating at 100 percent of its rated demand. Lighting power density (LPD) is not modified by reducing lamp wattage or installing controls. As a result, the real life energy savings of setups like Madison's that use those tools will likely be even greater. The Central Library's selective lighting system is designed to operate at a full electrical demand of 0.91 watts per square foot (sf), which is 30 percent below the energy allowed by the code in place at the time of design (2007 code, 1.3 watts/sf). But the lighting in study rooms, conference rooms, service rooms, offices, workrooms, storage rooms, restrooms, and kitchens and at computer and study tables is automatically energy and creativity our visitors can expect to find inside." The exterior lighting uses only 2500 kWh/year, equating to about $350/year.

Working together The most notable lessons learned from the process of redesigning MPL's Central Library emerged from integrating lighting into furniture, coordinating construction trade responsibilities, and managing the sequence of bidding. Furniture, fixtures, and equipment (FF&E) services are typically a separate contract from the architecture, negotiated after the bid for general construction. Lighting is part of the general construction, and electrical contractors are responsible for bidding, purchasing, installing, and energizing hard-wired luminaires. A process was required to allow each trade to bid, provide, and install their respective systems without voiding UL listings and warranties of either the furniture or the fixtures.

Making the MPL lighting scheme flexible and adaptable required close collaboration among the design team, furniture supplier, and lighting manufacturers. Because the table modifications were on a different bidding track from the lighting modifications, the sequence of engineering and specifying the luminaires for the general construction bid became a challenge. Ultimately, the table lights were taken out of the general construction bid and absorbed into the FF&E package. The lu-

electrical conduit, and fluorescent strips for up-lighting and to provide a solid location for attaching the mounting arms for the fixtures that would illuminate the collection. The channels were put into the book stack contract with the intent that they would be structurally attached to and become a seamless part of the completed book ranges for future flexibility, but the process was occasionally trying.

Lighting installation mock-ups and electrical inspections resulted in modifications to the channel, electrical wiring, up-light, and luminaire mounting arm. While the end product is one we're proud of, the road to it could have been simplified and less costly had the channel been specified as part of a complete lighting assembly provided by lighting manufacturers, a lesson that shouldn't be lost on libraries facing similar design decisions.

The coordination extended even to painting: the lighting strategy at the MPL relies heavily on high light reflectance throughout the interior, so white paint and bright surfaces are used wherever practical. In some areas, the light surfaces are at odds with the high use of the library, requiring increased attention to maintenance. Periodic repainting will be an important part of the library's operations going forward.

THE RIGHT LIGHTS
Top: Winona suspended lights help reduce the contrast on surfaces and provide comfortable levels for reading. Bottom: Lighting Services Inc. (LSI) provided track lighting for the third-level gallery. Color-corrected, low-voltage incandescent bulbs were chosen to highlight the art and can be replaced with LEDs as technology advances

Sustainable savings
To achieve this lighting strategy took about one-third more design and coordination time up-front as compared to a more conventional lighting approach, such as recessed direct/indirect lighting and a modest number of accent lights. It also cost more: the lighting itself cost approximately $11/sf in 2011 dollars, compared to a conventional lighting approach at $6–$7/sf. But in the long term, the 70 percent energy savings this will produce will recoup those up-front expenditures. For MPL, this equates to roughly $33,000 per year in savings. While energy costs and savings will vary with specific locations, it seems clear that taking a fresh look at library lighting can help save the pocketbook as well as the planet.

minaires were factory- modified as required for the table stands and fitted with cords and plugs. The furniture manufacturer then purchased them and installed the table stand, table attachment, and luminaire as part of a single table assembly.

Coordinating lighting installations on the book stacks required a considerable amount of building trade and design team coordination during construction. The lighting installation was designed with a channel attached to the top of the book range to conceal ballasts, junction boxes,

Traci Engel Lesneski is head of interiors and Principal, MSR. She spoke on library design at the 2013 American Library Association (ALA) annual conference in Chicago, has contributed articles to New Library World *and* LJ, *and is chair of the ALA LLAMA/BES Architecture for Public Libraries Committee. Carla Gallina is the Design Principal of Gallina Design LLC. She currently serves on the Illuminating Engineering Society of North America (IESNA) Library Lighting Committee. Her work has been published in* Architectural Lighting Magazine, EC&M Magazine, *and* LJ's Library by Design

Is Your Library Accessible?

Providing equal access to your historic building can spur
other crucial updates By Philip O'Brien

"Sure we're accessible, there's a handicapped sign on the boiler room door out back." Does this sound like your library's accessibility solution?

Making your public library accessible to the handicapped can be complicated and expensive, and it may even reduce your usable space, but getting it done is more important than ever, and it can improve the function of your library for everyone.

According to the American Library Association (ALA), there are nearly 17,000 public libraries in the United States. In its most recent (2010) Public Library Survey, the Institute of Museum and Library Services reports visits to public libraries totaled 1.5 billion, or 5.1 library visits per capita. These numbers are continuing to rise, and the recession has spurred demand even further. Given these trends, the aging of America's population, and the Americans with Disabilities Act (ADA) requirements, providing equal access to all is the right thing to do—and soon.

Where to begin? The town of North Brookfield, MA, is home to the beautiful Haston Free Public Library, which was donated to the town by Mr. and Mrs. Erastus Haston in 1894. Since then, no substantial renovation work had been done until a recent remodel and restoration project was completed in 2007.

The Haston library is an elegant, Richardsonian structure on a prominent site in the center of North Brookfield. The building encompasses two stories, with a full basement, and is clad in granite with a red slate roof. The site slopes steeply from front to back so that the front entrance is on the main level, while the basement exits at grade at the rear. Prior to the renovation, only one room was accessible in the basement at the rear of the building, but the floor itself wasn't safe to walk on owing to serious rot that disconnected it from the stone foundation. The children's department, housed in a nearby room on the basement level, could only be reached via a narrow stair from the main level. The main floor of the library was entered only via the original stone steps to the front door, and the upper floor was closed to the public. Where to begin?

Providing access that works requires three things: money to make the changes, space to accommodate the clearances required, and careful planning, which will also help reduce the money and space needed.

An effective access project can also help maintain, and in some cases improve, library circulation, security, and control. A successful plan grows from understanding the access upgrades required and how best to incorporate access effectively into your library's day-to-day operation.

Public libraries have very specific workflow and control needs, which are both integral to their daily operation and unique to these institutions. Maintaining security and command in this type of environment can be very challenging and has traditionally been accomplished through a combination of controlled access, monitored circulation points, and visual supervision. Accessibility upgrades should reinforce these control systems, not short-circuit them.

This, then, was the plan for the Haston Library: make every existing square foot count and provide additional space for collections, computers, and places to work and read. Maintain access for all, to all three levels, and do so in a safe and secure manner so that existing staff could maintain the library without a reduction of service.

And get the kids out of the basement.

Challenges and solutions The challenges in North Brookfield were not unlike those in many historic libraries. In fact, they read like a top ten list of small-town, historic library concerns: small site; little room for expansion; beautiful, historic exterior and interior finishes; no room for new stairs or an elevator; leaking basement and roof; antiquated heating, plumbing, and electrical systems; and only minor renovations over the past 100 years.

The solutions lie in focusing on library service to create a plan that not only provides access for the disabled but improves access for all, in an efficient, easy-to-supervise manner. In too many cases, libraries install accessibility upgrades as stopgap measures that seldom stand the test of time, often do not fully comply with access codes, and short-circuit security and control systems. After all, who is really watching your boiler room door?

Identify barriers Consider access strategies that are durable, maintainable, and integrated into the existing fabric and circulation of your building. Changes that accommodate both the handicapped and able-bodied reduce cost and consolidate supervision requirements and go a long way toward providing universal access.

The ADA, and many building codes, requires total access to all spaces, equipment, and materials in your building. Regulations extend from the size of doors to the slope of sidewalks, from the type of flooring to the furniture selected. Careful planning and decision-making is required to ensure that all patrons and staff can be served with little or no repetition in services.

Start with a barriers survey of your building and grounds. This will help identify current barriers to access and determine the severity of the access issues. The ADA has a checklist (see Further Reading) that can help you identify concerns and generate your survey. Historic libraries may have preservation restrictions, or other regulations imposed by a local historic commission, that limit options. Indeed, any library building can have important features that could be marred by access improvements such as a ramp or lift.

Winning solution for all users The best design solutions for identified access barriers address each of your project parameters in some way. It may not be possible to develop the "perfect solution" for every problem. The trick is identifying what works best for your library, your patrons, and your budget. This may mean reviewing a variety of solutions early on, vetting those that don't fit, taking the best from the remaining ideas, and combining and refining them until they do work for you.

At the Haston library, the winning remedy included a small addition off the two-story high-stack wing. This provided the needed square footage to accommodate accessible stairs, an elevator, toilets, and a new accessible main entrance. The rotted basement floors were replaced, and the entire basement was renovated and waterproofed and now houses the reference, nonfiction, and local history collections, as well as meeting spaces. A new "bridge" was constructed across the two-story stack wing to connect the floors of the upper level, resulting in a new, bright, and greatly expanded children's department.

Whether making your building accessible calls for simple upgrades to your existing entrance and toilets or a complete renovation and addition, keeping the focus on library service is critical. Tour other libraries in your area to see what they've done, and note what works and what doesn't work for your facility.

Access solutions that treat all patrons the same, able- bodied or not, are more likely to simplify workflow in and around your building; im-

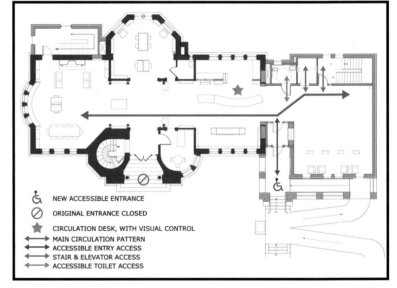

MORE ACCESS FOR ALL A much-needed update to the 1894 Haston Free Public Library created a more functional space for staff and patrons as well as better access on every level. The renovation and addition called for the original entrance to be closed in exchange for a ramped door, a single elongated service desk that allows for a seamless flow of activity and long sight lines, and more

♿ NEW ACCESSIBLE ENTRANCE
⊘ ORIGINAL ENTRANCE CLOSED
★ CIRCULATION DESK, WITH VISUAL CONTROL
→ MAIN CIRCULATION PATTERN
↔ ACCESSIBLE ENTRY ACCESS
↔ STAIR & ELEVATOR ACCESS
↔ ACCESSIBLE TOILET ACCESS

prove visibility, control, and security; and open up more space for library use by eliminating duplicate services.

Look to place your circulation or information desk in a commanding location, with routes for patrons nearby. Creating visual control over internal circulation patterns and access points used by all patrons consolidates tasks for staff, giving them more time for service. In the case of the Haston library, a modest addition effectively tripled the usable square footage inside the building simply by making spaces accessible.

A well-planned accessibility project, when executed with care, can reinvigorate your older or historic building and may even increase circulation. Just as important, it heralds your mission as a public service organization—and your boiler room door can stay closed.

Philip O'Brien (pobrien@johnson-roberts.com), a Principal with Johnson Roberts Associates Inc. in Somerville, MA, has been designing additions and renovations to public libraries and other municipal buildings for 25 years

4
green "LEEDers"

ENVIRONMENTALLY FRIENDLY AND AFFORDABLE STRATEGIES

From rethinking the first steps of the design process to living up to green goals long after the ribbon is cut, these leading libraries—shared from *LJ*'s design coverage since 2009 as originally published—demonstrate that sustainability is a core part of building a library for the future.

Light Done Right

The state of the art in lighting design is also dark sky lighting —
safe, energy efficient, and environmentally sound
By Carla Gallina & Jeffrey Mandyck

Tonight, after dark, go out and take a fresh look at your library. Notice how the lighting works, or works too hard. Is the walkway to the front door bright despite being empty? Is the parking lot, sans cars, aglow? Is light shining in your eyes from the building or grounds? Look up. Can you see stars? Then, imagine light when and where you need it, illuminating a path to the library entrance as you walk along it; a parking lot lit only when occupied; looking up from your screen or book to view the constellations, even the Milky Way. These are not mere futurist fantasies but realistic expectations for improved quality of life and energy savings enabled by the advancing exterior lighting strategies and technologies.

The haphazard lighting currently used to support our 24/7 lifestyles affects our natural rhythm, our physical and spiritual well-being, and our ability to see and study the stars. Continuous illumination also relates to the natural rhythms of animals, birds, reptiles, bugs, and, yes, even plants. More conscious lighting design can help us address these issues, and libraries can set the tone by modeling both appropriate architectural design and environmental stewardship.

Three culprits: light trespass, glare, & sky glow

The quality of night lighting depends on selecting appropriate light levels, reducing or, even better, eliminating glare, and minimizing stray light that involves neighboring properties and wildlife. In making fundamental design choices, visual performance, visual comfort, and energy efficiency all interrelate. If the objective is to improve public safety, security, and wayfinding, the design strategy will certainly include improving how well one can see at night. Eliminating glare will improve visual performance at lower light levels. Eliminating glare and lowering light levels will reduce our energy demand and our impact on the earth. Overillumination, glare, and stray light have an impact on our ability to see our immediate surrounds and tamper with wildlife. This is called light pollution.

Light pollution is defined by three terms: light trespass, glare, and sky glow. Light trespass is electric light that falls beyond property boundaries measured horizontally on the ground and extending vertically to ten feet above the highest structure on the site, such as a building or a light pole. Most local codes and zoning ordinances restrict the amount of light allowed to spill beyond property lines into neighboring sites. Glare includes direct or reflected light that is visually uncomfortable and in extreme cases disables vision altogether. It is a subjective response and is therefore difficult to define and measure. Sky glow results from any light in the sky, electric or celestial, that is reflected by particles in the air. Sky glow masks our clear vision of the night sky, disrupts astronomical observation, and disorients wildlife.

To understand sky glow it is important to note that we do not see light in clean air. We perceive light in the form of illuminated objects —

CALMING CONSISTENCY
Indiana's Carmel Clay Public Library's uniform lighting design looks beautiful as it heightens safety for both pedestrians and vehicles

more technically, objects that reflect light instead of absorbing it. At night, we see airborne matter such as vapor, smoke, gas molecules, dust, and other small particles reflecting the light in the sky. This is what we see suspended over large towns and cities and that defines a disturbing cycle of sky glow, air pollution, and energy production. Namely, excessive exterior lighting necessitates increased energy production. The increase in energy production raises the number of particles and the amount of greenhouse gas in the air, which in turn are amplified by reflecting the excessive light in the sky.

Light quality doesn't equal light quantity

So, how do we light libraries at night with minimal impact on the earth and night sky? The answer is very simple…improve light quality, and switch off the lights.

Light quality doesn't equal light quantity. The most common rationale for nighttime lighting in and around public buildings is safety and security. Our natural inclination to improve security is to increase light levels. However, uniform lighting at an appropriately low intensity is better at helping us see at night than nonuniform light at brighter levels. Consider the way our eyes function: when we walk into a building from bright sunlight, our eyes take time to adjust to the change in intensity.

The same thing occurs at night as we look from highly illuminated zones such as parking lots to less illuminated or nonilluminated zones like walkways or paths. The difficulty of adapting to light and dark zones is further exaggerated by glare, which is intensified by bright light in a

dark surround, much like the headlights of oncoming traffic while traveling a dark road. While glare at night is distracting to most, it is often disabling to the elderly, whose ability to adapt to bright light has diminished by the natural loss of elasticity in muscles that control pupil size.

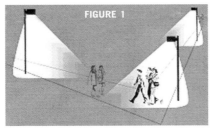

FIGURE 1

Areas of nonuniform light create "black holes" in the visual environment. People or objects located in a dark zone might be hard to see in general and even more so as our eyes adapt from brightness to darkness. People and object recognition is further impaired by silhouetting, which results if the object or person is in front of a relatively intense light or a glare zone. Figure 1 illustrates the effects of nonuniform lighting.

The intensity of light required to illuminate objects adequately at night depends on the site. Exterior lighting at a rural site will appear brighter than the same lighting system installed in a fully developed suburb or city center with a higher ambient light level. The contrast between illuminated and nonilluminated zones at a rural site makes it more difficult to see safety hazards than does the same lighting in a city. The international lighting commission (Commission Internationale

SHIELD OF DREAMS
Minnesota's Saint Cloud Public Library features large overhangs and canopies that offer shade and protection at the entryway and plaza. At the same time, light fixtures and indirect light from the building and the ground are screened, minimizing the amount of light directed into the sky

de l'Eclairage, CIE) developed the lighting zone classifications shown in Table 1 to define areas of high and low ambient light. This classification system has been adopted by the International Dark-Sky Association (IDA), U.S. Green Buildings Council (USGBC), and professional lighting organizations to identify appropriate nighttime light levels for various demographic regions and lighting applications.

Achieving light quality requires putting light only where it is needed. This practice addresses light trespass and sky glow and will be realized primarily through proper selection and placement of light fixtures. Selection of well-designed light fixtures will minimize glare, improve uniformity, reduce energy demand, and minimize uplight (the amount of light that a fixture emits directly into the sky). The Illuminating Engineering Society of North America (IESNA) classifies light fixtures as full cutoff, cutoff, semicutoff, and noncutoff based on the amount of light that is distributed above 80°, which is optimal.

The Leadership in Energy and Environmental Design (LEED) program developed by the USGBC and IDA in their *Outdoor Lighting Code Handbook* combine the CIE zone system with a luminaire classification system similar to that of IESNA's to identify criteria for minimizing light trespass and sky glow. Table 2 provides a summary of LEED criteria for light pollution reduction credits based on these two design metrics.

Applying dark sky design criteria There are numerous guidelines and much basic information available about dark sky design. When planning for a specific site, it is important to keep the big picture in mind as each library type has its own set of use and location circumstances that will direct the outcome of the final design. Local codes and organizations such as IESNA, IDA, and USGBC provide prescriptive criteria for generic installations and light fixture types. Focusing on the restrictive requirements of local codes and LEED criteria will result in an energy-efficient dark sky design. Yet this isolated approach will not

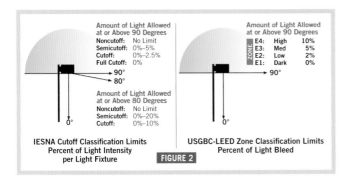

IESNA Cutoff Classification Limits
Percent of Light Intensity per Light Fixture

USGBC-LEED Zone Classification Limits
Percent of Light Bleed

FIGURE 2

ensure light quality, public safety, or an aesthetically appealing design.

In terms of exterior lighting performance, LEED addresses three measurable quantities that contribute to light pollution and energy reduction. Meeting these LEED criteria will ensure that energy demand and lighting controls meet current codes, light levels at a site boundary do not exceed a specified value, and exterior light fixtures emit little or no light above 90°, which is less stringent than the IESNA classifications. However, it is not the intent of the USGBC to define light quality, so it doesn't address the quality of light within the site boundary as expressed in terms of glare, visual comfort, uniformity, safety, security, and other library- and site-specific use requirements. Nevertheless, LEED has created a common vocabulary and set of tools for libraries and design teams to use to evaluate a design and its impact on the environment and the community.

The traditional "shoe box"—the black or dark bronze rectangular light fixtures mounted on a 25' to 40' pole—is without a doubt the most common and cheapest light fixture available offering full cutoff performance, but it is not the only installation type that will meet dark sky or LEED design criteria.

Take St. Cloud Public Library (SCPL), MN, for example. Decorative post-top pedestrian luminaires define a daytime site aesthetic and line the allée along the site entry, while shoe box fixtures mounted on 25' poles are relegated to the parking lot. Post-top luminaires are also located on the pedestrian plaza, downlights are installed in the entry, and pedestrian canopies and recessed step lights define the front edge of the building illuminating the walkway leading to the main entry. This library was designed to be a high-performance, low-energy building. The exterior lighting demands less operational energy than allowed by code, and the decorative luminaires are managed by the building lighting control system, which switches them off one hour after the library closes.

These strategies exceed the intent of a basic LEED design. All of the light fixtures, with the exception of the decorative post-top luminaires and step lights, emit zero percent of their initial fixture lumen into the sky. Each of the 17 post-top luminaires emits 26 percent of its initial fixture lumens above 90°; each of the ten low-wattage step lights emits 50 percent of its initial lumens above 90°. The result of this light fixture mix is that seven percent of the total site lumens are distributed above 90°, above the limit for LEED criteria.

If St. Cloud were a major metropolitan, high–ambient light zone LZ4, this design would easily meet the LEED-allowed uplight criteria of ten percent. However, St. Cloud is a moderately active college town with an ambient light level assigned to LEED zone LZ3, which allows five percent of the total initial designed fixture lumens to be emitted above 90°. If this library had been designated as a LEED project, the design team might have selected a step light with full cutoff shielding from the many aesthetically pleasing styles available. The team might also have selected a decorative post-top luminaire with 19 percent uplight in place of 26 percent, or reduced the lamp wattage of the decorative fixtures, which in turn would reduce the individual fixture lumen, or reduced the number of decorative light fixtures in the design. Any of these minor adjustments would have led to the LEED criteria easily being met without impacting the visual appearance of the site during the day or the light quality at night.

The affordability of quality lighting

The application and construction costs for LEED-certified buildings can sometimes exceed the cost of buildings designed to meet basic high-performance and/or energy- efficiency criteria. This is not necessarily so for site lighting. While high-performance light fixtures will cost more than mediocre light fixtures, the overall site costs may be lower owing to the number of fixtures required for equal light performance of the two fixture types. For instance, while the shoe box is not the most aesthetically pleasing lighting instrument available, it is certainly one of the least costly; if properly designed, a shoe box system will provide good performance without trespass or sky glow.

It is very difficult to estimate general costs for lighting systems because of how they are specified, purchased, and bid. Just as energy costs vary by client, site, and region, so do light fixtures. There are numerous costs added to the price of a basic light fixture such as overhead and profit (O&P) for the manufacturer, the distributor, the electrical contractor, and the general contractor; delivery charges based on location; secure site storage; and the bidding environment. To make the system even more complex, the cost of the hardware is difficult to extract from the total system of installed costs after the bid has been accepted. The exact price of an individual fixture is often buried in the lump sum of the interior and exterior lighting package. Packaging is a lighting industry practice developed to protect the distributor's ability to provide all of the lighting specified for a project and to safeguard distributor and electrical contractor profitability. Lighting professionals request manufacturers' guaranteed pricing in an effort to document cost comparisons and remove the fixture from the lump sum price. However, in the end, prices are not guaranteed until the actual bid has arrived.

The cost savings for implementing dark sky strategies are significant. Though exact cost savings will vary by installation, the sources of the savings are universal. Limiting light intensity and locating light fixtures only where they are needed will reduce costs of energy and initial installation. Switching lights off will reduce energy and long-term lamp replacement expenditures.

Strategies to light by

Light within and without libraries finds its way into the night sky in a variety of ways. Interior light emitted through windows either directly or indirectly contributes to the measured light in the exterior surrounding. After-hours activities such as community gatherings and Internet café operations require parking, paths, and walk-

---

TABLE 1 LIGHTING ZONE CLASSIFICATION SYSTEM

ZONE*	DESCRIPTION	EXAMPLES
E1	Areas with intrinsically dark landscapes	National parks, areas of outstanding natural beauty, areas surrounding major astronomical observatories, or residential areas where residents have strictly limited light trespass.
E1A**	Dark sky preserves	Areas close to major active astronomical research facilities and within and near dark sky preserves or parks that have identified the preservation of the darkest nighttime sky a priority.
E2	Areas of low ambient brightness	Suburban and rural residential areas
E3	Areas of medium ambient brightness	Urban residential areas
E4	Areas of high ambient brightness	Urban areas that have both residential and commercial use and experience high levels of nighttime activity.

* The U.S. Green Buildings Council zones are identified as LZ1, LZ2, LZ3, and LZ4, respectively.
** E1A was added to the CIE list by the International Dark-Sky Association.
SOURCE: Commission Internationale de l'Eclairage (CIE)

TABLE 2 USGBC GREEN BUILDING RATING SYSTEM VERSION 3 LIGHT POLLUTION REDUCTION CRITERIA

ZONE	AMBIENT LIGHT	MAX LIGHT INTENSITY ALLOWED AT THE SITE (FOOT-CANDLES*)		MAX LIGHT INTENSITY ALLOWED BEYOND THE PROPERTY LINE (FOOT-CANDLES)		PERCENTAGE OF FIXTURE LUMENS ALLOWED ABOVE 90°
		HORIZONTAL (FC)	VERTICAL (FC)	LIGHT LIMIT	HORIZONTAL (FC)	
LZ1	Dark	< 0.01	< 0.01	at the property line	< 0.01	0%
LZ2	Low	< 0.1	< 0.1	at 10' beyond line	< 0.01	2%
LZ3	Med	< 0.2	< 0.2	at 15' beyond line	< 0.01	5%
LZ4	High	< 0.6	< 0.6	at 15' beyond line	< 0.01	10%

Foot-candle: the amount of light of one candle measured at a distance of one foot from the flame

PAVING THE WAY Dark brick pavers along the walkway leading to Carthage College's Hedberg Library, Kenosha, WI, are shaded by tall trees, reducing heat gain. The pavers absorb the electric light that illuminates the path at night, limiting light reflected back into the sky

ways to be adequately lit for nighttime use. Lighting above entry doors and at loading docks offers safety for staff and security of the building. After-hours book drops should be well illuminated to help safeguard people and library property. Signage, flags, and architectural details are often illuminated at night to reinforce the importance of the library within the community.

With the exception of illuminating signage, flags, and architectural details, exterior lighting is typically designed to direct light downward to horizontal surfaces such as parking lots and walkways. Even fully downward-directed lighting systems create a potential of adding reflected light into the night sky. Flags, signage, and architectural details are often lit by floodlights on the ground and aimed upward. Most building codes don't require exterior lighting or interior egress lighting to remain on when the building is unoccupied or closed to the public, and herein lies a significant strategy for reducing both energy demand and light pollution.

SWITCH LIGHTS OFF This will reduce the amount of distracting night light released into the environment, save energy, and reduce toxins such as air pollution and greenhouse gases. People are naturally attracted to illuminated areas. Switching interior and exterior lights off signals to the public that the library is closed, discouraging pedestrian and vehicular activity on library grounds after hours. Controlling exterior lights via occupant sensing systems illuminates people when they are present, providing safe paths and parking, alerting neighboring properties and security personnel to site activity. Where switching lights off is not

appropriate, consider dimming the lights when unoccupied. Occupant sensors and time clocks can be used to switch lights on, change light intensity, and trigger a camera response to the location.

IMPROVE LIGHT QUALITY Set goals for light quality based on location, climate, and public use. Lowering light intensity to appropriate levels, improving light uniformity, and reducing glare will enhance security and safety around the library at night and reduce the environmental impact. If designed properly, this can also reduce energy demand. Minimum light levels for parking and pedestrian paths are often identified in local building codes. In its most recent library lighting recommendation RP-4 (to be published in spring 2010), IESNA will document minimum light levels and uniformity ratios for parking areas (see Table 3). It is important to note that adequate light must occur at least 60 inches above the ground surface in order to illuminate people and other vertical objects. Note that lighting energy requirements measured in watts per square foot are not the same as light quality measured in intensity and uniformity. The exterior lighting at Carmel Clay Library, IN, on the cover, provides an example of glare-free uniform light on the library grounds.

REQUIRE TWO POINT-BY-POINT LIGHTING CALCULATIONS FROM YOUR LIGHTING PROFESSIONAL One will show initial light levels, the other will show maintained light levels reduced by age, dirt, and light source depreciation. To document light trespass, request an Outdoor Site Performance (OSP) calculation to show light levels on a horizontal plane located ten feet above the highest element on the site and vertical light levels at the site boundaries. This calculation should be provided for both initial and maintained light levels as well.

REDUCE GROUND REFLECTANCE Lowering the ground reflectance in and around your library will reduce sky glow caused by indirect light emitted from surfaces. Light-colored, hard surfaces such as concrete are typically specified for walks, steps, ramps, and parking areas. The light color is attractive during the day, and because it reflects rather than absorbs radiant energy from the sun, it will reduce heat islands. A natural concrete surface reflects 40 percent of the sunlight, but it also reflects 40 percent of the electric night light, thereby increasing the amount of light that has a potential to become sky glow. Dark surfaces reduce the amount of

| TABLE 3 | MINIMUM REQUIRED LIGHT LEVELS & UNIFORMITY RATIOS FOR PARKING AREAS |

AREA	LIGHT LEVEL MINIMUM (FOOT-CANDLES*)	LIGHT LEVEL VERTICAL AT 60" ABOVE GROUND SURFACE (FOOT-CANDLES)	UNIFORMITY RATIO MAX FOOT-CANDLES/ MIN FOOT-CANDLES
Parking Lots—Basic	0.2	0.25	20:1
Parking Lots—Enhanced Security	0.5	0.25	15:1
Parking Garage	1.0	0.25	10:1

Foot-candle: the amount of light of one candle measured at a distance of one foot from the flame

Reduce Your Footprint

Few libraries have a facilities budget that allows changing lighting for the sole purpose of reducing light pollution. Yet, in many instances reducing light pollution will also result in reduced energy and maintenance costs, which may justify a larger modification program. The following provides a process for identifying lighting requirements and potential operating modifications.

1 **Identify potential lighting improvements. Yes means it needs improvement.**

■ Does your site lighting extend beyond the edge of your property, disturbing neighboring properties?

■ Is your library in a suburban or rural community; near water, parks, or observatories; or at the edge of a nature reserve?

■ Do you have light fixtures that are aimed above 90° or emit light above 90°?

■ Is your entire site illuminated all night?

■ Do you have interior lights located near windows that remain on all night?

2 **Document pedestrian and vehicular use patterns after dark.** Know when neighboring establishments close and how that affects your library's parking and walkways. Identify areas where public safety is threatened; this will be a daytime issue as well as a nighttime issue. Identify any other library- or site-specific vehicle and pedestrian night use.

■ Zone parking lot, walkway, and feature lighting so that they can be controlled separately. This is easy in new construction. Existing libraries may require new relays, wiring, and/or lighting control panel.

■ Install lighting controls and ballasts to dim safety-critical incandescent and fluorescent lights throughout the night. Begin with lights operating at 100 percent until 10 p.m. and reduce light output to 50 percent by midnight or when use is expected to be low.

3 **Identify critical and noncritical lighting.** Critical lighting will be required for public safety at staff entrances, along walkways, in parking areas, and at book drops. Noncritical lighting will illuminate objects and amenities such as flags, architectural features, water features, and benches. Locate lighting only where it is needed. If light fixtures exist in nonessential locations, remove or disconnect them.

■ Outside, switch off lights in noncritical areas. Light only parking and pedestrian areas that should be used throughout the night. This may require control and wiring modifications if existing lighting is not zoned.

■ Inside, where appropriate, switch safety-critical incandescent, fluorescent, and LED lighting off after hours. Install occupant sensors and emergency relays to switch on lights and cameras when the area is occupied.

4 **Program or modify your lighting controls to switch off lighting where and when it is not needed.**

■ Inside, program night lighting near windows to switch off when the building is unoccupied. Install relays to ensure that lights will switch on in an emergency and install override switches for staff use after hours.

■ Outside, program lighting located at staff entries to switch off after normal operating and cleaning hours. Install occupant sensors or override switches to enable exterior lighting for after-hours use by staff and for emergency access.

5 **Replace or remove offensive and inefficient lighting where appropriate.**

■ Instead, use light fixtures that shield glare, minimize uplight, distribute light where it is needed, and are more energy efficient. Select light fixtures with a "house-side shield" when located at or near a property line. Verify performance via lighting mock-ups and light plots prepared by a lighting professional. Beware of sales rhetoric.

light reflected into the night sky but increase the temperature at night by radiating the sun's energy absorbed during the day. This catch-22 requires a balanced response. Trees and bushes can be used to shade dark surfaces during the day in an effort to limit the amount of radiant energy reaching and absorbed by the dark surface. Inversely, plants could be used to block indirect electric light reflected from light-colored surfaces. This might include locating trees and lighting standards side by side against parking lot medians or along walkways. Trimming tree branches up to seven feet and pruning bushes to three feet will clear sight lines for pedestrians and address the public safety issues typically associated with planted material.

IDENTIFY DESIGN TRADE-OFFS If it is important to illuminate the building exterior, trade that lighting for signage lighting and allow the building to become the sign. Instead of illuminating a flag, retire it at night, once standard practice for public buildings especially in rural communities. Consider lighting only those areas that require nighttime illumination, such as a book drop and the parking spaces immediately around it.

INCORPORATE LIGHT SHELTERS Night lighting located below overhangs and canopies has many benefits. These structural elements provide daytime shade and shelter for pedestrian travel, exterior events, and reading/lounge spots. They also provide locations that fully shield direct and indirect light from the sky. The pedestrian plaza and entrance canopy at SCPL are examples of lighting in people shelters.

SCRUTINIZE LUMINAIRE CHOICES Not all light fixtures are created equal. The key criteria to look for when presented with light fixtures are position, cutoff classification, distribution patterns, and efficiency. Lamps installed vertically in pole-mounted area lights cannot be appropriately shielded and at the same time provide efficiently distributed illumination. Vertical lamps are usually identified by a drop or sag lens. The result will be visible lamps, bright reflectors, or both—almost always resulting in visual and sometimes disabling glare.

INCREASE MOUNTING HEIGHTS Mounting light fixtures on tall poles and using lower wattage lamps will diminish low-level glare, improve horizontal and vertical uniformity, and reduce the number of locations required. By using low-wattage lamps and concentrating on light uniformity, the installation will provide better light and reduce the overall energy demand. For white light, consider metal halide light sources between 150W and 250W mounted on 20' to 25' poles. If more light is required, consider high-pressure sodium in the same wattage range and at the same pole height. New LED sources designed for pole mounting are becoming more readily available. However, the lighting industry has not yet developed a consistent method of documenting LED performance. If performance information is not available, request a sample, a mock-up, or a site visit to verify glare and distribution performance.

INFLUENCE PUBLIC POLICY Library administrators and staff are representatives of one of the most important public buildings within each community. As such, they should influence public policy regarding exterior environmental criteria, and they should certainly make their voices heard in any debate regarding public policy that directly affects library grounds. Each town, city, region, and state has a unique set of exterior lighting and environmental criteria. To begin any discussion, these criteria must be identified, thoroughly understood, and documented. The IDA's *Outdoor Lighting Code Handbook* presents detailed discussions on lighting code topics, issues, and choices to be made when it comes actually to writing and influencing exterior lighting codes. Being informed and joining in the debate is a first step toward improving the night environment.

A library's influences extend beyond its walls. By taking lighting to the next level, we will enhance our libraries and our environment in many ways…seen and unseen.

Carla Gallina (carla@msrltd.com) is In-house Lighting Designer and Jeffrey Mandyck (jeffreym@msrltd.com) is a Principal Architect, Meyer, Scherer and Rockcastle Architecture and Interiors, Minneapolis

San José's Green Art

By Lynn Blumenstein

The Pearl Avenue Branch Library (PABL) in San José, CA, is one of 20 new or renovated libraries that will display public art as part of a $212 million bond approved by voters in November 2000, but it is the only one to boast an installation that melds beauty with green-powered practicality. "Solar Illumination I: Evolution of Language," created by artist Lynn Goodpasture and fabricated by Peter Glass Studios, features art glass panels embedded with photovoltaic cells that power a lamp at the library's entrance.

The artwork explores cultural differences and at the same time celebrates what we all have in common. Each of the four panels, forming the building's southwest corner and facing the children's room, holds characters in different ancient scripts, forerunners of Latin, Russian, Vietnamese, and several Indian alphabets. The color-changing lamp is engraved in cuneiform with the message, "We are all one." According to Goodpasture, the artwork links the past with the present by celebrating the writings of humanity while incorporating today's solar and LED technologies.

A commitment to green, and to public art How did PABL decide on such a unique project? "It's not an easy process," Deputy Director Richard Desmond told *LJ*. "When it comes to art and architecture, everyone has opinions." Every branch project begins with a community meeting, where library officials gather feedback to include in the design process. "Every neighborhood tells us they're unique," said Desmond, "but they all say the same thing—they're diverse and formed in agriculture. We try to avoid fruit." He considers PABL to be one of the more successful collaborations.

The City of San José has a green building policy that has influenced the evolution of the project. Originally, all buildings were designed to meet LEED Certified status, although the San José Public Library (SJPL) didn't pursue certification owing to cost considerations. Now, SJPL has decided to do so, said Desmond, and all buildings larger than 10,000 square feet will seek LEED Silver status. PABL is 14,000 square feet.

Art isn't the only up-to-date feature at SJPL facilities. Each branch has self-checkout capability, a quiet study area, and a "living room" concept area, complete with fireplace, according to SJPL spokesperson Lorraine Oback. SJPL recently opened another café, now totaling six. It's not much of a moneymaker, admitted Jennifer Easton, a senior project manager with the city, but more of a convenience for the customer.

SJPL's bond-funded construction project is near completion, as 13 facilities are now open to the public, four are currently under construction, and two are in the design phase. Project managers will begin seeking design input this summer for the final facility, bolstered by the knowledge that two percent of the budget has been designated for public art.

Lynn Blumenstein, formerly Editor, Library Hotline

State of the Art in Darien

A long, flexible process helped the new Darien Library become the Northeast's first projected LEED Gold library building, while truly reinventing the public library By Louise Parker Berry & Alan Kirk Gray

The new Darien Library opened on January 10, 2009, a snowy day in our corner of Connecticut. After the speeches, the governor's proclamation, and the ribbon cutting, 7200 revelers headed toward the building (the crowds were so large, it took them more than 20 minutes to make their way in). Some 10,000 people visited that weekend.

When we first started thinking about how to provide new services to our community ten years ago, we had no idea how long it would take us, how much it would cost, or how, exactly, our plans would be realized. Certainly we had no idea of the technology involved, or that we would end up pursuing LEED (Leadership in Energy and Environmental Design) certification. And we could never have imagined the extraordinary building into which we'd eventually be moving.

We knew our project had a great pedigree. We already enjoyed strong community support—the library's use statistics were off the charts—and have for several consecutive years been ranked by Hennen's American Public Library Ratings among the country's top ten libraries. The library's trustees had created a long-range plan that set forth the community's need for additional services, concluding that a new building would have to be constructed. The subsequent building program was authored by Princeton

Public Library, NJ, director Leslie Burger, also head of Library Development Solutions and later president of the American Library Association. Written in 2002 and significantly updated in 2005, it defined our new building needs clearly, including the need "to reduce maintenance and operating costs as much as possible...utilize efficient building systems and...achieve LEED certification."

We decided to work with Peter Gisolfi of Peter Gisolfi Associates in Hastings-on-Hudson, NY. Peter is an architect whose work we respected, someone who realized, as we did, the importance of a significant public building at the center of a New England community. Peter likes "heavy" buildings, but he imbues them with light and transparency, and we wanted our new facility to be open and accessible while also having a heavy, i.e., permanent, presence.

As it happened, our early planning was derailed in 2002 when our first idea—to acquire neighboring property and expand the existing 22,750 square foot library—fell through. In retrospect, it was a stroke of luck. On our initial trajectory, we would have built a better Darien Library, but we would have missed an opportunity to take our building vision, and our service vision, to the next level.

After several frustrating years spent looking for a suitable site in Darien, our perspective gradually changed. We shifted our focus to the future instead of trying to improve on the past. We stopped thinking about ourselves and about what we wanted and looked around the cor-

ner to a future we couldn't clearly see—a future in which we envisioned our patrons approaching us with entirely different concerns and values. We visited new libraries looking for takeaways and saw lots of great architecture but found few ideas we could use. So we decided to design a library entirely our own.

Considering what the future might look like We knew the building would have to retain the small-town look and feel of the existing, 50-year-old library, which many of our users did not want to lose. We would be fanatical about making sure that every space in the new building worked exactly right. And we would place a big bet on technology as the means to allow us to provide an expanded array of services to each patron as an individual.

Our working partnership with Peter and his team was the most important element in the success of the project, because it was a true partnership. In a sense, we designed the library from the inside out, space by space, while Peter, as an architect does, designed the building from the outside in and from the ground up. At our request, he was a participant in every design meeting for the first three years.

We agreed on the building's core structure early on—a three-floor facility, plus a mezzanine, with an active main level, classic library functions on the upper level, and technology and computers on a lower level. When Peter first proposed this idea, he referred to Charles McK-

im's 1887 design of the Boston Public Library, a "palace for the people" with a busy main floor and a grand staircase that pulled people up to the second level.

That idea resonated with us, and it anchored us to hallowed library tradition, even on so much smaller a scale, but we had a different reference point: Ray Oldenburg's vision of libraries as described in his 1991 book, *The Great Good Place*. There, Oldenburg foresees libraries as "the third place," that "heart of a community's social vitality, the grassroots of a democracy." We wanted our library to be less what he referred to as "exacting, complicated and expensive internal arrangements," i.e., less like a hospital, and more like a café or a bookstore, so that it would be at the heart of our community's social vitality.

With this perspective in place, we probably had a clearer view of what we wanted to accomplish than many other library clients do at the early working stage. This was sometimes to Peter's disbelief and sometimes to his dismay but often to the benefit of the project.

Roadblocks along Main Street In a couple of areas, we were breaking new ground as far as we knew, with our concept of a "Main Street"—an active central area with all our new books, DVDs, and audiobooks on CD arranged as though in a store, with sidewalk displays, café tables, connecting the Children's Room on one side and the Community Room (a 170-seat auditorium), café, and fiction stacks on the

A "POWER"-FUL PRESENTATION (clockwise from far left) An interior view of the second-floor stacks taken from a perch study space. The exterior view of the new library when it opened, with the biofiltration system in the foreground. The four-level structure (including the mezzanine) blends both traditional and modern architecture. On "Main Street," which staff call "the heart of the library," patrons can find holds, return/check out materials, browse the fiction collection, consult with staff trained in readers' advisory, or hang out in the café. The flat-panel screens on the brick pillars behind the welcome desk announce new releases and upcoming events. An open staircase leads to the entrance of the basement's "Power Library," equipped with 32 public access computers and including a room dedicated to office needs. Also on this level are an adjacent Teen Lounge, technical services, the materials handling system, and space for future expansion

other. But it took more than nine months to agree on how the space would be laid out.

That's partly because we didn't have the same understanding of space as architects do. Architects know how big a space is just by looking at plans. We needed to see what the space was actually going to look like. We found a basketball court and bought a lot of blue painter's tape to lay out spaces like Main Street, to see how they would really work, where shelves would be, and if we could walk in and use it as our patrons would. In some cases, we were able to reduce the size of spaces when we realized what they were really like when they weren't on paper in 1/8" scale. We did it alone once but then included the architects, which was very helpful. Working together in a neutral environment, though not exactly a breeze, did promote the sense of us being on the same team.

We knew what we wanted to achieve on the lower level, where we placed most of the building's patron technology: a Power Library. The Power Library is as close to a learning commons as we could make it—a central space with PCs, a tech training center, a SO/HO (small office/home office) copy and binding center, two smart conference rooms that can be upgraded to allow for videoconferencing, and the Teen Lounge, which is a hangout space with books, chairs, and some fairly robust computers that can drive a flat-panel wall display.

We're much more comfortable than most libraries in putting computer users close together and letting them drink coffee while they do their work. We're also prepared to give a lot of help to users, so we saw the Power Library as an active, not a private, space, where users have a sense of being together. The values there are tech, not library. In a community where more than 95 percent of households have high-speed Internet access and nearly everyone has his/her own technology—a PC, at the very least—things get pretty busy. Kind of like a great good digital place.

Why is the Teen Lounge there, too? Someone said early on that we needed to put the teens next to either the coffee or the computers. Someone else said if they were close to the computers they'd be more likely to get into Harvard. Case closed.

Funding a higher price tag
Perhaps unique to Darien, the library board always knew the building project would be paid for with privately raised funds, as the existing library had been. The cost of the expansion, originally estimated at $10 million, jumped significantly when it became a stand-alone building. We ended up with a design for a 54,000 square foot structure (including 7000 unfinished square feet on the lower level) and a project cost of $28 million, including land acquisition and remediation. It is a library built to last a century, with steel columns and concrete block walls, brick and aluminum-clad windows, and a slate roof. The interior combines timeless New England and modern finishes.

George Wyper and Kim Huffard, as cochairs of the capital campaign and successive board presidents, took on the task of raising the $24 million needed once we factored in the $4 million proceeds from the sale of the old building. Their success is a tribute to their hard work and tenacity as well as to the community's widespread and longstanding support of our library. Though it didn't hurt that Darien, with a per capita income of over $77,000, is one of the most affluent communities in the United States, this was a much larger fundraising effort than had ever before been attempted here. The citizens of Darien really took to heart the motto, "Once in a lifetime a community builds a library."

The site we eventually chose was comprised of three properties, including a former gas station at which there had been several major spills. The environmental remediation project, which involved close coordination with the Connecticut Department of Environmental Protection, was complicated, lasted three years, and cost $1.5 million. Dot Kelly, a socially aware community member who first joined our building committee, then later the board, played a major role in guiding us through the excavation and contamination cleanup. She also enabled the library to receive a nearly $1 million reimbursement from the state as a partial offset to those expenses.

The importance of materials handling
We decided early in our planning to use RFID technology as a means of rebalancing the services we could provide to patrons. We'd already invested in touch screens and omnidirectional barcode readers to make our circulation desks more efficient but still had to address that 90 percent of staff–patron interactions in the old building amounted to books and DVDs being pushed back and forth across desks.

After we studied RFID for several years, we realized that we needed to be thinking about materials handling—the automatic return and sorting of items—since that's where the potential savings lie. Because we were early enough in the planning process, we were able to avoid the problem we've seen with other libraries when RFID materials handling systems are put in as an afterthought, without getting much benefit for the expense they incurred.

We felt that the right way to approach the process was to involve the RFID vendors as active participants, not as passive respondents to a request for proposal (RFP). Out of the eight vendors with whom we'd consulted, we asked three to review our plans and propose the system they would install. Each examined our circulation statistics, a review of our operations, and the plans for the new building to make their proposals, which were then refined by a technology committee. At that point we asked each to make a financial proposal. On the basis of all this, we chose 3M to provide the RFID tags and self-check machines and FKI Logistex to provide the automated returns, conveyors, and sorting system.

Since the whole point of adopting RFID/materials handling technology was to allow us to provide better service to our patrons, we opted against having a circulation desk, which we felt has kept other libraries from achieving high patron self-check usage. Instead, we planned for a Welcome Desk, essentially a concierge desk for the building. But we didn't just dismiss our circulation staff. Instead, those among them who were readers began a three-year education process to become readers' advisors (RAs). We sent them to conferences as well as brought in speakers from bookstores and publishing companies to share their insights, and we gave them the responsibility of purchasing all our fiction books. Main Street is their bookshop—they acquire the stock, and they handsell it. The remaining circulation staff, those who did not have futures as RAs, are mainstays in the materials management area, involved in the care and feeding of our automated return system and in organizing the shelvers who take the sorted return items and get them back on shelf.

Our adoption of materials han-

CLASSIC RIFFS The Reference Room exemplifies one of the building's driving design principles: transparency. The windows look out to other areas of the building

A Sustainable Library, Inside and Out

By Peter Gisolfi, AIA, ASLA

Because the Darien Library board committed early to a sustainable site and building, we were able to integrate sustainable strategies into all aspects of the design.

Green on the inside The building is intrinsically sustainable. It is made of heavy materials such as concrete and concrete block, which provide high thermal mass and help to maintain a comfortable interior environment. This construction enables stable temperatures that complement the functioning of the geothermal heating and cooling systems. The building is constructed with high-resistance to heat transfer and low air infiltration at the building envelope. Other features include daylighting in all spaces, multilevel lighting controls, and a building management system that further help to save energy. Materials used within the building include porcelain tile, carpeting, wood paneling, and gypsum board, which are nontoxic and easy to maintain.

Green on the outside The building forms three sides of a reading courtyard shaded by honey locust trees. To the west of the courtyard is the parking area, shaded with native plant materials.

The formerly toxic land on which the building sits—previously home to a gas station and car wash—was fully remediated and is now a sustainable green site. Four "standing-column" geothermal wells provide ground water for the heating and cooling system as well as irrigation water for the site. To manage stormwater, bioswales, vegetative landscape elements that remove silt and pollution from surface runoff, filter the water and direct it to retention basins under the parking area. The

A GREEN PLAN Peter Gisolfi (l.) works with a model to demonstrate design elements. Part of the library's stormwater management system (above) uses bioswales to remove impurities from surface runoff water

filtered stormwater is then gradually released into the ground water beneath the site.

The building's exterior materials, including brick, slate, aluminum-clad wood windows, and copper flashings and gutters, are permanent and require virtually no maintenance.

The proof is in the points The new library is slated to achieve LEED (Leadership in Energy and Environmental Design) Gold certification, obtaining nine out of 14 credits for the site, four out of five credits for water efficiency, nine out of 17 credits for energy and atmosphere, five out of 13 credits for materials, ten out of 15 credits for indoor environmental quality, and five out of five credits for innovation.

The metrics for the building are equally noteworthy. For instance, 85 percent of the stormwater infiltrates on the site. The building saves 48 percent in energy costs when compared to a baseline building of the same size that meets all energy codes. It also uses 41 percent less potable water. The landscape requires no irrigation from the potable water supply. Of all materials used, ten percent are from recycled sources, and 20 percent are local; 84 percent of the waste was recycled.

The new Darien Library was envisioned, designed, and constructed with the idea that life cycle costs are more important than initial savings. It is a beacon of sustainable design, serving as both an educational tool for the community and an inspiration for all.

---

dling technology caused us to consider the future of other critical inter-action-based services like reference. In 2005, we asked ourselves: How long before patrons start IM-ing us their reference questions? How should we organize the library to manage IM and other kinds of internal and external e-reference services?

We spent the next four years trying to answer those and many other questions, and the resulting dialog influenced our thinking and design choices. For instance, we decided on "pods" as a way of describing the nature of our reference desk structures (meaning they would be collaborative spaces) but didn't have a clue what they'd look like. And we came up with "glades" as a way of expressing our plan to reorganize the nonfiction collection into browsing areas somewhat divorced from Dewey.

By 2007, on track to build a library we knew would be extraordinary, we put off design decisions on furniture and shelving while working department by department on what services we would deliver and how we would do so. Throughout, we kept reminding ourselves that the new Darien Library was not our library but our patrons' library, the center of their community. This drove innovation, and change. We reconfigured our plans for children's services three times, for example, and our nonfiction shelving strategy four times.

Using technology to redefine user experience We always knew we'd have an opportunity late in the project to decide on technology, since new generations of technology tend to follow closely on one another's heels. Leading up to that, we asked such library tech luminaries

as Michael Stephens, Aaron Schmidt, and Jenny Levine to speak to our staff, we hosted conferences, and we made sure to stay current on the latest thinking and trends. We also attended conferences other libraries typically don't, such as InfoComm, which bills itself as the world's "largest information communications" conference.

It wasn't until we convinced John Blyberg of Ann Arbor District Library, MI, to join us in 2007 that we began actively planning the role of technology in our library. Technology ultimately became an integral part of the services we provide, and we attempted to infuse it into the library experience in ways that aren't glaring when they don't need to be.

This attitude led to a major innovation: Blyberg's concept of a UX (User eXperience) team to oversee all the technology-based interactions between patrons and the library, whether virtual or onsite.

Say you ask an information services librarian a question about the Crimean War—you might not recognize it's an ASUS EEe PC subnotebook she's using to access a database for you, you're just grateful to get the information you want. Similarly, if you're in the Technology Center taking a class on Excel, you don't care that you're looking at an 82" Samsung flat-panel display, you're just enjoying seeing all the details. And if a book you want is on the shelf, you might not give a thought to the role the materials handling system played in getting it there. The aim of Blyberg's UX team is to address the reality of these and other patron experiences and continually seek better ways to deliver the appropriate services.

We also wanted technology to create a contrast between the timelessness of the building and the immediacy of the digital world. To that

LOOKING FORWARD "We'd decided we wanted to build the first of the new libraries, not the last of the old," write Berry and Gray about the new Darien Library. The staff reconsidered how users would interact in the library of the future when designing vital services like the nonfiction collection (at left). They reorganized nonfiction into browsing areas envisioned as "glades," with Dewey taking a bit of a backseat. As part of its green initiative (the library is projected to receive LEED Gold certification this month), the entire building is infused with daylight via massive windows, as in the periodicals room, above

end, we installed flat-panel displays driven by a neat piece of InfoComm software called Sedna Presenter to lighten our Main Street area. To make the statement that the library is committed to providing patrons access to the latest and best technology, we put 24" monitors on the ASUS EEe PCs in the Power Library and a Microsoft Surface in the children's room. (The former was a relatively inexpensive statement to make; the latter, at $15,000, a costly one.)

The next generation library In 2005, we'd decided we wanted to build the first of the new libraries, not the last of the old. We felt a responsibility to do something more than just expand on the success of the existing Darien Library. Our goal was not bravado, just a way of saying, "We haven't figured everything out yet, but we will."

What we've learned in the intervening years is that we haven't figured everything out yet—and that we're not likely ever to. That said,

when we unveiled the new Darien Library in 2009, we opened the doors to a wonderful building that fulfilled its ten years in the making. It is all we ever dreamed it might be—a library that will stand for generations as a tribute to this community's commitment to knowledge and learning and, we hope, a library to meet the opportunities and challenges of the future.

Louise Parker Berry is Library Director and Alan Kirk Gray is Assistant Director, Operations, Darien Library, CT

DATE LIBRARY JOURNAL, SEPTEMBER 15, 2011

A Whole Systems Approach

Why Integrated Building Design spurs better, more sustainable projects from start to finish By Rebekkah Smith Aldrich

What if I told you there was a potentially smarter, better, and faster way to build a new library—a process that could maximize innovation and deliver on long-term sustainability goals? Sounds pretty good, right?

What if the same process could possibly decrease the cost of your project? Integrated Building Design is such a process.

As library leaders we have a responsibility to make the most of any building project. For many, it is the once-in-a-lifetime opportunity to have an impact on the library's physical space. It is a singular opportunity to address long-standing concerns and hopes for the future, and it is an amazing chance to solidify the library's place in the community.

Those library leaders who think out of the box during their construction projects (e.g., Darien Library's customer service–focused design or DOK's library concept center in the Netherlands) have been rewarded with increased visibility and, more important, greater viability in their communities. However, this drive for maximum benefit is tempered by our charge to use every dollar wisely. We are beholden to our taxpayers and donors to stretch the dollars they place in our trust as far as we can.

That stewardship of the public and private dollar is resulting in a steep rise in the number of libraries that are looking for long-term performance issues to be addressed through their building projects as well as through operational solutions—consider, for instance, the Chrisney Branch Library, IN, the first net-zero energy building in the United States. Literally every day there is a news story about the grand reopening of a library that has sustainable design features—energy conservation, water conservation, healthy materials used in construction (see Facebook.com/SustainableLibraries).

Libraries have caught on quickly to the "green wave" sweeping the construction industry, not because it is a fad but because it makes sense. It makes sense because a green approach lets you reduce operating costs, which creates savings that last long after the punch list is completed.

Nonetheless, the drive for library innovation and sustainable design adds to the complexity of a project. It puts a lot of pressure on library leaders to verbalize, coordinate, and deliver projects with big impact, especially in this time of economic hardship. Luckily, we are not expected to do this alone. We work in partnership with design professionals, engineering professionals, consultants, construction firms, and tradespeople who translate our vision to the physical form. This is nothing short of a monumental, sometimes miraculous effort for many libraries and a fairly intimidating one for the uninitiated.

Collaboration that optimizes solutions
Integrated Building Design (IBD), also known as Integrative Building Design and Integrated Project Delivery (IPD), sounds fairly simple, as it takes one of those things you learned in elementary school and applies it to our grown-up

THE RESULTS Using IBD principles, Judson University's ventilated Harm A. Weber Academic Center in Elgin, IL, came to life with PSA-Dewberry's design and a UK architect who specializes in natural ventilation working in conjunction

life: when you work together with others, you can accomplish more than you can alone.

I like the IBD definition from the American Society of Heating, Refrigerating and Air-Conditioning Engineers (ASHRAE) best, but it goes on a little long so I've boiled it down:

IBD is a collaborative process, resulting in optimized solutions from an engaged team that is committed to the process from start to finish.

IBD breaks down silos in the traditional building process and brings the experts to the table from the very beginning of the project to look at the project from a "whole systems" perspective. A "whole systems" approach or "systems thinking" assumes that individual parts/roles are better understood in relation to others. So, with IBD all the players involved are asked to work together rather than on their own, from the inception of the project. This can better engage everyone in the library's goals, and in one another's goals, which can ratchet up commitment to the project—to getting it done cost efficiently without compromising the library's vision—and spur earlier, more comprehensive problem-solving.

"We believe strongly in the collaborative approach to a project as an effective way to optimize and integrate the efforts and abilities of the owner and all the other team members," says Victor Canseco of Sandpebble Builders in Southampton, NY, builders of the Westhampton Free Library, an *LJ* New Library Landmark honorable mention. "This integration becomes a prerequisite on high-performance building projects where the traditional linear method has been shown to be very ineffective. In addition, this approach has proven to be very suc-

FIGURE 1 Traditional Process vs. Integrated Building Design

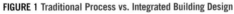

Traditional Process	➡	Integrated Building Design
Linear	➡	Whole Systems Approach
Team members involved only when necessary	➡	Team members included throughout
More decisions made by fewer people	➡	More decisions made in teams, iteratively
Emphasis on up-front costs	➡	Emphasis on full life-cycle costs and benefits
Systems considered in isolation	➡	Systems considered in relationship to others, allowing for full optimization
Less time, energy, and collaboration exhibited in early stages	➡	Front-loaded—time and energy invested early

SOURCE: U.S. DEPARTMENT OF ENERGY (IBD ONLY)

Embracing Austin, Inside and Out

By Marta Murvosh

With a rooftop reading garden and reading porches on three floors, the new Austin Central Library, TX, in the city's downtown will embrace the community's love affair with books and nature. "Austin is an outdoor kind of city," says John W. Gillum, Austin Public Library (APL) facilities process manager. "We tried to bring the outdoors indoors in this building."

Construction started in May on the as-yet-unnamed $90 million, 198,000 square foot new Central Library, which will be built of wood, metal, and native limestone. (Gillum says that the APL Friends Foundation, a merger of the Friends and the foundation, is working on getting a large donation and that may result in a name.)

Features include a 350-seat event center with a flat floor and flexible seating, a used bookstore, a movable demonstration kitchen, a level devoted to children and teens, and at least a dozen technology-rich meeting rooms for smaller gatherings, accommodating from four to 12 people. Plus, of course, many places to curl up inside and outside to read or enjoy the views of the city, natural trails, and waterways.

A $90 million bond passed in 2006 and a land sale will fund the $120 million effort, which includes extending streets and improving infrastructure. The new Central Library will replace the technologically outdated 33-year-old, 110,000 square foot John Henry Faulk Central Library, which will become archival and display space for the Austin History Center. As the 18-branch system grew, Faulk's meeting room, auditorium, and other programming space was sacrificed for administrative and behind-the-scenes functions. "We just outgrew it," Gillum says. Faulk was built for a community of 350,000, Gillum says. Austin reached almost 842,600 residents in 2012, according to the U.S. Census Bureau.

An Austin State of Mind Input from community meetings held by library leaders and the design team at Shepley Bulfinch Richardson and Abbott of Boston and Lake|Flato Architects of San Antonio guided decisions. Shepley Bulfinch is the architect of record, though Lake|Flato took the lead on the exterior.

"People were saying, 'Give me a place where I can read books,'" says Lynn Petermann, an Austin project team member at Shepley Bulfinch.

Austinites also asked for sufficient vehicle parking, bicycle storage, a café, and a well-lit, unique, green building. Lighting was particularly important because it is lacking in the existing Faulk Library, where the poor lighting in the stacks generates complaints from customers and pages who can't see the labels. "We have lanterns that we put on the carts that [pages] can shine in the direction of the shelving," Karen Baker, Central Library services manager, says.

Community members also asked for a library with an Austin vibe. The liberal enclave's unofficial slogan is "Keep Austin Weird," and that includes thriving food and music scenes as well as outdoor pursuits. "They wanted it to be beautiful and look like Austin and be an icon they could be proud of," Gillum says.

Baker expects to offer extensive programming at the new Central Library and to build partnerships with other organizations to enrich library events on topics such as rearing urban chickens, organic farming, beekeeping, and Texas cuisine. Baker says, "We want more programs that have the Austin vibe."

That Austin vibe will inform the collection as well: when it opens in

2016, the new Central Library Austin will feature collections of CDs recorded by Austin musicians and cookbooks filled with Texas and Austin cuisine, as well as traditional library offerings, says Baker. The library also hopes to rebuild its zine collection.

Even Greener The city aimed for a Leadership in Energy & Environmental Design (LEED) Silver certification but is on track to earn a Platinum, says Sid Bowen, principal architect at Shepley Bulfinch. The new library will offer electric car charging stations, a bike corral near a popular biking and hiking trail, and an underground cistern (converted from a vault left on the site) to collect rainwater for irrigation and toilets. According to Jonathan Smith, Lake|Flato project architect, the new library is expected to employ 60 percent of the power used by a similarly sized building. A photovoltaic cell designed to generate 13 percent of the library's power

DATE ACADEMIC NEWSWIRE NOVEMBER 4, 2013

Nova Scotia Sustainability Center Gives New Life to Library Discards

By Roxanna Asgarian

Dalhousie University's library system was in a bind. Bound books, mostly out-of-date academic journals that had since been uploaded to online databases, had been piling up for years. At nearly 50,000 volumes, the library was running out of space.

"Any university that's subscribing to a lot of academic journals, you're challenged to house them, because they grow exponentially," said Patrick Ellis, the director of Dalhousie's health sciences library. "So space that looked copious in 1967 is jammed to the rafters in 1987."

The library rented an off-site warehouse to house the journals. But they were seldom, if ever, asked for by students. The library was squeezing an already-tight budget for books that were no longer needed, so eventually, the librarians decided to let many of the books go.

The first thought was to shred them, and recycle the paper. However, this proved difficult, as the covers needed to be stripped manually before they could be shredded, and the journals needed to be fed very slowly into the shredder because the textbook paper, which contained clay, had a tendency to gum up the machine. Because the shredding truck needed to be running in order to operate the machine, there were also issues of fumes and noise.

"While trying to shred to be environmentally friendly, we were creating all these gasses and noise pollution," said Nicola Embleton-Lake, the facilities planner who coordinated the project. "There were offices above and next to us, and it became an issue because it was really a nuisance to them."

After complaints of noise, and with only a tiny fraction of the books shredded, Dalhousie gave up on that solution. The library considered using the books as fuel, but glues and other components they contained made that option environmentally hazardous.

Stumped, the university began to seek ideas.

When builder and inventor David Cameron heard of the problem, he began to think. His work has focused on finding creative ways to deal with waste. He'd previously come up with a way to remove traces of gas from propane tanks to declassify them as hazardous waste and instead crush and recycle the steel, while using the extracted propane as the energy source for the whole operation.

Cameron's main project these days is the Blockhouse School, an abandoned schoolhouse that's now a community center focused on sustainability. The school is old, and the nonprofit doesn't have the money to to heat the minimally insulated building. So when he heard about the books, he hoped to solve two problems at once.

"I built three straw bale homes, so I have some experience working with cellulose—books are made of cellulose," Cameron said. "They don't have the insulating value of straw bales because they don't have the air pockets ... but there would be some value there."

Dalhousie University paid to deliver 10,000 books to the Blockhouse School, and Cameron and his team got to work. He stacked a wall of books, and covered the result with a mixture of clay, sand, and straw, called earth plaster.

Building the book wall at the Blockhouse School

He cut costs by having students, who were paying to take a course in earth-plastering, help him complete the wall.

"My modus operandi is to turn everything into a learning experience, which at the same time is something people would pay to learn," Cameron said. "It's a bootstrapping operation, where you spread these useful skills throughout the community at a very low cost, and also get the job done."

Beyond insulation, the Blockhouse School recently ran an exhibit called "New Life for Old Books," in which they called for community members to come up with uses for old books in "art, craft, garden, construction, installations, performance" and "anything else you can think of!"

Ellis was simply glad to make a dent in the pile of books that have increased as the needs of students dictated that Dalhousie's libraries devote more space to study room.

"This was a very unique solution. It got rid of a lot of stuff we have no need for, and the books are a viable insulating material," Ellis said, and then laughed. "Too bad they're not building a bigger building!"

Ellis said that Dalhousie is working in conjunction with other universities in Nova Scotia on a long-term plan for waste and space management, but the immediate problem isn't fully solved. Embleton-Lake has been coordinating a plan for the remainder of the books that includes paying for "processing"—manually removing the covers and recycling the paper.

"Blockhouse School has been a really successful project in and of itself because it's shown really valuable uses of books and of what can be done," Embleton-Lake said. "It's a scientific exercise, though, not something that is going be easily assimilated in the construction industry. But it's a step in the right direction, of asking what can we do with them? Because we aren't the only ones with this problem."

Roxanna Asgarian is a freelance journalist based in New York City

Living Up to LEED Silver

By Lynn Blumenstein

The new B. Thomas Golisano Library at Roberts Wesleyan College (RWC) in Rochester, NY, debuted in September 2007, designed and built with the intention of becoming the first academic facility to achieve LEED Silver certification. The efforts of architectural firm Leo A. Daly and SWBR design were successful; that status was conferred the following summer.

Performing as designed Two years later, *LJ* spoke with library facilities director T. Richard Greer about how the library is operating. "It's been performing as designed," said Greer. "It comes down to planning and making sure the people have the knowledge to install things properly." With that in mind, the building team invited 35 construction personnel to an all-day seminar on LEED building practices.

Builders faced many first-time scenarios, like drilling a series of wells ranging from 49' deep to 340' deep. They regulate the temperature of the two-story, 43,000 square foot facility through geothermal methods. Water is either heated up or cooled off as it is pumped through varying depths of wells.

The LEED "commissioning" process makes it even more important that the building "operates as designed," said Greer. A LEED representative reviews construction throughout the process and turns in a report at the end as well as a six-month follow-up.

Efficient features Greer considers LEED practices as "just commonsense things we should be doing anyway." In addition to LEED qualification, the library's features make it 40 percent more energy-efficient than New York State Energy Code recommendations.

The features include renewable materials such as cork flooring, carpet squares made of highly recycled content, and sunflower board cabinetry; efficient T-5 fluorescent lighting; energy derived from wind or bio fuels purchased from Hess Energy; natural light leveraged throughout to extend energy efficiency; optimal north-south building footprint orientation; solar shades to reflect the direct rays of the sun and bounce light to specific areas; and locally harvested materials, saving gasoline and transportation costs and resources.

A place for interaction Like many new facilities, the library features a 3000 square foot Information Commons comprised of a café, computer lab, group study rooms, and large meeting rooms and having wireless capability. In the words of the architectural firm, the space serves as an example of the "architecture of interaction." The commons allows students and staff interaction, encouraging increased use. It is a dynamic space where students can come to study but also "hang out" in the coffee shop, by the fireplace, or in the reading lounges.

Function trumps form Ultimately, function must be the most important criterion. Because of shelving, the library wasn't able to achieve a daylighting credit in its LEED certification. Despite large windows, natural light is only able to penetrate one-third of the way into the center from all sides, said Greer. The standard is total penetration.

Overall, however, without a designated student union on campus, the library is one of several buildings that serve as "student gathering places around campus," said Barry Smith, VP of student life. Students immediately see it as a place for studying and socializing. It's spacious and "appropriately placed on campus" as a destination. LEED characteristics are often unnoticed to the untrained eye, but the internal lights are sensitive and respond to outside conditions. The overall aesthetic is one of a "sense of place and balance."

Lynn Blumenstein is Contributing Editor, LJ

5
kids & teens

NEW SPACES AND PLACES

Kids of all ages have never had it better, as more and more design creativity is focused on them, from tiny touches to entire destinations dedicated to the demographic. These strategies—shared from *LJ*'s design coverage since 2009 as originally published—show how making spaces delightful, comfortable, and engaging bring libraries to the next level while adding elements of whimsy and play for everyone. Many of these projects are already getting time-tested by little feet, but the insights here will inspire any design process.

With Kids in Mind

Do more than punch up the palette and shrink the seats so kids can benefit from surprisingly sophisticated choices By Traci Engel Lesneski

When creating special spaces where children can experience joy in learning and investigation, public and school libraries often are inclined to produce primary-colored themed spaces that may appear on the surface to be kid-friendly. These spaces, however, can be a flat experience for children. Children appreciate good design, subtlety, and nuance. We should avoid talking down to them with the spaces we provide just for them.

By considering the following principles, libraries can create children's areas that provide a layered experience that works for youngsters of many ages and that provides multiple ways for children to learn, interact with other children or their caregivers, and achieve a sense of accomplishment.

Create simplicity, directness, and delight

Design your building to be easy for parents and caregivers to use by making the spaces interesting for children and offering both caregivers and children a place to rest the body, soul, and mind. Include comfort rooms where children can calm down, or nursing mothers can have a quiet, private space. Offer aspects of surprise to allow children to discover something new on each visit. Make the ordinary extraordinary. For example, set windows and doors at child height to signal the space is just right for them.

These windows at this Dallas Branch library are just the right height for children—signaling that this is their space ▶

Provide layered experiences

Offer a variety of areas—active and quiet, social and private—that encourage a range of experiences with multiple levels of challenge for different ages and abilities. Use technology to teach and engage. Simple interactive installations such as projected art that responds to movement will stand the test of time and will be enjoyed by all age groups. Allow the space and activities to grow with the children and provide enough complexity to engage children on more than one level.

Offer refuge within the building

Children need places where they can regroup to rest their eyes, their bodies, and their minds. These spaces can be pockets with soft seating and books or puzzles to settle in with or spaces with views to the outside.

Design to foster wonder

Today's children are more scheduled than ever before. They have precious little opportunity to explore the world around them on their own terms. Your children's area can be a space for fostering wonder, through interactive early literacy fixtures or aspects of the architecture itself.

▲ The Madison Public Library, WI, Central Library features reading caves with floor sensors that turn on the lights when children climb in

This popular reading area ▶ at the busy Ramsey County Roseville Public Library, MN, lets children get out of the fray

Allow children to fill in the blanks

Children are more sophisticated about design than adults often give them credit for. They are keenly observant and interested in their surroundings. Design to allow children to fill in the blanks rather than prescribing what they see or how they engage with a theme or literal interpretation. Children are among the few in our society who look up in a building, so give them something at which to look.

▲ These seats in Mount Prospect Public Library, IL, are appealing to children and designed for adult and child to sit together comfortably

Offer paths to pride and accomplishment

Children thrive when accomplishments are visible and acknowledged. This accounts for the popularity of summer reading programs. Celebrate milestones both in learning and life.

▼ A child using the McAllen Texas Public Library, TX, marks his growth progress

Create a beautiful building

Consider the aspects of space design that offer comfort and encourage learning, such as access to daylight, the use of natural materials, comfortable seating, and places that provide shelter (e.g., booths or nooks) and are composed of environmentally healthy finishes. Recognize that children appreciate those things, too.

Remember that kids need to move

Provide space where it is okay to do so, and set out fixtures that encourage movement and activity, while fostering imagination. For example, a play kitchen lets children use gross and fine motor skills.

▲ The Dakota County Wescott Library, MN, offers reading nooks for children to get the wiggles out or curl up with a book

Engage all the senses

Simply put, the more senses we use in a learning activity, the more we remember. Create a memorable experience by getting children to use all of their senses—sight, smell, touch, hearing, and even taste. Positive memories will increase learning and the desire to return.

▼ This flexible room at the Ramsey County Roseville Public Library, MN, is filled with tactile and interactive fixtures when story times are not in session

Create a sense of anticipation

The journey and path to the children's area are just as important as the destination.

Traci Engel Lesneski is Principal and Head of Interiors, Meyer, Scherer & Rockcastle (MSR) Ltd., Minneapolis

Inspired To Climb Higher

A clever design for children's spaces is top of the trees
By Dennis Humphries

"Trees and tree houses reflect exploration and risk-taking…going higher and challenging yourself to do things that may be uncomfortable or seemingly beyond your ability." —Barbara Mitchell Hutton, Director, Rocky Mountain School for the Gifted and Creative

When Humphries Poli Architects (HPA) suggested to the Rangeview Library District, CO, a.k.a. Anythink™ libraries, that its four new branches feature tree houses in the children's areas, it took almost a full two seconds for the administrative staff to embrace the design team's idea. Since then, there has been no looking back—the tree houses have become symbols to spark the imagination and inspire a sense of wonder for both young and older library users.

Above it all The design concept was initially inspired by a *Denver Post* article by Sheba Wheeler that describes the appeal of tree houses: "When the stress and strain of everyday life become overwhelming, it can be hard to find a place to get above it all. So people are increasingly turning to an iconic childhood getaway—the tree house—for a new kind of grown-up escapism."

Rangeview director Pam Sandlian Smith noted in her monthly report to the board that the tree houses were a perfect symbol for the rebranded Anythink libraries; they would give patrons a sense of nature and bring the peacefulness of the outdoors indoors. She emphasized that having patrons perceive the library as a place for retreat and renewal was central to their vision. The entire staff drew on this picture when they began developing concepts for the new facilities.

Idea to reality The design team crafted different types of tree houses for each of the four Anythink branches. The rural 6000 square foot Bennett Branch was intended as a kit for the outdoor children's garden.

The architects created an "assembly manual" illustrating a step-by-step construction to be built by volunteers; it is expected to be completed later this fall.

The 25,000 square foot Huron Street Branch features soaring vertical slabs covered in bark siding from poplar trees, allowing children to explore among the trees, or climb through the "holes." One of the trees simulates a nocturnal experience, combining the sound of insects and frogs with images of the constellations projected in the tree canopy. The 20,000 square foot Brighton Branch will feature a literal connection from the interior to the exterior program space, while the 45,000 square foot Wright Farms Branch offers the excitement of crawling through a fallen tree.

SENSE OF PLACE The Western aesthetic stands tall with trees spurring grand dreams at (clockwise from top left) Anythink's Wright Farms and Huron Street branches

Of course, the design and construction team had to face issues of keeping costs down and ensuring an accessible and safe experience—so no elevated platforms. Instead, children, and adults who read to them, can sit under the green canopy. But, most important, the tree houses stimulate the mind in order to reinforce the notion of climbing higher.

Even though the new facilities incorporate tree houses in the children's areas, the view of libraries as places full of possibilities, exploration, and creativity holds true for all ages.

Dennis Humphries, AIA, is Principal at Humphries Poli Architects, P.C. (www.hparch.com), Denver

The Theatrical Library

By Janice Davis

As libraries around the world today adapt to the new parameters of the Information Age, what used to be rooms full of book stacks are now centers for digital information, community meeting places, film and lecture halls, and—oh, yes—book stacks. A library is no longer just a place to look up information or find an enjoyable novel; these days, a library needs to draw patrons in with a wider range of services and attractions, and suddenly style and aesthetic appeal are more a part of that draw than ever before.

Touch customers What's going to entice two-year-old Emily away from *Sesame Street* or 12-year-old Tim away from his X-Box? The next generation's appreciation of reading is riding on the answer. In order to meet the challenge, libraries are taking a page from retail stores and themed restaurants: get them in the door *just* because it's a cool place to be, and *then* sell your product. Entice them inside and there the books—and their minds—can begin to open. The greatest opportunity for imaginative fun is, of course, the children's section.

Janice Davis Design LLC (JDD) started off in the business of theatrical set design, segued into exhibits, and finally into theatrical décor for public spaces, including libraries. Theatrical décor designers are called upon to pick up where architects and interior designers leave off, as theatrical elements require different skills, construction methods, and materials than traditional interior design. Combining theatricality with practical needs can therefore result in all manner of magic, such as a forest (of display cases), a castle (activity room), a cave (for video viewing), or a pirate ship (as a quiet reading nook). Theatrical décor can happen in tandem with new construction or renovation or can be installed in existing spaces for an entirely new look without the expense of total renovation.

Magic in the making Recently completed in November 2008 was JDD's work on the children's section of the Bay Shore-Brightwaters PL on Long Island, NY. Library director Eileen Kavanagh and head of children's services Linda Clark were excited about the renovation for their whole building as designed by New York architects Beatty, Harvey & Associates, but they wanted something that went beyond beautiful interior design to capture the fancies of local children—they wanted fantasy and magic that children would relate to.

Fundraising efforts were ongoing, with ultimate results still uncertain, so the early planning stage designs had to have flexibility to fit a budget that might wind up being smaller or larger than projected. This meant prioritizing the décor elements involved. The top priority for everyone was the entrance arch to the children's section, the design of which would be echoed in various places once inside.

A concept was chosen: famous children's book characters were to be tumbling out of and scrambling around their books. For this nonprofit purpose, copyright allowed use of the characters—without alteration. It was surprising how many illustrations easily lent themselves to our theme. The tumbling books and characters create an entrance arch, at the top of which is the largest of all the

open books, proclaiming the long-standing motto of the children's section, "The Magic Lives Here."

Originally, the support columns in the children's area were to be surrounded with sculptural books and characters in continuation of the entrance arch theme, but by the time plans were drawn and bids came back from several theatrical construction shops, fundraising would not allow much more than the arch itself. Nonetheless, it was important to bring some of the sensibility of the entrance inside, so the solution became to design custom digitally printed "murals" to surround the lower portions of the columns on all sides. And so, as did their friends on the entrance arch, Pippi Longstocking, Peter Rabbit, and a dozen or so others could escape from their books as well to mingle with young readers seated nearby.

A continual process Because theatrical scene shops never have the luxury of missing a deadline (opening night *is* opening night), theatrical décor installation tends to go remarkably smoothly. In the case of the Bay Shore-Brightwaters installation, the only thing that needed to be altered on Beatty Harvey's original plans was that the entry into the children's area had to be raised by one foot in order to accommodate the tent-like book that tops the arch. Chris Howard, project manager from Springboard, Inc., the fabricator of the décor elements, built the piece in sections so that installation and touch-up took only three days.

The total design, construction, and installation of the dimensional arch and printed column surrounds cost approximately $75,000. Initial discussions included ways to build on the design concept and enhance it with additional sculptural elements and murals in the future as funds allow. The hope is that each new element will be a new reason for kids to be excited about coming back to pick up a few more books.

Janice Davis, originally a theatrical set designer, is President and Founder of Janice Davis Design LLC (www.janicedavisdesign.com), a company that designs theatrically styled interiors

DATE SCHOOL LIBRARY JOURNAL, APRIL 2014

Look, a Nook!

Create a cozy haven for reading with inventive space design
By Chelsey Philpot

Why is it that people "curl up" with books? Whether a bibliophile chooses to fling her legs over the side of an armchair, huddle close to a friend, or make a haven from a large cardboard box, the places she chooses all reflect the same idea: There is something about the act of reading that calls out for a safe, snug, and comfortable spot.

Perhaps it's only when your body, whether you're five or 85, feels sheltered that your imagination is free to inhabit the world you find in the pages of a novel.

In the reading areas and nooks pictured here, some spaces and furniture are the products of complex architecture plans and methodical design. Others, such as window seats and bean-bag chairs, are seemingly simple in comparison, but no less welcoming. You'll find a wide visual range of all types of spaces in this sampling—along with DIY tips and notes from architects and librarians about what makes a great reading spot for children and teens.

Inspired by Nature

Bringing the outdoors indoors is a reliable strategy for creating appealing spots to nestle and explore, as these designs show.

A tree grows in the children's department of the Central Library building of the Ohio Township Public Library in Newburgh, IN ▶

◀ Environmentally friendly "reading nests" at the Madison (WI) Children's Museum, created by Kubala Washatko Architects, Inc.

In "The Trove," the new children's library at the White Plains (NY) Public Library, a video-viewing cave by Janice Davis Design LLC encourages kids to engage with books and media ▶

Sensational Structures

Child-scaled shelters—such as the pirate ship and mini house pictured here—feed the imagination while providing an appealing refuge for young patrons.

Left: a house made of books at the Iowa City Public Library invites young readers to move right in ▶

Right: the pirate ship at the Trove Children's Library at the White Plains Public Library accommodates both storytime and active imaginations. Janice Davis Design LLC ▶

▲ Left: Nicolette Lennert, a former teacher and a co-creator, with Karen Whiteside, of "The Classroom Creative" (theclassroomcreative.com), made this forward-facing "book sling" for less than $20. Add some brightly colored pillows and you've got yourself a nook. Right: Whiteside built this teepee using PVC pipes and clearance fabrics. Best of all, reading time can be portable

Do It Yourself

You don't need a large budget to create reading areas with a big allure, as Karen Whiteside and Nicolette Lennert, co-creators of "The Classroom Creative" blog, prove. Inviting interiors "can be done on a dime," says Lennert. "Ask parents, shop clearance racks, and, of course, hit garage sales and thrift shops for books."

Eight DIY Tips

1 "Score carpet squares, giant pillows, bean bags, and, especially, kid-sized lawn chairs and kiddie pools on summer clearance!" suggests Lennert.

2 Have kids bring sleeping bags in for D.E.A.R (Drop Everything And Read) time. Lennert did this with first-graders, and the classroom was "pin-drop silent."

3 String holiday lights and sheets between bookcases to create a comfy tent.

4 Add a few pillows to a blow-up pool to create an oasis.

5 Decorate using old hardcovers.

6 In general: pillows, pillows, pillows!

7 Check out independent bookstores and children's museums for ideas.

8 Comb Pinterest for inspiration.

Caves and Pods

An innovative overhaul transformed a portion of the Madison (WI) Central Library into a sleek, sprawling children's area with naturalistic motifs. Meyer, Scherer & Rockcastle Architecture's (MSR) reconstruction of the 45-year-old, 95,000 square-foot facility earned the American Public Works Association, Wisconsin Chapter, Project of the Year Award for 2014.

These pods at the Madison (WI) Central Library are made of bent willow and were designed and fabricated by artists Tom Loeser and Dave Chapman ▶

Echo Your Environment

Does your library reflect a sense of place? This range of designs by CK Design International, based in Sydney, Australia, takes note of neighborhood and regional features, whether cultural or natural. "Our clients like us to find something that adds to the local identity and is different from other libraries," says director Cecilia Kugler.

▲ The curved horse bench and stools in the Margaret Martin Library in Randwick, Australia, celebrate the nearby Royal Randwick Racecourse. "All projects are like our 'babies,' but Randwick and Katoomba are [two] of our prettiest," says Kugler

▲ The youth space in the Ku-ring-gai Library at Gordon, in New South Wales, Australia, draws inspiration from local parks. Its architectural elements and colors make it a distinct area, attractive to teens

◀ The West Ryde Library, located in a Sydney suburb, was completed in 2005. A local miniature train park inspired the theme

For the Katoomba Library in the Blue Mountains of Australia, Kugler says, "We designed the cocoon-like enclosures in reference to Katoomba's most iconic tourist attraction— the Three Sisters rock formation." ▶

Carving out a Haven

It can be a challenge to create reading hideouts in a high-traffic public area, but the Queens (NY) Library has accomplished just that—and achieved "what I call 'nookdom,' or creating the feeling of being in a nook," says Queens Library operations project manager Gillian Miller. For instance, "We try to include deep window seats where we can." The right lighting and colors also make spaces feel inviting. "For every child, there is a different 'great' space," adds Miller. "It may be the ability to gather their friends around a good picture book. Or, it is the feeling of being able to disappear into the text and block out everything else."

▲ Top, left-right: A cheerful reading cave for one… or two, if you don't mind squeezing. This window seat has a sleek, modern look and a come-perch-here feel

Lots of natural light and calming blues make this space a reading oasis ▶

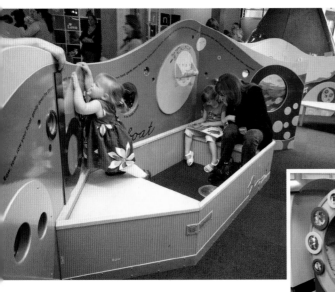

Going Mobile

For grown-ups, a vehicle takes you somewhere else. But for many kids, a boat or passenger car or truck is a destination in itself. What better place to park one's self and crack open a book!

▼ Left-right: All aboard the "Passenger Car" of the Mitzvah Train at the Levi Yitzchak Children's Library in Cedarhurst, NY. Truck reading nook at the Fremont (IN) Public Library

▲ Children in the "b is for boat" nook at the Vancouver (WA) Community Library

A Core Design Element: Books

In these reading areas at New York City libraries, playful design features create the sense of delineated areas within large, flowing spaces. Books are always the anchors, however. "We love books and we love to read," says architect Jennifer Sage of Sage and Coombe Architects, which has designed numerous reading rooms for the New York Public Library (NYPL) system. "And anything that encourages children to do the same will surely enrich their lives, offer them intellectual satisfaction, and prepare them to meet challenges ahead."

▲ The reading room of NYPL's Hamilton Fish Branch includes tables and chairs for studying, along with "a carpeted 'landscape' with foam blocks that [allow] the children to read on the floor and stretch out to share a book," says Sage

For the award-winning design of NYPL's Fort Washington ▶ Branch Library, the architects felt that "to be most effective, the space would benefit from an articulation of areas that to add a smaller scale," Sage says. So they created a series of reading "gardens" with oversized "lampshades." A carpeted area by the windows was kept open for read-alouds and group activities

▼ Bookshelves serve two purposes at NYPL's Melrose Branch: They hold titles and they're great for leaning against

DATE SCHOOL LIBRARY JOURNAL, APRIL 2014

Mural Magic

A class assignment becomes an artistic gift

By Mahnaz Dar

When Missouri University of Science and Technology student Lara Edwards, a senior studying biological sciences, took an Art in the Community class last summer, she wasn't just fulfilling a school assignment—she also took the opportunity to give back to the Leola Millar Children's Library, part of the Rolla Public Library in Rolla, MO. Both Edwards and another student, Michael Crabtree, decided to create a mural in the children's library and worked on the project together, with Crabtree taking measurements and sketching out the mural on paper (planning the scale of the mural), and Edwards coming up with the color scheme and deciding what to draw.

Missouri University of Science and Technology student Lara Edwards sits in front of her mural

Though a great deal of planning went in, both Edwards and Crabtree were flexible, adding a nighttime scene later on, although they had initially planned only daytime scenes.

"... while we were painting, Michael said he thought we should include night scenes," said Edwards on the Discover Missouri S & T website. "So we picked one scene to be nighttime. This decision didn't change the characters or landscape in that area, but it changed the color scheme a lot."

Time was another matter the two had to be flexible about. The two students had originally planned to devote 40 hours toward finishing the mural, but when the class ended in August 2013, they were still not finished. They continued working, devoting more than 100 hours total to the project, between their other classes.

Edwards even worked in details at the request of children visiting the library, including an image of a penguin for a boy who was initially disappointed to see that she was painting an owl.

"...he thought I was painting a penguin and when he realized it was an owl, he was disappointed," said Edwards on the Discover Missouri S & T website. "So the next day, I painted a penguin on the wall for him."

Edward's efforts paid off. Her lavish mural includes planets, jungles, deserts, dinosaurs, and more.

This isn't the last project for Edwards on the horizon. She is finishing a comic book about endangered cheetahs, which her Arts in the Community professor, Luce Myers, has plans to publish upon completion.

"When you find a student who has this kind of vibrating gem inside them, it's so exciting and you don't want it to go unnoticed," Myers said on the Discover Missouri S & T website. "You don't want to miss the opportunity to shine a light on them."

Edward's published comic book will be publicly displayed at the campus student center.

Mahnaz Dar (mdar@mediasourceinc.com) is an Associate Editor for School Library Journal *and can be found on Twitter @DibblyFresh*

Over 13 Not Admitted

Stockholm's TioTretton library gives tweens a space of their own
By Sarah Bayliss

At the unique TioTretton library in Stockholm, Sweden, children between the ages of ten and 13 are the only patrons allowed to enter. No parents. No teachers. TioTretton—translation, "Ten Thirteen"—makes tweens feel at home while providing some distance from the grown-ups who direct so much of their lives. "Our goal is that every visitor can feel like they can shape their visit that day," says Amanda Stenberg, an educator who works at the library.

In tune with this non-rule-bound atmosphere, architect Ricardo Ortiz wanted to "create a place where a child could find his or her own mood." That could mean nestling in one of several red-cushioned pods and selecting a book from a nearby shelf or suspended from an overhead coil. It could involve making ravioli from scratch in the library kitchen and browsing through cookbooks; putting together a costume with one of the sewing machines and leafing through books about textiles; making music; or sharing a film made on one of the library's iPads.

DESIGN ELEMENTS OF SURPRISE Books are integrated into all areas of the TioTretton library (top), even hanging from the ceiling. Hammock seating next to the plate-glass windows provides a place to climb and curl up with a book

Giving tweens what they want Located on the second floor of the Kulturhuset building, a large cultural center in Stockholm that is also home to other library spaces, TioTretton opened in fall 2011. It was the brainchild of Katti Hoflin, the former director of Stockholm's libraries. She'd seen that kids this age weren't interested in the city's existing library options.

"Instead of saying, 'How can we change kids to get them to come to the library?' she said, 'How can we change?'" according to Stenberg.

To discover what tweens want in a library, Hoflin initiated a pre-study, carried out by Ylva Ågren of Stockholm University's Centre for the Studies of Children's Culture and Lena Thunberg, now an educator at TioTretton. The poll asked 125 Stockholm tweens about "their thoughts concerning reading, what they liked to do in their free time, and about their dream space," Stenberg says.

"They wanted a place of their own," the study revealed. Stenberg adds that kids this age are "really used to always being told by grown-ups what's right and what's wrong." They "wanted grown-ups who knew what they were talking about who were not teachers." TioTretton librarians act as this "third adult" figure, she says.

Space for TioTretton was carved out of an adult library area and renovated with funds from the city. Like Stockholm's other libraries, its operations are fully supported by taxpayer money, says Stenberg.

Planning this new space, Hoflin was adamant that it have a kitchen and that the architect make the most of the large windows. She also wanted "a place to climb," says Stenberg.

While Ortiz planned how to achieve these goals within the 1,200-plus square foot space, he kept in mind the ideas of Danish philosopher and family therapist Jesper Juul. Ortiz says, "A child will do exactly what you want if you present it in a way that suits him. It's a matter of how you present a problem."

Ortiz also wanted every library activity to circle back to reading. "The whole idea is to create a space where you catch their attention and give them a book," he says. But the impetus must come from the child, not from authority figures. "The more you push, the less they will read in the future," he says. As such, the activity areas always have themed books nearby. TioTretton, he says, is "not just a place with books. It's a place to be well. Once a child had found a place to sit and be well, he is receptive to reading."

Ortiz's design embodies his conviction that "everything is a progression of the mood of the child." "If you are an introvert, you go to the cocoons," he says, referring to hammock-like seating slung at varying heights next to the plate-glass windows. Nestled there, a child "can see in and be protected at the same time."

However, "If you feel more open, you can sit in a red soft furniture area" constructed like stairs that ascend pyramid-style, Ortiz says. "I've carved little spaces inside this foamy area for a child to find protection, look out, and mingle but not too much."

"If he feels a bit playful he will find a soft 'sausage' seating area in the middle of the room where he can sink in," Ortiz says. He continues, "The more extroverted part of the design is this funky little bar outside the theater."

The third adult, from cooking to crochet While TioTretton's design empowers kids to discover their own experiences, its staff strive to make them feel unpressured and free. The kitchen meets many of those goals, says Stenberg. Concocting recipes at the large kitchen table, kids can experiment and make mistakes without consequences. "At this age, kids are thinking about performance and that things should be perfect," Stenberg says. "The kitchen is a place to mix things and see what happens."

TioTretton's librarians are trained in specific ways to be that "third adult" who is neither parent nor teacher and avoid setting the agenda for their charges. "We work so much on how we talk to our kids," says Stenberg. "For example, we don't use gender-specific pronouns. We don't ask where they're from. We try to create an atmosphere where they shape their own identities. A place where you can come and experience stories. We don't ask people their names."

Out in the main library space, the librarians are present while also hanging back. "We sit with a book or crochet or draw something," says Stenberg. "We try to let the kids take the initiative." While refraining from making personal inquiries, "we ask questions regarding what they are doing" or what kids are reading to engage with them.

Being an anti-authority figure is useful in other ways, too. Though Stenberg is an accomplished cook, "I'm not very good at music programs," she says. But some tweens view her lack of experience as a plus. The young patrons usually do not want experts helping them with music and film, she says. "I sit down and learn with the kids. It creates an open atmosphere."

Notes Stenberg, "One of the biggest things is the philosophy that this is a work in progress that will never be finished. We should always try new things. TioTretton should shape and reshape itself."

It has already done so. When the library opened, "we had this idea that the more grown-ups in the library, the better," she says. "It was too messy. We started too many projects at the same time." During school visits, for instance, librarians used to host "really long digital and drama workshops." The kids would look at the cocoons by the windows and say, "Can we just climb up there and read?"

Sarah Bayliss (shbayliss@gmail.com) has written for LJ*'s Movers & Shakers feature and* Library by Design *supplements*

DATE SCHOOL LIBRARY JOURNAL, MARCH 2014

Chicago Public Library Expands YOUmedia Labs

By Karen Springen

Chicago teens can thank the John D. and Catherine T. MacArthur Foundation and Mayor Rahm Emanuel for an expansion of YOUmedia—an innovative digital-learning program with several programs in the Chicago Public Library (CPL) system that embrace food, noise, and video games such as Guitar Hero.

Five CPL branches currently have YOUmedia labs, including the original 5,000 square-foot lab in Chicago's main Harold Washington Library Center, where the initiative started in 2009. With an additional $2 million from the MacArthur Foundation and $500,000 approved by the Chicago City Council, CPL will open and staff YOUmedia programs in six more branches this summer, along with temporary "pop-ups" in 12 branches. Teens may tackle challenges such as building a robot or making a movie in two days, says Andrea Saenz, first deputy commissioner of the CPL, who is overseeing the expansion.

More than 1,500 teens currently participate in Chicago YOUmedia programs, which meet President Barack Obama's previously stated goal of empowering kids to become "makers and creators of things, rather than just consumers." About half of the participants are African-American teenage boys living in at-risk neighborhoods, according to a press release from the Mayor's office and a report on YOUmedia from the University of Chicago's Consortium for Chicago School Research.

"YOUmedia initially was a place," says Saenz. "Now we're seeing it as a service model and an approach and a philosophy that allows us to engage teens regardless of the space or the technology."

The newest YOUmedia centers' computers were sponsored by a Chicago Public Library Foundation endowment.

"It's really inspiring—this idea that a library can be so many different things," she adds. "It's about being responsive to what your community wants."

For Violet Urban, a 15-year-old high school freshman, that means making jewelry with the 3-D printer, recording podcasts, and—yes—checking out lots of books, especially manga.

"I'm here like every day," she says. "When I first saw YOUmedia, I said, 'This place is my sanctuary!'"

Her friend Isaiah Fernandez, a 16-year-old sophomore, became a regular more than a year ago, when he stumbled upon the program during a rare visit to the Harold Washington Library for a school project.

"I thought, 'Oh, my gosh, what is this place?'" he says. "It was basically a room full of teenagers with PlayStations, Mac computers—really cool. Now I'm kind of here every day."

If it weren't for YOUmedia, Fernandez would "probably go home and finish my homework by five o'clock and be bored for the rest of the night." Now he checks out books and looks at ACT college admissions exam prep books—"feeling scared while trying to prepare myself," he says.

Teens visit YOUmedia for different reasons, according to the consortium report. It classified 18 percent of teens who visit YOumedia sites as "socializers" who mainly hang out with friends, play cards or board games, and attend open mic sessions. Twenty-eight percent are "readers and studiers" who check out books and use the computers and space to do homework. Twenty-one percent are "floaters" who try everything, while 11 percent are "experimenters" who use the computers and keyboards outside of the studio to practice and write music, but rarely interact with adults in the space. The 22 percent of teen "creators" come together with staff around interests such as music, video, poetry, gaming, writing, or graphic design.

The Consortium report found that teens saw YOUmedia as a "welcoming space, where they feel emotionally and physically safe and where they feel they belong." Participants reported more involvement in their chosen interests, improvement in at least one digital media skill and in their academic skills, and better understanding about opportunities after high school.

Forty percent of those early users were male African-Americans who may have initially come into the library to create videos and music using the program's digital technology, but often ended up "using the library as a library," says Penny Sebring, co-founder of the Consortium and principal investigator on its YOUmedia study.

YOUmedia teens also loved working with special "youth-oriented" mentors and librarians who were part of the YOUmedia program.

"It's the combination of the space, the people, and the equipment, Sebring says. "In the inner cities, there are just not as many after-school activities for kids." The expansion to more branches will let more kids take advantage of "these very positive experiences," she says.

Karen Springen teaches journalism at Northwestern and spent 24 years as a Newsweek *correspondent*

Climbing the Shelves

Niños Conarte in Monterrey, Mexico, takes kids' engagement to the next level By Ryann Uden

Monterrey is the third largest city in Mexico and an urban area rich in history and culture. It is also home to Fundidora Park, a Museum of Industrial Archaeology created from a steel foundry established in 1900. The expansive park includes recreation areas, auditoriums, convention centers, theme parks, hotels, and museums, along with the historic industrial structures from the foundry (blast furnaces, chimneys, and more).

On July 2, 2013, the complex added a library to the mix. The children's library Niños Conarte provides a unique, interactive space to encourage reading and art education.

The Council for Culture and Arts of Nuevo Leon (Conarte) commissioned architectural firm Anagrama Branding to build the reading center and cultural theater. Anagrama was tasked with creating the space while also preserving the 11,000 square foot historic factory structure. (The architects can't release the total cost of the project owing to nondisclosure agreements, Roberto Treviño, architecture director of Anagrama, told *LJ*. It was funded by Conaculta, Mexico's National Council for Culture and Arts.)

Looking outside the library As the design process began, the architects made a concerted effort to leave traditional library designs behind as they planned a fun and inviting space for children. They looked to other child-friendly spaces such as pavilions, playgrounds, and parks for inspiration.

They also gave a nod to the Sierra Madres foothills that surround the city of Monterrey for the shape of the imaginative reading space. The peaks and valleys offer children the chance to climb and explore while enjoying the books that surround them. The "mountains" are asymmetrical shelves covered in grey artificial grass. The color scheme makes use of primary colors with a neon twist to engage the children while complementing the industrial environs. Interior colors are replicated in the logo for a coherent theme.

Money or a library card are not necessary in order to visit Niños Conarte, but people who come had better bring socks: shoes aren't allowed in the reading area. The space is intended to bring about the feeling of being surrounded by books, with tall shelves lining one wall. Approximately 4,300 titles are available to enjoy and share on-site but are not loaned. Selected by Conarte's cultural development manager, a book editor, they cover a range of reading and age levels.

The topmost shelves hold historical items not for use by visitors. Children are welcome to share and enjoy the volumes on the bottom shelves. At some point, the topmost shelves may be appropriated for works in other languages (English, French, Portuguese, and German). If so, a special ladder will be installed to make them accessible.

Niños Contarte also meets a need in the community for art-related education. Anagrama designed the theater and art room with a more functional focus than the whimsical reading room. Design elements extend into the auditorium, with neon-red beams and blue pipes. Suspended tube lights illuminate the space while still revealing the historic framework of the building. Recently, Anagrama Branding was awarded the Architizer 2014 A+ Awards for Popular Choice and Jury Selection for this project.

Anagrama is familiar with presenting unexpected designs to surprised clients, and this project is no different. Treviño likened the

A LITERARY LANDSCAPE Niños Conarte's unique climbable shelves

experience to a roller-coaster ride, with clients both excited and nervous as they take the plunge. After a few weeks of discussing minor adjustments to the plan, Conarte staff approved the design, and their risk paid off.

Serving a destination population Niños Conarte opened to very positive responses from the public, according to manager Ana Lucía Aguilar. Thousands explored the space during the summer of 2013, and the 20-person staff added weekend tours to meet demand. An estimated 30,000 children visit the space on a monthly basis. Feedback is then gathered from teachers who come with school groups; a more formal survey of public needs and opinions is being considered.

Niños Conarte is geared toward children from birth to age 13, parents, families, and educators. Some ten monitors, four of them children's literature experts, help supervise the children and guide their experience through readers' advisory. Groups frequently visit from area schools and organizations. Programs at the space include weekly storytelling sessions, bebeteca (a program for babies under two), plays, summer day camps, and more.

Aguilar describes two recent author visits as her most memorable experiences so far. When Javier Sáez Castán and Francisco Hinojosa stopped by, children were given the opportunity to ask the writers questions and have books signed. Aguilar was impressed by how the children's questions displayed their developing literacy, critical thinking, and empathy skills.

Playing off its culturally rich surrounding in Fundidora Park, reflecting the topography of the Sierra Madres, and encouraging the love of reading and learning make Niños Conarte an innovative example of a library reflecting its community while also meeting its needs.

Ryann Uden is Head of Youth Services, Barrington Area Library, IL. Find her on Twitter @ryuden. Special thanks to Ana Lucía Aguilar of Niños Conarte and Lucía Elizondo of Anagrama Branding for assistance with this article

6
strategies

SMALL SOLUTIONS FOR SMALL BUDGETS

It's rare that a community will have endless resources to design and maintain its library—hence the inevitable prioritization based on needs, goals, and strategic outlook. The projects here—shared from *LJ*'s design coverage since 2009 as originally published—illustrate how small steps can make all the difference in design, maintenance, and the critical community engagement piece that any library needs as it builds investment in projects small and large. Many of these projects are well under way or now reinvented themselves, but the learning captured here along the way will inform any design process.

Expert Makeovers

In New Jersey, a SWAT Team of Library Transformers brings savings and smarter design to four libraries By Gary Cooper & Kathy Schalk-Greene

As in many areas of the country, New Jersey libraries are struggling to meet higher demand and maintain critical services in the face of reduced state and local funding. And library space is at a premium without a lot of renovation money to go around. This gap prompted the New Jersey State Library, on the recommendation of State Librarian Norma Blake's Blue Ribbon Task Force on the Future of Libraries, to create the "SWAT Team of Library Transformers." This group of four librarians, all of whom had addressed similar challenges in their own facilities, shared their expertise with four New Jersey public libraries in dire need of affordable makeovers.

"All of our libraries have shown a dramatic increase in traffic over the past two years," says Blake, *LJ*'s 2008 Librarian of the Year. "More and more job-seekers, reading program families, and people on tighter budgets are coming to our libraries, meaning our older libraries need to become more welcoming and more efficiently utilize every available space. When taxpayers walk into their libraries, they want them to be attractive, inviting, and easily accessible. Our SWAT Team worked with libraries to ensure each got the most out of their budgeted money."

The team Mount Laurel Library director Kathy Schalk-Greene led the team, tapping lessons learned when she transformed her building into a nationally acclaimed bookstore-style library. Other team members were Jayne Beline, director of the Parsippany-Troy Hills Library; Cheryl McBride, director of the North Brunswick Library; and Gloria Urban, director of the Vineland Public Library.

HARDHATS AT WORK SWAT Team members (l.–r.): Jayne Beline, Gloria Urban, Kathy Schalk-Greene, and Cheryl McBride

The team worked with the selected libraries—Caldwell, Matawan-Aberdeen, Midland Park, and Gloucester County Library's Glassboro Branch—as expert consultants regarding their projects. The team visited each library and collaborated on a detailed transformation plan. Throughout the process team members were available for consulting, advice, and moral support.

Libraries were chosen for the program based on applications detailing their needs and transformational goals. Each had to commit at least $5000 to the makeover, with all projects completed within 11 months. State funding paid for the team members' consulting time.

"With the guidance of our experts, these libraries were able to show dramatic, visible transformations in their floor plans that resulted in improved customer service," says Blake. "I hope this program will serve as a demonstration project for other libraries, both in New Jersey and nationwide, that library interiors can be transformed without a lot of money."

The 2010 SWAT Team Project worked so well that four new libraries have been selected this year: Atlantic County Library–Mays Landing; Clifton Public Library–Allwood Branch; Passaic Public Library; and Sayreville Public Library.

More information is available at swatteam.njlibraries.org/index.html. Here's what they accomplished.

Gary Cooper is the Public Relations & News Media Contact for the New Jersey State Library. Kathy Schalk-Greene is Director of the Mount Laurel Library and leader of the SWAT Team of Library Transformers

GLOUCESTER COUNTY LIBRARY–
GLASSBORO BRANCH

Let in the Light

The Gloucester County Library's Glassboro Branch was once a circa 1950 grocery store with few windows. The library wanted to brighten the dark paneled interior, arrange library materials in a more inviting and easily accessible way, and make better use of the interior space. Staff removed old shelving, weeded materials, and rearranged the furniture to create a more welcoming space for users. Project funds were spent on painting the entire interior, with the assistance of design and sign artists, significantly brightening the space. More comfortable, updated furniture was added with financing from the Friends of the Library. A bonus to the SWAT project was the transformation of the only meeting room thanks

BEFORE

BEFORE

to a local Boy Scout who saw an opportunity to earn his Eagle Scout badge. He secured donations of materials and labor to install new flooring, cabinetry, and custom painting and coordinated it with the new look of the library's interior.

COST $14,178 (COMPLETED OCTOBER 2010)

CALDWELL PUBLIC LIBRARY

Grandeur Plus Functionality

The Caldwell Public Library opened in 1917 as a small one-story brick structure, but expansion had compromised the original charm of this Carnegie Library. The transformation goal was to restore the grandeur of the original library, organize the space to reflect the warm "heart of our town" feeling, and optimize available space to meet user needs. Changes included removing shelving to make the entryways more welcoming, moving the circulation desk for greater visual impact, relocating all printed library information onto slatwalls, and reducing clutter throughout. Funds were spent painting the first floor, rebuilding and highlighting a historic window, adding new shelving for media, and installing slatwall. The library doubled its original commitment with matching funds from the local women's club.

COST $13,690 (COMPLETED DECEMBER 2010)

BEFORE

BEFORE

MATAWAN-ABERDEEN LIBRARY
A Major Housecleaning

The Matawan-Aberdeen Library showed a 257 percent increase in DVD circulation over the previous year, with demand for new and old movies increasing. The challenge was to find space for this popular service in the 9,880 square foot library. Improvements included buying new DVD shelving, realigning the shelving for better sight lines, and categorizing the DVDs. New library catalog computers were installed on space-saving end panels.

Although the staff met its goal, other needed changes were made. A corner with a microfilm reader was cleaned out and reconfigured to support computer job searching and one-on-one computer tutoring. The basement was cleared of years of accumulated books, furniture, and other clutter (two dumpsters' worth!); the local newspaper was digitized, and old local journals were donated to the historical society. The technical services department was moved out of the basement. The basement will be used to expand the public meeting room.

COST $6000 (COMPLETED DECEMBER 2010)

BEFORE

BEFORE

MIDLAND PARK MEMORIAL LIBRARY
Clarifying Overhaul

The Midland Park Memorial Library was built in the knotty pine style of the 1950s and expanded over the years. Its renewal plan addressed both the main circulation area so that new materials would stand out and sought to update and improve the overall ambiance of the library. Improvements included weeding of almost 20 percent of the collection. Shelving that was blocking access was replaced with new shelving that was arranged to make the area more open and accessible. The makeover also installed shelving to highlight the fireplace and removed excess furniture and tables that were obscuring sight lines.

While completing these goals, the Midland Park staff and SWAT Team identified larger needs. Staff then worked with an architect to develop an expanded plan. Funded by the Board of Trustees with dedicated reserve monies, the expanded plan's goal was threefold: to provide

BEFORE

BEFORE

a more cohesive entrance into the library, better delineating the adult and children's areas; move the circulation desk to a central area, allowing staff better views of both the front and back entrances; and remove a public restroom from the middle of the library, replacing it with separate restrooms for men and women in a less central spot. "People walk into the library now and say, 'Wow!'" says Director Melissa Hughes.

COST $200,000 (COMPLETED JUNE 2011)

Library Inside Out

Exceptional lighting ups the impact
By Sarah Bayliss

The goal of the new Tenley-Friendship Neighborhood Library in Washington, DC, which opened in January 2011, was to give neighborhood residents a "grand, well-lit, inviting" place—a "fantastic library where people would want to spend time," says Kim Fuller, District of Columbia Public Library's (DCPL) project manager, who oversaw the library's construction.

The 22,000 square foot library's architecture, with floor-to-ceiling windows overlooking busy streetscapes and trees, provided the framework for this concept. Strategic lighting design did the rest, with $600,000 from Tenley-Friendship's budget of $11 million.

"The intent was to have it feel transparent," says Hayden McKay, principal at Horton Lees Brogden (HLB) Lighting Design, which conceived the lighting scheme. "We wanted the library to be as daylit as possible and also have a connection to nature."

The lighting strategy also provides a model of energy efficiency, thanks to strategic sunlight harvesting, sun control, occupancy sensors, and other features that helped propel the library to Leadership in Energy & Environmental Design (LEED) Gold certification.

Designing in views Mindful of DCPL's commitment to creating a community icon with an urban street presence, McKay and colleagues strove to enhance the library's open, inviting architecture and to bring in the natural cycles of daylight. HLB installed vertical, copper-colored fins along some façades to shield patrons from the sun, while also framing dynamic views onto the street that shift as patrons move through the space. The copper hue also enhances sunlight differently depending on the position of the sun.

These vistas also "allow you to redirect your focus after you've been looking at a computer screen," says McKay, a switch that relaxes and refreshes the eyes. "It's not just daylight itself that's important to people but the view. The windows tell you about the time of day, the weather, the climate, what's happening on the street."

In the center of the library, an enormous, bow tie–shaped skylight above a large atrium feeds light to the main reading room. Direct light makes one area "feel like an outdoor patio," McKay says, an ideal environment for sun-loving patrons (though the collection throughout is shielded from damaging UV rays).

For a more whimsical effect in the children's area, "we use circular fluorescent fixtures in varying sizes—three-, four-, and five-foot diameter, scattered in a playful way," says McKay.

Open for business Multiple photo sensors in the library reduce electrical light output depending on the level of natural light. McKay estimates that the library lights typically dim to five percent during the day. Photo sensors automatically turn off the lights in empty conference rooms.

Throughout the library, HLB envisioned "indirect, soft uniform lighting" to complement the library's airy design and provide visual comfort. Cantilevered fixtures over the stacks offer a diffused sense of light, as does indirect light that bounces off the open ceiling. Collectively, McKay notes, this "illuminates the whole space so you

don't get a feeling of being in a CVS, with exposed lights all day long."

There is one catch to all this energy efficiency, though: because so many lights are off, "people aren't always sure the library's open" during the day, McKay says. To "make it inviting," HLB installed six long, candle-shaped pendants in the stairwell that stay on during library hours. Though only 13-watt fixtures, they add a critical "little bit of sparkle."

"People can stay inside for extended periods of time as long as they have the connection to the outdoors," observes McKay. As testament to this, Fuller notes, "people are there every hour that the library is open. That was not the case with the old [building]."

"It may sound elementary, but people are grateful for well-lit spaces," adds Fuller, noting that "deferred maintenance" in the previous branch led to poor lighting. Now, "you don't have go to around the corner and worry that the light is out."

Sarah Bayliss has written for LJ, *the* New York Times, *Boston* Globe, *and* ARTnews *magazine, among other publications*

Let "Green" Creep

Ten steps to sustainable library operations By Louise L. Schaper

You've heard the buzz about building green libraries, but what about green library operations? You know, the things we do every day to give our customers a great library experience, like cleaning the floors, registering new cardholders, and leading a story time. In each area, we can do a better job being stewards of the earth's resources, and, in the process, we can redeploy the money saved to things our customers want.

Green libraries cost less to operate, and, if you plan it right, you might find out that your library has more to spend on items like books.

My experience with green libraries began back in 1998 when, under my leadership, the Fayetteville Public Library (FPL), AR, decided to build a new facility. After a very public planning process in which residents voiced their desire for an environmentally efficient library, FPL became, in 2001, the first building in Arkansas to be registered for the U.S. Green Building Council's LEED (Leadership in Energy & Environmental Design) certification, the nation's most used and respected standard for green buildings. In 2004, the Blair Library opened. It later received LEED-NC (new construction) Silver certification.

When bids were opened in 2002 and, owing to a building boom, came in higher than expected, some people suggested cutting those "green things" from the budget. The finance administrator first uttered and then persuasively repeated a definitive "no." She knew the long-term value of those "green things"—money saved every year in utility and maintenance costs. Those "green things" stayed intact, and the library ended up saving about 19 percent in gas and electric costs in the first full year; savings increased to 35 percent in the third year (see table, below). The cost of going LEED-NC Silver was paid back in the first few years.

Aligning values and practice After the Blair Library opened, I became acutely aware that our "green library" was designed and built on a set of values that were not being carried out in day-to-day op-

Energy Performance of Fayetteville's Blair Library 2005–2009

	Gas (CCF)	Electric (kWh)	Total kBTU**	Total $	kBTU/sf	$/sf	% savings kBTU	% savings $
Industry Standard*	19,567	2,092,106	9,151,710	$154,960	104.0	$1.76	0.0%	0.0%
Design Budget (2003)	16,312	1,744,093	7,629,350	129,183	86.7	1.47	-16.6	-16.6
Actual 2005***	20,539	1,785,280	8,204,838	124,972	93.2	1.42	-10.3	-19.4
Actual 2006	10,821	1,516,080	6,286,346	116,025	71.4	1.32	-31.3	-25.1
Actual 2007	13,528	1,510,800	6,546,881	100,829	74.4	1.15	-28.5	-34.9
Actual 2008	13,121	1,276,960	5,707,138	106,192	64.9	1.21	-37.6	-31.5
Actual 2009	13,931	1,274,160	5,780,934	98,506	65.7	1.12	-36.8	-36.4

Total Gas and Electric Use in kBTUs**

Total

(y-axis: kBTUs, 0 to 10,000,000)
(x-axis: Industry Standard*, Design Budget (2003), Actual 2005***, Actual 2006, Actual 2007, Actual 2008, Actual 2009)

*ASHRAE 90.1-1999: American Society of Heating, Refrigerating and Air-conditioning Engineers; an international organization that establishes standards for the uniform testing and rating of heating, ventilation, air conditioning, and refrigeration equipment. ** kBTUs: British Thermal Units (thousands)—a measure that serves as a common energy use denominator. *** **Commissioning Period.**

erations. The building's design team, MS&R, Ltd., produced a gem to which legions of visitors came to learn about green buildings. But with each tour, I thought, "If they noticed how un-green we were in routine functions, they'd question our commitment to sustainability." When I looked around at what we were doing, I kept hearing the values that community members clearly articulated during the planning process and could see that we were not carrying them out as we should. For example, we were:

1 Nurture the champions
The most important step on the way to green operations is identifying and nurturing staff members with the commitment and skill to go green. Directors, don't worry that you have to know everything. Your job is to lead, empower, and support.
1. The facilities manager must be a champion. If you don't have a green-leaning facilities staff, share your expectations; support learning time but get commitment in return. Make clear that going green requires abandoning existing notions of how things are done.
2. Personality also matters when considering champions. Sam Palmer, my quintessential

FPL Champion: Sam Palmer, Director of Facilities and Sustainability

director of facilities and sustainability, had the skills, respect, and a natural bent to share and spread the "wealth" of emerging knowledge about green strategies. Plus, he is a joker, a bonus! Making "green" fun encourages participation.
3. Give champions room to succeed and fail. They need a commitment of resources, whether for training or time to visit or read about green facilities or to explore new products and processes.
4. Encourage champions to network. Relationships formed with other entities and vendors are invaluable. They can result in real benefits

like receiving free or heavily discounted green products and technologies.
5. Update titles, job descriptions, interview questions, annual objectives, and job evaluation forms to reflect green operational responsibilities or tasks.

2 Transform cleaning
Every director is challenged when it comes to housekeeping. I used the motto "keep the building in opening-day condition" to inspire the staff. Green cleaning requires learning new habits, but it also offers an easy win on your path to a greener facility.
1. If you use contract cleaners, find those trained in green cleaning. FPL took cleaning in-house, reallocated that budget, and was able to afford an assistant facilities manager, automated janitorial equipment, 2.5 housekeepers, and supplies—enough to keep 90,000 square feet exceptionally clean.
2. Hire cleaners with little experience but a strong desire to clean—old habits die hard.
3. Begin cleaning early, around 6 a.m.; finish just after closing. Limit after-hours work to infrequent jobs, like waxing floors. This strategy decreases electricity use and light pollution and provides

1. Giving away plastic book bags.
2. Lighting up the sky and using lots of electricity with night cleaning services.
3. Printing thousands of monthly newsletters.
4. Gluing ads for library programs to foam core for display at service desks.
5. Using bottled water and plastic cutlery, cups, and dishes for events.
6. Serving candy and other unhealthy foods at programs.
7. Driving to meetings and restaurants, even if only a few blocks away.
8. Leaving PCs and monitors on 24/7.
9. Adding cooling units and fans to address server and CPU overheating.
10. Offering library cards that couldn't be recycled and wouldn't decompose.

How could we align the green values inherent in the building with operations? With so many of our actions, including mine, I saw activities trending upward in carbon emissions instead of down. What could we do? We were overwhelmed by all the critical things you do when moving into a new building, like tweaking work processes and ensuring that residents get every bit of value for their $23.4 million. Isn't serving a rapidly growing base of customers drawn to a facility that one young adult said was "just like a New York City library" enough? How would we ever have time to make operations greener? Was I sufficiently committed?

Driving home my personal embarrassment were customer complaints, with at least one in the newspaper, that the library claimed to be green but was leaving its interior lights on all night. The lights were on late for the cleaning crews, but the customers were right: we were wasting electricity!

Instill it in the mission When I retired at the end of October 2009, operations at Blair Library were green and getting greener. We were saving money and natural resources. The building was more comfortable. More staff members than ever before were proactive about green procedures on a professional basis. I laughed when my successor, Shawna Thorup, told me that one trustee called her plan to go for LEED-EB, the certification for existing buildings and operations, "mission creep." I said, "update the mission to reflect the library's responsibility to provide services in a sustainable manner." Don't we want our libraries to be there for future generations? Don't we want to reduce carbon emissions, save money, and give our customers additional materials and services?

Operating green means more than recycling. It's a change of perspective that makes your library stronger, richer, and healthier for your staff and the public. Operate your library in ways that don't compromise the ability of future generations to meet their needs. That's sustainability.

Being green is also a commitment to (1) discover best practices; (2) innovate when solutions don't exist; (3) reduce waste and inefficiencies; (4) adopt and embrace new habits; and (5) measure and celebrate progress. You do this every day; now just wear a green lens.

Be a green pioneer Your community needs visible and tangible examples for inspiration and ideas. There is no more visible entity than the library, so go ahead and be a green pioneer and a champion. You can start small or large. In the process, a lot more people will be visiting your library and asking questions. Ultimately, you'll be changing lives in more ways than you thought possible.

The FPL journey to green actions did not begin with a written plan or a consultant telling us what to do; it started with open eyes and self-examination. But ten steps emerged that made all the difference. All of us working toward being green are in the early stages of what someday will be best practices. But for now, we're all learning. These steps just might be what your library needs to get greening.

---

for on-demand help during open hours like cleaning up spills and setting up meeting rooms.

4. Get rid of harsh chemicals. When going green, think less is more. All you'll need is a few spray bottles, water, and several cleaning solutions.

5. Use a simple and effective basic cleaning product. A good one is hydrogen peroxide in dilutions from one percent to five percent. It breaks down easier than most substances, and, while great as an antibacterial, it is kinder on the environment than bleach. Cleaning with commercial-grade concentrated hydrogen peroxide costs about 3¢ a gallon. FPL's cost for its 90,000 square foot facility is under $100/year.

6. Buy specific cleaning agents that are certified green, e.g., a nonacid bathroom cleaner, a spray disinfectant, wood polish, and a carpet spotting solution. Spartan Chemicals makes GreenSeal certified cleaning products.

7. Use microfiber cloths, which have a super ability to pick up tiny particles. Not all microfiber is created equal, however, so you'll need to experiment.

8. Always look out for new ideas. I recently noticed that the water at a restaurant tasted exceptionally good. Ends up they electrolyze city water and use the alkaline portion for drinking and the acid portion as a cleaning agent. Even actor and environmentalist Ed Begley Jr. electrolyzes his own home's water. Who knew?

3 Deploy energy-savings lights and controls
Beyond turning lights off whenever possible (remember night sky and energy drain), think about light bulb replacement and lighting controls. Lighting is an easy fix with tangible and documentable cost savings. In many cases, lighting will be improved. Any new library should come with a lighting control system that automates on and off times and dims fixtures when sunlight is available. Motion and light sensors, timers, and energy-saving dimmers can be easily and inexpensively retrofit to existing buildings. Light bulb replacement is an easy savings opportunity. The benefits of compact fluorescents are well documented, but there is great news about LED bulbs.

The greatest electricity reduction comes from using LED bulbs because LEDs reduce consumption by 50–90 percent and emit 90 percent less heat than conventional bulbs. They produce much more light than heat, so they have maximum energy efficiency. Furthermore, the ten- to 20-year life span of an LED bulb means you'll rarely have to change them, and fewer bulbs will go to the trash. The cost is high (about $54 to

replace a T-8 bulb), but factor in that labor costs for changing a bulb are in the $100–$200 range, and over ten years an LED bulb will only cost around $200, while a compact fluorescent will cost up to $1200 and a T-8 up to $450.

With such longevity, LED bulbs also give your facilities staff more time to spend on pressing projects. Plus, you can change the color of the bulbs. FPL's donor wall can be programmed to display any color, including those of the Stars and Stripes.

First, find a good vendor partner with expertise and excellent sources of reliable LED bulbs. Be sure to assess wattage needs of under- or overlit areas; this is a great opportunity to address any issues. To get the fastest return on your investment, start the conversion with bulbs located in difficult-to-reach places or where there are specialized, expensive traditional bulbs. LED bulbs may actually be cheaper than or similar in cost to specialized bulbs. FPL found it cheaper to replace cold cathode tubes with ribbon LED lights because of the high cost of shipping the tubes.

4 Lighten IT energy use

Computers consume a lot of electricity and generate a lot of heat, thereby increasing cooling costs. To make matters worse, libraries, like many other organizations, often leave computers on 24/7. The good news is that it's easy to reduce IT electricity use, resulting in more money to buy more computers.

When I hired Lynn Yandell, MCSE, to be FPL's IT director in 2008, I knew I had a green champion. It wasn't just his exceptional education and experience; he was drawn to the job because of the library's commitment to being green. He soon crafted and began implementing an energy reduction strategy.

Here are some procedures for green IT, but, as with all things green, keep in mind that newer and greener technologies and software are always emerging.

1. Deploy thin clients in place of PCs where appropriate, i.e., public access catalogs and walk-up Internet stations. Thin clients are low-power, inexpensive, small-footprint PCs with a scaled-down version of Windows. Small, fanless units with a solid-state hard drive, they use one-tenth the power of regular PCs—think 25 watts vs. 250 watts. Replacing PCs with thin clients cuts power consumption by a minimum of 75 percent; Fayetteville saved 97,200 watt-hours per day. Plus, they are a lot cheaper than PCs, in the $200–$450 range.

2. Automate power down. When procuring new PCs, buy those with Intel VPro. They'll let you remotely set power cycles for all your PCs. Blair Library's 200-plus computers automatically shut down for 12 hours each night, saving 537,000 watt-hours daily. Monitors that are not turned off go into a power save mode that draws less than one watt.

3. Find efficient CPUs. Computer companies are producing far more energy-efficient CPUs. New models can save approximately 130 kilowatt-hours a year per PC.

4. Have a server strategy that guarantees power reduction. If you can't implement it all at once, do it piecemeal. Servers not only use a lot of energy, they put out a lot of heat, which increases cooling costs.

Sustaining the library and the earth: sell reusable bags

a. If your library is truly innovative and bold, figure out how to divert the heat from your server room to heat the water in your café. Let me know if this works.

b. Consider switching to blade servers. Made by various companies including Dell, IBM, and HP, blades are about half as expensive as traditional servers and employ 66 percent less energy. They are small-footprint, superreliable, fault-tolerant machines.

5 Use sustainable materials and processes

You'll need the help of everyone on the library staff to adopt more sustainable materials and processes. Collaboratively identify ideas and build commitment. You may be asking people to be much greener than they are in their personal lives.

At one point in the FPL journey, I suggested that employees be encouraged, like Wal-Mart workers, to develop their own "personal sustainability plan." That idea never made it out of administration after someone nearly choked on what they termed a corporate-like invasion of personal life. I gave up too soon. I think an optional program to learn and think about how to green one's life would be valued by many staff members. Who doesn't want to save money?

Here are some ideas to get you started:

1. Switch to recyclable and/ or biodegradable library cards. Even better, invent virtual library cards. Think of the money and resources that could be saved.

2. Sell reusable bags. Find one that is manufactured close to home and made of sustainable materials.

3. Switch to LED holiday lights, if you must have them.

4. Print less often; teach everyone how to make double-sided copies. Buy paper with high recycled content and low-chlorine bleaching. Encourage vendors to make recyclable tags and labels.

A thorough recycling center

5. Use attractive, large tabletop or freestanding reusable sign holders. While FPL's signs were attractive, using spray adhesive is a hazard, and putting foam core in the trash is not green. Too many libraries have too many paper signs taped onto walls and doors. Less is more.

6. Implement an e-newsletter, and cut the paper one. Consider an e-newsletter service like Constant Contact. As an interim step, keep your print newsletter, but decrease its frequency to a few times a year, and offer a simple but attractive half-page monthly listing of events.

7. Rid your library of bottled water. Do this for your health and the environment. I did this by dictum but in conjunction with the installation of water filters on many faucets. Our purchasing agent found great "water coolers" at Sam's Club to use at events.

8. Rid your library of plastic cups, cutlery, and dishes. After an event, just look at the size of your trash. Instead, buy, rent, and use the real stuff for events. At the very least, use products made of recycled content that can be recycled. Yes, I know what you're thinking. I've done my share of dish washing.

9. Offer healthy and sustainable food at events. If you do offer food and drink, be sure it's natural. Partner with a local natural food store or farmer's market; locally grown food is the most sustainable. Model good food choices and eating practices.

10. Organize recycling and reuse efforts and train staff. Make bins attractive, label them clearly and keep them clean. Find sources for items not taken by your local recycling office.

11. Add bike racks and consider initiating a bike-lending program.

12. Create a smoke-free campus. In Fayetteville, this meant no smoking up to the sidewalk. This is hard to enforce but much appreciated by those who want to enjoy those spaces.

13. Acquire hybrid or electric vehicles and recharging stations. Hybrid vans and bookmobiles are already available; electric vans with a 100-mile radius are about to debut.

14. Deploy remote returns to reduce traffic and use of fossil fuels. FPL's bins were donated by a bank and located at its branches.

15. Make building alterations and maintenance sustainable. Consider registering for LEED-EB (existing buildings) or start small by ensuring green materials are used in alterations or maintenance projects, e.g., paints and other finishes with low volatile organic compounds (VOCs) and use Energy Star appliances in staff and meeting room kitchens.

6 Adopt alternative energy solutions

Someday your library, home, and vehicle will be powered by alternative energy sources. By starting now, your library could reap significant savings (and have more money for collections) and get a leg up in knowledge.

At Blair, we dreamt about going alternative but stopped with technologies that were top-of-the-line energy efficient yet relied on fossil fuels. The dream didn't die. While contemplating applying for a Public Library Innovation Grant from the International City County Management Association (ICMA), I ran into Alan Mantooth, an electrical engineering professor, at a holiday party, where a plan was hatched. The library and the city would partner with the university, an electric utility, the state, a think tank, and a local start-up with some cool patents that made solar power systems more efficient. The Solar Test Bed project was born and then enabled by the good folks at ICMA.

It will result in a solar photovoltaic system mounted on the roof of the library to generate a small amount of electricity, ten to 20 kilowatts, saving about $5000–$10,000 a year. Student designed, the system will eventually be a platform for testing locally invented superefficient inverters that convert solar energy into a usable form. The project will help develop the region as a "green valley," serve as an incubator for local business, educate citizens, and promote private and public partnerships. Most important, it is a deep learning experience that will lay the groundwork for future efforts.

Get started now with understanding these technologies, and take advantage of opportunities as they present themselves.

1. Start by becoming aware. Tour projects, network, and read articles. Learn how other types of entities are deploying alternative energy systems, e.g., "Wineries Draw on Wind Power" (Wine Spectator, 4/30/10).

2. Start with the right project. If you are a Texas library, go solar!

3. Start small. Solar hot water can have a fast payback especially if you have a café. Small, inexpensive solar photovoltaic projects can have a positive impact on the bottom line and the community.

4. Ensure the right players are assembled, e.g., mechanical engineers, electrical engineers, solar experts, and the power company.

5. Think alternative when it comes to funding.

a. There are companies that lease solar systems. The library could use its energy savings to carry the cost of the lease. Or, consider third-party financing and repay the loan with the savings.

b. Find partners for public tests. You'll get the equipment, and the partners will get lots of publicity.

c. Seek private and public dollars. Is there a rebate program? Will a foundation provide funding if matched by local government?

7 Continue commissioning

When your library moves into its new energy-efficient building, you'll want it to deliver the maximum performance and, thus, savings. Commissioning is a process by which your facilities manager learns how the library's building systems work and fine-tunes them for maximum performance. It is a key step in opening a new building, especially LEED buildings that come with energy use projections.

It takes training, time, and continual updating and tweaking to get the best results from your library's automated lighting and HVAC systems, as well as from its plumbing, refrigerant use, irrigation, water capture, and air quality monitoring systems. Because conditions like weather and large events affect the building's interior climate, regular system adjustments are needed throughout the building's life span.

Ongoing commissioning is critical; it saves money and reduces the building's carbon footprint.

8 Invite community support

Enable your customers to help make the library greener so that you can add services for them. Consider whatever wild ideas might arise and give them a whirl.

One idea FPL implemented emerged from the "carbon credit"

concept. Carbon credits are sold by organizations that develop or invest in clean energy or other environmental solutions. Corporations and individuals buy them to offset their use of carbon-based energy. The carbon credit company gets capital to continue its work, and the buyer has a cleaner green report card.

Riffing on that idea, Fayetteville created the "eco-fan card," a library card composed of biodegradable material that customers can buy instead of getting a free card. The beautiful card appeals to

Author Schaper with FPL's "eco-fan card," launched in 2009

library supporters and those who care about the environment. All proceeds go directly to efforts to make the library more sustainable, like buying more LED bulbs or solar panels. If the cards are successful, the library could raise $100,000 for green efforts.

9 Educate and be a leader

There is no better institution to educate the community about green buildings than a public library. We're open to everyone, relatively transparent, and are always looking to promote what we do.

1. Incorporate green initiatives into your public and media relations; keep your board and elected officials fully informed. Use all your regular routes, including Twitter and Facebook. A power outage at Fayetteville's announcement for its Solar Test Bed project offered a surprise media opportunity and a funny anecdote to heighten awareness of the project.

2. Offer speakers and programs that educate the community and your staff. Some hugely successful programs included talks by Amory Lovins, CEO of the Rocky Mountain Institute, and actor/green advocate Ed Begley Jr., as well as youth programs like "Solar Bug Tug," in which young adults made solar-powered toy boats, and a screening of the Academy Award–nominated documentary Food, Inc.

3. Conduct tours of your green facility or green operations. Let this be known via your web site, Chamber of Commerce, builders associations, or civic groups. Broadcast green tours on your local community access channel or YouTube. Set your green champions free on the civic club circuit.

4. Partner with other organizations and libraries to do great things.

5. Don't forget book displays. Practical books and DVDs on living simply or building green homes fly off the tables.

10 Put it in writing

Build "green" into your strategic and HR infrastructures. I didn't do this but should have. A year after we moved into Blair Library, we began a strategic planning process, and the light bulb mentioned earlier had not gone off for me. The plan barely mentions the word "sustainable" and only in the context of funding.

Actor Ed Begley Jr. espouses going green to a library crowd

Whether you're just starting or well on your way to sustainable tasks, create a strong foundation with the support of staff and stakeholders.

1. With stakeholders, amend your values list with the words to express sustainability, for example, sustainable choices, and green practices in all that you do.

2. Build sustainability into your strategic plan. It ensures buy-in from stakeholders, assuming your library uses a broad input process.

3. Incorporate green values into your policy manual by amending existing policies or developing new ones. If you have purchasing policies, amend them to clarify decisions—paper must have at least 50 percent recycled content or cleaning products must be certified green. Or, be bold and develop a carbon-neutral policy that must be met within, say, a decade.

4. Consider measurable goals for each green step in this article, e.g., reduce electricity use by five percent in 2011. Then clearly articulate how your library will achieve that goal, e.g., the light bulbs on the second floor will be replaced with LED bulbs by the second quarter 2011.

Remember, you won't know if you go green unless you know how much was consumed before you went green and how much you consume after. If the goal is to reduce paper use, brainstorm ideas with staff, develop a plan, and implement. But first record how much paper your library used in the previous year as a baseline. Then begin your effort to reduce paper use. Record use at specific intervals, then compare the same time periods. Success? Celebrate and share the news. Little progress? Look at what's happening and adjust the strategy. Eventually, you'll manage by the numbers, just like those hybrid car owners who adjust their driving habits because they see in real time how much, and how little, gas they are consuming.

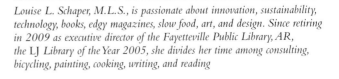

Louise L. Schaper, M.L.S., is passionate about innovation, sustainability, technology, books, edgy magazines, slow food, art, and design. Since retiring in 2009 as executive director of the Fayetteville Public Library, AR, the LJ Library of the Year 2005, she divides her time among consulting, bicycling, painting, cooking, writing, and reading

Keep Excitement High, Costs Low

Building plans on hold? You can still respond to needs in the short term while keeping stakeholders engaged in the future vision
By Henry Myerberg, AIA

In this economic climate, many libraries that have developed extensive plans to renovate or expand are now finding themselves unable to execute their capital projects. They face fewer and overtapped donor sources in both the public and private sectors. This contraction of support collides with greater demand for library services and shifting expectations for the services and experiences at the library. With a little creativity, libraries can respond to the most pressing needs while keeping stakeholders engaged in the long-term vision for the library.

Shifting patron needs The library has evolved from a place where information is stored and retrieved to a place where information is exchanged and created. Gen Y is now surprisingly the largest growing demographic user group of public libraries. Look at colleges, social networks, hotels, and markets to imagine the future of the public library.

As such, the library is an active mixed-use community center for groups to study, meet, and attend events and conferences while employing various media and information technologies. At the same time, the library is a quiet oasis for individuals to work, compute, relax, read, and contemplate. However, the fixed spaces and outdated furnishings of many libraries conceived in the 20th century were not designed for the mixed and flexible uses of the 21st century. Often groups cannot find available or suitable places to collaborate and socialize, and individuals cannot find an empty seat at a computer table or at a program.

Poised for the future During lean times, how can libraries respond to needs in the short term and remain poised for the future? How can a library keep big visions and big plans alive in the minds and hearts of its constituents and supporters?

Westport Public Library (WPL), one of the busiest libraries in Connecticut, is addressing these issues head on. Some 1,600 visitors per day cram into every bit of its 50,000 square feet. Concept plans completed two years ago responded to the library's ambition to provide more welcoming and flexible spaces for gathering, working, and socializing for a 21st-century-minded community, but the funding to realize plans for the 80,000 square foot expansion and renovation is not all in hand while the needs are mounting. Doing nothing is not an option, and neither is spending a lot of money. Instead the library will leverage scarce dollars wisely, with furnishing and technology improvements that create and demonstrate:

An engaging periodical room

EXISTING CONDITIONS The periodical room is an enclosed 500 square feet with river views, with tables and chairs flanked by periodical shelves.

PROPOSED Transform space into an adaptable setting that invites talking and sharing—a kind of café for conversation—that at any given time can be a game room, conference room, or comfortable place to relax and read. Configure four-person square and round Allsteel Merge tables for individual or group activities. Use brightly colored Metro Top Mobile chairs that swivel and roll like task chairs but feel like lounge chairs. Convert a section of periodical shelving to an interactive whiteboard like the Steelcase ENO System here.

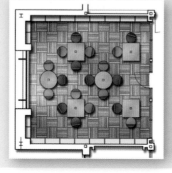

- a fresher look and feel
- collaborative and flexible uses of key spaces
- more capacity and choices of seating
- integration of current technologies and power outlets
- energy savings and green design

In addition, by showcasing how the library is addressing some pressing needs, WPL hopes to garner donor attention and foster public discourse of its intended expansion plans.

WPL has identified about 5,000 existing square feet to implement and test these improvements, which Director Maxine Bleiweis characterizes as an opportunity to perform a "preoccupancy evaluation." Three key areas are a periodical room, a quiet corner room, and an alcove of reading/work tables. These proposed cosmetic and furnishing improvements, potentially costing under $250,000 and targeted to be completed over the next year, are sustainable investments. They can be reused when the larger scale renovation and expansion plans are enacted.

Henry Myerberg, AIA, the principal of HMA2 architects, based in New York City, focuses on the design and planning of academic, school, and public libraries. Among the libraries he is currently working on are those in New York; Washington, DC, where he did the LJ makeover of the Southeast Neighborhood Library (LBD, Fall 2007); Elon, NC; and the American University of Central Asia, Kyrgyzstan

Contemplative corner

EXISTING CONDITIONS A 1,400 square foot room with generic reading tables, chairs, and lounge seating.

PROPOSED UPDATES Create a "contemplative corner" that welcomes individual study and relaxation. Line one end of the space with inviting high-back Nienkamper Turnaround Swivel chairs, to enjoy views or avoid glare, with a portable Bix Metro side table to hold laptops or coffee cups. Anchor the middle of the room with six movable Worden Stance tables equipped with state-of-the-art Worden LED reading lights (long-life, low-heat, low-voltage fixtures not requiring hard wiring) that elegantly define personal space without blocking open space.

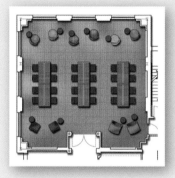

Rooms within a room

EXISTING CONDITIONS In this area of tightly spaced carrels and reading tables collaborative groups can disturb others and discourage solo table users.

PROPOSED Transform this alcove into a mix of single and group work and study spots. Increase seating and improve acoustics with a row of diner-like booths built from AGATI Hampton High-Back Banquette and tables, with sound-absorbing upholstered high-back benches and Tretford-Wild Rice carpet-like wall treatment. These welcome teens doing group homework, adults preparing media presentations (the Steelcase Mediascape System is pictured), or those seeking semiprivacy. Fit each booth with an LED task light. Add movable Danko Atmos chairs with comfortable seat and back straps made from colorful recycled seat belts.

Same Budget, New Branches

Plan to meet growing demand with static or decreased funding to the next level By Louise Levy Schaper

Can your library afford new branches or even operate existing facilities? Many libraries still struggle to meet increasing demand with flat or falling budgets and outmoded facilities.

The situation of Emily Baker, director of the Olathe Public Library (OPL), KS, exemplifies the problem many libraries have faced over the last five years. In 2008, her library completed a 20-year master plan that recommended two new branches, relocating the main library, expanding the existing branch, and doubling the number of staff. Baker moved forward to accomplish the service improvements, but recession realities put the facilities portion of the plan on hold. Finally, in 2011, the Olathe City Council appointed a task force to reexamine the library's ability to expand access but more affordably.

Don't leave your library in the dust Every librarian knows that changes in the economy, technology, demographics, and user habits continue to impact libraries. These changes teach us that while our core values remain steadfast, we can't look back to the way we used to provide services and there won't be a steady state of service we can provide.

However, that is no reason to leave your library in the dust of the early 21st century. You can plan for the future, and, if your library is not severely underfunded, you might be able to expand access. Rethink the old adage that bigger buildings and more hours require bigger budgets.

In fact, it's never been a better time to refresh your master plan and get going on its implementation. A fresh approach to the planning process might yield effective solutions to the increased demands on your library that are within the limits of your operating budget.

One architect and planner, David Schnee, principal with Group 4 Architecture, Research and Planning in South San Francisco, proves it. His work on the Otay Ranch branch—a heroic effort on the part of Betty Waznis, director of library and recreation in Chula Vista, CA, was included in an *LJ* piece on libraries in retail spaces (*Library by Design*, Spring 2013, supplement to *LJ* 5/15/13). That effort built a new branch despite the heavy toll the recession took on the library budget. The result wasn't the stand-alone facility specified in the prerecession scheme, but the mall-sited express branch filled a need and opened a new world of service opportunities.

I learned that Schnee's firm steps went beyond the classic master planning goal of identifying the need for more space. Instead, Group 4 focuses on helping libraries maximize service and access within available resources, aka a sustainable library planning approach.

One customer, Paula Miller, executive director of Colorado's Pikes Peak Library District (PPLD), sums up a common theme these days in her introduction to the library's 2010 Sustainable Services and Facilities Study by saying, "Taxpayers want and deserve efficient, accountable agencies serving them." PPLD faced a major reduction in funding, so a planning process that looked at how to move forward and improve

services and staffing despite difficult funding scenarios was appropriate. The resulting plan fully integrated programming, staffing, and facilities by meshing the funding realities and an out-of-the-box perspective of 20 years ahead. It created a model 21st- century service design. Although the worst-case scenario didn't happen, the planning framework guides PPLD's work as the library continues to make service and facility upgrades.

Schnee says that planning and building sustainable libraries isn't just about libraries, it's about the library's role in envisioning, leading, and facilitating sustainable communities. The planning process is really about identifying goals for the community's future and building a network of partners that will work collaboratively with the library toward achieving those goals.

Classic master planning In the classic master planning model, "more" is better—more space, more facilities, more staff. A typical classic planning process is directed by the library board and/or library director and in simple terms consists of seven steps:

1. Gathering and summarizing community input, usually via focus groups and questionnaires
2. Calculating population projections
3. Analyzing and presenting benchmark and peer comparative data about service measures, square footage, collection size, reader seats, and hours open
4. Assessing current facilities
5. Recommending needed changes to existing facilities and additional square feet, often in the form of neighborhood branches
6. Identifying service improvements
7. Estimating the cost of needed construction or renovation.

The outcome of classic master planning, i.e., more space and facilities, may produce great results in a good economy. Yet when the economy fails, hours are likely to be cut and branches may be closed. Therefore,

ENVISIONING THE WAY FORWARD Olathe Public Library's (OPL) current branch (l.) and a look at how it might appear following future changes (inset). OPL's Strategic Visioning Workshop (above), a daylong event at which community leaders gathered to discuss how OPL could align its services and facilities planning to support a shared view for the future of the community. Participants were guided through a series of focused activities to develop ideas and encourage visionary thinking

we must learn how to plan sustainable library systems that can weather the natural ups and downs of the economy.

Sustainable master planning In Group 4's work, a community task force is established to oversee or play an active role in the planning process—this allows for more viewpoints, forges partnerships, and places the library's planning more visibly in the context of the community's future. Representing a broad cross-section of the community, task force members ask the tough questions that their fellow community members might also have in mind.

The consultants focus more heavily on strategic visioning, patron use and transportation patterns, analysis of service trends, and service offerings of a range of library types. They combine new design strategies and analytical approaches to streamlining operations to recommend a system of destination libraries that can be built and sustainably operated long into the future.

Olathe abandoned its prerecession plan owing to cost issues. In 2012, the library hired Schnee, who came with library futurist Joan Frye Williams. The pair were focused less on new buildings and more on "what's happening now and what we can afford to operate in the future," according to OPL director Baker. She says it was a "much larger planning process—more aspects of planning, bigger picture with more elements."

Many libraries are looking for a bottom line–based but expansive perspective on planning for a sustainable future. Sustainability has been a major focus in five of Group 4's recent master plans. A move toward a more sustainable master planning process—based on a realistic budget picture, as well as efficient service models that maximize access—is a logical response to the painful realities of economic vicissitudes for many communities.

Shelly Holley, director of the Frisco Public Library, TX, says she's read too many master plans where cost of operations aren't mentioned. Her library's plan will include the projected annual operating budget for recommended facility types. "If you put operating cost in the design process, you think about design differently. I don't want a pie-in-the-

sky master plan that looks fabulous but when it comes to action and affordability in the long run, it sits on the shelf. Facilities should follow a master plan, not be the master plan."

A philosophy for planning libraries Schnee speaks enthusiastically about his approach to planning 21st-century libraries that draw residents in but are more budget friendly, aka sustainable, to operate than those of the past. He readily shares his wisdom and approaches, as well as those of others that have influenced him.

Schnee says we must take a new system because there will always be another economic challenge, and cutting hours will not work in the long term: patrons will stop coming. He starts from the reality that libraries are busier than ever but asks why customers will come to the library in person when they meet all their transactional needs online. At least a partial answer is that libraries are rapidly evolving from a supermarket role to the kitchen role, i.e., from a place to get materials to a place to create content, collaborate, support learning, serve as a "hyperlocal archivist," and engage workers. In future, he believes that one-third of libraries will evolve into 21st-century libraries, one-third will be so well funded and loved that the strength of the book will keep them at status quo, and one-third will disappear.

Among the goals he urges as part of the design process is to have library staff helping customers with valued added services, not spending time directing people to find things or executing routine tasks. As such, he says libraries should strive for 80 percent to 90 percent nonstaff-mediated transactions. This will allow libraries to pull money from within, redirecting cash from administration and materials flow to value-added impact services. He suggests libraries go for small locations if they offer an express service tailored to the needs of the immediate local area, running efficiently with a nontraditional staffing model for longer hours. For general service, he suggests fewer, larger facilities that create more vibrant destinations with more resources, better staffing, and more hours. Says Schnee, a small, poor-quality, minimally open branch is not worth the drive.

Eight ideas to expand services sustainably If the idea of sustainable planning is appealing, check out these ideas for your next master planning process:

1 Hire a great planning team. Think deeply about what your library needs from a master planning process and put it into the request for qualifications. Consider specifying a library futurist along with an architect planner with plenty of library experience. Some larger library systems are bringing IT, marketing, demographers, and economists into the planning process.

2 Establish a task force. Consider a task force or advisory group to oversee or be engaged in the planning process. This will ensure that the master plan meets community needs and can be implemented. Be sure it's a broad mix of community leaders including government, business, education, arts, community, and social service entity leaders. They'll likely become strong ambassadors for the plan's implementation. The task force approach in Olathe was, according to Baker, a much better process because of the variety of people and viewpoints. "We unearthed so much more to make a good decision," she comments, "and we built up good relationships among ourselves."

3 Evaluate current services and facilities.
The planning team looks for what needs to happen to your services and facilities to deliver an evolving library service model.

4 Collect data.
Be sure to specify knowledge of GIS mapping as a requirement for the planning team (Olathe's map at left). That's important for successfully interfacing with

city government, the library, and data firms like CivicTechnologies and OrangeBoy, Inc. These mapping and data analytical tools, plus customer surveys, are used to map customer use, identify transportation and circulation patterns, and assess community needs. Transportation patterns and branch use can be leveraged to provide services more efficiently.

Baker says sustainable planning [as opposed to classic master planning] means "digging deeper for data about your customers and community, questioning all former assumptions, and looking at the future as carefully as possible. Times have changed and much more thought and input are required to get closer to what is really warranted for your library and community." For instance, the finding that Olathe residents have highly mobile lifestyles resulted in a recommendation for two destination libraries rather than one main and three branches, as in its previous master plan.

5 Understand the operating budget.
Schnee is a firm believer that more services can be provided by streamlining the workflow. He invites library staff to watch a video of the Brooklyn Public Library's 2011 quest to expand hours despite years of cutbacks and a three-year hiring freeze. The effort, called the Open Library Initiative, carried out an exhaustive study of work tasks, undertook needed efficiencies, and resulted in an increase of service hours of about one extra day per week per branch. BPL, according to its director and chief librarian, Richard Reyes-Gavilan, "was largely successful in eliminating labor-intensive back-end processes that didn't have tremendous public value. Now that we're not sitting in back rooms counting change for the cash register, or sorting books to be sent back to their home branch, or a host of other activities about which our public doesn't care much, our frontline staff now spend most of their time involved in activities that provide some value to our users—that could mean delivering a program, offering a book recommendation, or something similar."

Schnee then asks library managers to break out the amount of time employees spend staffing a desk, delivering programs, and working in materials flow and administrative or nondirect service work. The result is that they will see how little of the budget goes to direct service, as well as notice opportunities to fix existing inefficiencies and reallocate resources to direct services, e.g., more hours, more outlets. Schnee says that automated materials handling systems make return on investment sense for high or growing circulation situations, but where they don't, there are still plenty of opportunities to achieve efficiencies in the manual equivalents.

6 Hold a daylong visioning session
with community, educational, industrial, and political leaders, along with artists, social service groups (i.e., potential partners), and Millennials. The goal is to get a lot of different people thinking differently, using techniques like metaphor games, taking on avatars, mock blogging, and backcasting to imagine a library in a future community.

7 Create a robust system design
of different library types that fit your community's needs. Destination libraries are full service, conveniently located, optimally sized to deliver most of the place-based service. They can be flagship-sized or large or medium-sized because they are sized according to the number of

people likely to visit them. They have more resources and seating, better staffing, and longer hours to provide an engaging quality experience. The destination library model is built on the concept that fewer, larger libraries can be operated less expensively than a larger number of smaller facilities, even if they comprise roughly the same amount of space. Express libraries are smaller facilities that provide convenient options tailored to the specific location. They extend the reach and convenience of the destination libraries. Express libraries can be variations of:
- Small outposts providing access to library resources.
- Materials vending or lockers for picking up items placed on hold.
- Embedded service collocated with a community or retail partner.
- Mobile service such as a bookmobile, library fleet, farmer's market table/tent. Special purpose libraries are repurposed to focus on specific needs like job training, homework place, or literacy— all with a targeted staffing model and hours.

8 Create design strategies
for efficient operations. Two buildings with the same square footage and hours are likely to require different staffing levels. That's because floor plans, number of service points and levels, and services offered determine staffing requirements. To maximize efficiencies, Schnee recommends:
- Easy and intuitive wayfinding
- Flexible zoning to allow independently operating areas of the library. Most libraries have one open zone or perhaps two. Schnee's four operating zones at Contra Costa County Library's Walnut Creek Library offer ultimate flexibility for efficient functionality (shown in the diagram below). At this library, meeting rooms, catering kitchen, and tech area can open independently as a conference center. A "marketplace" zone can open for a late Friday night or a Sunday morning at a low cost per hour for access to popular collections, technology, and the café.
- A single point of service with flexible and ergonomically adjustable service desks or "perches," to provide for a more Apple Store–type customer interaction. Aid communication with hands-free, voice-controlled wireless voice communication systems, e.g., Vocera, for staff.

FLEXIBLE OPERATIONAL MODES

WALNUT CREEK LIBRARY, GROUP 4

- Maximum self-check at 80 percent or higher by effective design strategies and customer training. Kiosks must be prominent, visible, and accessible. The technology must be easy and quick to use.
- Good sight lines to minimize staff needs and extend staff effectiveness.
- Commissioning or fine-tuning your building systems. Building green is nearly the norm now, but to ensure the building delivers on its promise, Systems like heating, cooling, lighting, irrigation, and plumbing must be operating efficiently and that takes a concerted effort.

Schnee also advises librarians to plan for a "wow" experience. Nothing, he says, is more important than a beautiful, well-lit space where you can see outdoors. Space, comfortable noise levels, and light are essential to creating a destination where people feel comfortable gathering.

Give more without paying more? Can you give your community more without additional operating funds? It's possible. With the current economic situation reverberating into the future, it's not likely you'll find entirely smooth sailing ahead. Skidding into the future is an option, but sustainable master planning is a better one. Its bottom line approach to creating great library experiences may help your library survive and thrive now, as well as in the next worst-case scenario. With a sustainable master plan in hand, Olathe Public Library now knows it can afford to operate the recommended expanded facilities. All Director Baker needs now is capital funding for the construction.

Louise Levy Schaper, retired Executive Director, Fayetteville Public Library, AR, is a library consultant and freelance writer

DATE SCHOOL LIBRARY JOURNAL, MARCH 2014

Kickstart a School Library

Berkeley eighth graders raise over $78K

By Mythili Sampathkumar

Eighth-grade students at REALM charter school in the Berkeley Unified School District in Berkeley, CA, have designed their own crowd-funded library, complete with geometric shelving and furniture units built by students and teachers, along with new books and technology purchased with donated funds.

The "X-Space," as students have named their new library, was the brainchild of students in a REALM class called Studio H, an innovative design program run by Emily Pilloton, the school's director of creativity. The three-year-old charter school is located in a former commercial space that had no library area. The seeds of the X-Space were planted when Hallie Chen, an eighth-grade instructor, sent a simple survey to about 100 of her students asking, "What is a traditional library? What would you like to learn?"

That produced a wish list of what they wanted in terms of design, books, and technology. In addition to Wi-Fi, the students also asked for lots of books, with an emphasis on history. "Most of them know you can't trust everything on the Internet," Chen says.

REALM's students were hoping to raise $75,000 through a campaign on the crowdfunding site Kickstarter. When the month-long drive ended on March 27th, they had $78,843 in donations. On top of that, the Quest Foundation of Danville, CA, a private grant-making organization, had pledged an additional $30,000 if the school reached their project goal. In total, REALM will receive $108,843.

The $75,000 Kickstarter target money covers the costs of "approximately $30,000 for books—3,000 volumes; $20,000 for construction materials, lighting, fixtures, hardware; $15,000 for technology, and $10,000 for software, subscriptions, periodicals and ebooks," according to a statement on the Kickstarter page. The Quest money and extra Kickstarter funds will allow the purchase of an extra 3,000 books as well as additional shelving and technology.

Pilloton and Chen wanted to conceive a design concept that would be affordable and easy for the students to work on collaboratively. The group came up with the idea for a building-block "X" shape that could be used over and over to create bookshelves, table legs, seating, and desks and dubbed their design concept "STAX."

As a charter school, REALM has a board of directors but no school board to provide or approve funding for projects. Chen and school administrators decided to turn to Kickstarter because it "the school is like a start-up where innovation and entrepreneurship [are]

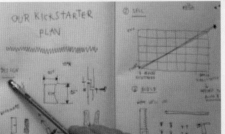

STAX: Student-built prototypes of bookshelves for a new school library; students brainstormed a design scheme for the new library at the REALM charter school; the student-invented STAX building system uses hundreds of X-shaped units; eighth-grade library builders

at the heart of everything," Chen says.

In addition to raising funds, Chen and Pilloton sought local support for the X-Space from Carl Bass, CEO of Autodesk, a company that designs software for entertainment, engineering, and construction purposes. Bass has a personal workshop in the school's neighborhood where he uses computers to cut materials to exact specifications.

Bass offered to support the X-Space by cutting their building materials—13-ply plywood—to the exact size the students needed for the STAX units. This enabled the eighth-graders to calculate the precise amount of wood they would need to furnish their allotted space. "He and his shop mate put in probably 80 hours of their personal time to help us cut over 900 pieces," says Pilloton.

Chen says that Bass's support was critical to the project's success. She notes that "If you can demonstrate competence," tap into local resources, provide a realistic time line, and accurately determine costs, people will see a project as feasible and will be more likely to fund it.

The Studio H crew had undertaken a previous Kickstarter campaign to help their school. In that case, high school design students raised $15,000 to buy old shipping containers, which they used to house additional classrooms on the REALM school lot.

While enriching the school, crowd-funding student-driven projects is also a good way "to hack the education system," says Chen.

10 Steps to a Better Library Interior

An interior designer weighs in with tips that don't have to cost a lot
By Traci Lesneski

At a time when many of our country's libraries need an update owing to age and higher-than-ever expectations from patrons, available dollars for renovations are all too scarce. Fortunately, there are simple, effective, and inexpensive steps that can be taken to reinvigorate your library interior.

1 See with Your Customer's Eyes You are in your building every day, so you probably don't even see the interior anymore. Take a step back, and view your library with fresh eyes. Walk through the building as though it were your first time. Can you identify the areas of your library easily from the entry point? Is it clear where to go for help? Can you find the bathroom? What visual noise is in the way of these goals?

Left: at Dakota County's Wescott Library, MN, customers entering the building were confronted with the overflowing holds section, long lines for self-check blocking their way, and little clarity about the library's overall layout

Above: with the holds and self-check stations pushed off to the sides, and the entry opened up to exterior views, with products and services beyond, the library now has a welcoming entry and intuitive flow. Much of the impact was achieved using mainly elbow grease to move collections and reorganize the interior. Additional changes include paint (40¢/sf) and carpet ($3.50/sf)

2 Remove Barriers Find ways to remove visual and physical impediments to using your library and easily accessing the resources within. For example, if tall shelves are blocking sight lines from the entry, find ways to consolidate materials in order to remove shelving or lower the height. If built rooms close off an area that would get more use if opened up, remove the rooms.

Left: these study rooms are underused and out of sight from customers. Consider what a simple move such as removing the doors and reorganizing the fixtures could do to create a more welcoming area, as in this mock-up for a study in the Bayport Public Library, MN

Above: suggested changes include paint (40¢/sf), door and wall removal and touch-up ($1500), new interior window ($15/sf), and new furniture ($25/sf)

3 Use Less for More Impact
If displays are taking over your library, consider paring them down so remaining fixtures have more impact. If you have painted walls to enliven your interior, did you use too many colors and lose the effect in the process?

Below: unify items such as displays through consistent use of materials or color, as in the Roseville branch of Minnesota's Ramsey County Public Library—one of *LJ*'s New Landmark Libraries

4 Unclutter
Visually chaotic surroundings intimidate many library users. Where should customers focus their attention? Resist the urge to add signs about every service or rule for using the building, and ask yourself why it isn't intuitive in the first place. Then address the core issue. Chances are, customers are going to ask a person rather than visually sift through a series of notes anyway; each interaction is an opportunity to add value to the customer's experience.

Left: many libraries collect but forget to purge, leaving patrons to sort out what's important visually, a problem Mt. Prospect Library, IL, faced before a renovation

5 Consider the Whole
Don't accept every cast-off piece of furniture, fixture, or other item that comes your way. Instead, consider the whole. Find ways to unify furnishings and fixtures through material, color, and form. Consolidate free materials and community notices with other self-service items, such as change machines, self-check stations, or copiers.

Right: prior to renovation, St. Paul's Central Library had three different shelving types with different materials and finishes, as well as mismatched study chairs and tables. The result was visually jarring

Above: a major role of the library's $16M renovation was to simplify and clarify the interior, which involved jettisoning the mismatched furniture and keeping only the pieces in harmony with one another and the building itself.

6 Support How Humans Use Space
People seek out natural light and views and want to be sheltered. Look for existing opportunities in the interior architecture to create reading nooks. Evaluate whether your seating takes advantage of natural light or views to the exterior, and think about whether shelves could be rotated or moved to let more daylight into the interior of the space. Make the most of interior brick by organizing the furniture to work with the cadence of the panels and add to the range of textures. Do the same with a sheetrock interior box by adding subtle or bold vinyl films to create visual texture.

Left: organizing shelving to work with—and not against—sources of natural light and views to the exterior can create magical little spaces like this one in the Louisville Free Library's Newburg Branch, KY. In an existing space, this may require nothing more than a fresh eye and elbow grease

7 Zone Your Interior

Examine the space with noise in mind: find the sources of noise and activity within each area and seek to avoid conflicts in privacy, sense of security, sociability, and acoustics. You might own the most comfortable lounge chair ever manufactured, but if you locate it near the copiers or with its back to a main aisle, no one will sit there.

Left: locate quiet reading areas away from the fray. Use the building's architecture or library shelving to create a sense of enclosure and help signal how to behave. These pendant fixtures at the Rancho Mirage Public Library, CA ($400–$800 ea.), also help bring the scale down and foster a sense of place

8 Create a Variety of Experiences

One size does not fit all. Allow customers to decide what type of social interaction they want, on a scale of none to lively collaboration. Don't assume that seating is seating is seating—provide variety and choice.

Above: teens, in particular, appreciate choice in how to study or collaborate, which is playfully accomplished at the Bud Werner Memorial Library in Steamboat Springs, CO

9 Light to Shape Space

When lighting is done well, we tend not to notice it; when it is done poorly, it can ruin an interior. In fact, many buildings actually are overlit. Our eyes need variety in light intensity so they can rest, but one must be careful of too much contrast as well—our eyes tire quickly when they must constantly adjust between, for example, a dark wall next to a bright window.

Left: vary lighting levels for visual interest and to cue behavior. At Hennepin County Library's Maple Grove branch, MN, lower light levels in the lounge area—but still plenty bright for reading—signal that this is a quiet area in the wide-open floor plan. More light over the collections encourages exploration

10 Embrace Color

Strategic use of color can direct attention toward an asset or draw it away from a liability. Color can help give boundaries to a space and signal how to behave. It can add warmth or liveliness or gravity. And, especially when applied through paint, it is easy and inexpensive to change, so you can alter your library interior over time.

Right: simple use of color can direct attention to amenities, such as the enclosed study room in the small Newburg Branch of Louisville Free Library. Paint costs about 40¢/sf when done by a professional

11 BONUS ITEM

Hire a design professional to help you with bigger moves or a comprehensive plan, which can be broken into smaller projects. Many professionals are willing to charge by the hour. If you come to them with ideas about your goals, they can very quickly help you define the areas that have the most impact. Reputable design professionals in your area can be found on the website of the International Interior Design Association (www.IIDA.org) and the American Institute of Architects (www.AIA.org). And don't forget to ask around for referrals from colleagues who have worked recently with design professionals.

Traci Lesneski (traci@msrltd.com) is Principal and Head of Interiors for MS&R Ltd., a leading national library design firm based in Minneapolis

One Step at a Time, Turning to the Future

Building in increments in rural Indiana By Sarah Bayliss

When Mary Hougland took over as director of the Jennings County Public Library in rural North Vernon, IN, in January 2008, she wanted to turn the nearly 34,000 square foot, modern pole barn structure, a characterless building erected in 1997, into a "user-friendly" destination that would be "someplace where people wanted to hang out."

Her first step: add color. She rebranded the grey-and-white structure with a gold, magenta, and blue scheme, visible on signage and library PR materials. Second step: a renovation to bring the library in this farming community of 28,000 into the 21st century.

The Plan Hougland had $600,000 in library savings to put toward the project. In 2009, she hired library consultant Kimberly Bolan Cullin, an LJ 2004 Mover & Shaker, to conduct studies and conceive of a plan.

Space was not an issue; using it well was. There was no teen area, nor was there any kind of youth center in town. Hougland and Cullin envisioned a teen destination with five new computers and room for recreation, education, and study. They proposed an expanded children's section with zoned spaces for different ages as well as literacy-enhancing equipment and flexible furniture. The plan included two small meeting rooms for tutoring and other purposes, a quiet study area, self-checkout equipment, improved technology, and upgraded heating and electrical components. Reconceiving the bulky main desk was key, as was adding more color and new furniture. Total cost: $1.7 million, $1.1 million of which would come from a proposed 15-year property tax bond measure.

The Setback Hougland and Cullin planned to present their ideas to the community in standard focus groups, but the library board saw this as an unnecessary expense. Only one public forum took place, in July 2010, at the request of the Jennings County County Council. At that meeting, 85 percent attending were in favor of the renovations, Hougland says, and two newspaper polls in June and July also showed majority favor. But when the council voted on the proposal that August, it was turned down by a vote of four to three.

"The council said, 'Use the money you have,'" Hougland recalls. "I felt like we were being punished for being fiscally responsible." In Cullin's view, the absence of planned community meetings and therefore awareness of the renovation's benefits was the bond's death knell. While the board's decision "saved a few thousand dollars," it cost the library the $1.1 million, she believes.

Hard lessons learned; time to move on. After "mourning," Hougland decided to "jump back on the wagon and use the money we had." She garnered an additional $14,794 in donations, including $5000 from the local OnSpot Foundation. An additional $18,206 came from the library's operating budget.

A New Solution With this $633,000 in hand, she thought hard about what would make the most difference to Jennings County—including those residents who disapproved of the bond measure. Work started on August 15, 2011, and finished on October 30.

Instant impact was key. Almost $240,000 went to furniture. "The furnishings, color scheme, and layout of the main area are the most eye-catching and what patrons notice first," Hougland says. The teen area came next. Using some of the $143,352 construction and demolition budget, she carved up a 10,000 square foot storage room to create a 4500 square foot teen area with an industrial look, comfortable seating, and a collaborative study area. Another $7,683 went toward an acoustical ceiling. Other storage space was turned into one small meeting room.

Next, Hougland replaced the large service desk with a smaller service point near the adult computer area. She added $26,000 in digital signage and laid down electrical work for future expansion, spending $89,200 on electrical work and $48,742 on HVAC.

Postponing the grand plans for the children's area was a strategic budget decision. "It will be an easier renovation down the road, as people are typically more supportive of children's spaces than adult and teen areas," says Cullin. In the meantime, she and Hougland installed a new children's rug, built an office for the children's librarian, and expanded the area slightly by building a curved wall. Hougland also kept the work local: 75 percent of the furnishings were made in Indiana, and the construction was done by nearby contractors.

Her goal now is to fund the rest of the renovation through donations. She has created what she calls a "Dream Big" brochure and is speaking with community organizations about her ideas. Plans include the installation of self-check kiosks, more technology, another small meeting room, a quiet area, and additional elements to the teen space, as well as a new kids' area.

For now, people like what they see. "I came across a 14- or 15-year-old laid out on the chairs in the teen area, Hougland reports. "He looked at me and started to get up, and I told him he didn't need to; this area is for him. He said, 'I never thought I'd have a place like this to go to.'"

Sarah Bayliss has written for LJ, the New York Times, Boston Globe, and ARTnews magazine, among other publications

7
top trends

ITERATIVE SPACE, LEARNING COMMONS, MAKER SPACES, AND MORE

From high-tech discovery zones to hands-on places to get back to literal meat-and-potatoes basics, libraries are adding spaces, here shared from *LJ*'s design coverage since 2009 as originally published, intended to provide the tools for patrons to create new content themselves, not just consume preexisting information.

...And the Kitchen Sink

Innovative library designs around the country are adding kitchens, the next (and original) Maker spaces By Sheila Kim

It's not news to anyone who follows library design that the mission is expanding from one of providing room for reading and research to a more complex, community-driven model that serves as a hub for a much broader range of activities. Hospitality-influenced amenities already permeate newer libraries and renovations in the form of lounges, cafés, and multipurpose event spaces. Now, some (literally) cutting-edge libraries are taking it a step further, adding kitchens for demonstrations and patron use.

Mike Zuehlke, an architect at Engberg Anderson (see Meadow-ridge Branch Library), says, "Food is one of those things that we all share—across cultures, races, economic, or educational level. Few things promote gathering and interaction as well as a shared meal."

While a kitchen in the library may seem a surprise or a luxury, these trendsetting buildings are using their new kitchen facilities to help patrons connect to their community, learn more about healthy living, feed their families better, express their creativity, and even make a little much-needed money—all core to the library mission.

MADISON, WI

Meadowridge Branch Library and Meadowood Neighborhood Center

Madison's Meadowridge Public Library occupies one end of a strip mall, right next door to the existing Meadowood Neighborhood Center; on the other end of the strip sits a now-closed Ace Hardware store. But thanks to $2.4 million in city funding, exciting changes are under way for this site. In musical chairs fashion, the library will move into the Ace space; the neighborhood center will shift into the former library; and a new, shared zone—featuring a community kitchen to be used by both entities—will reside in between, becoming the literal and figurative hearth of the project.

"Kitchens fall neatly into the [Meadowridge] library's mission of supporting community interests. Like other library spaces, kitchens are places to be informed, entertained, to learn by doing and observing, and all of this in a collaborative, social setting," says Mike Zuehlke of Engberg Anderson, the architects of the currently under-construction Meadowridge and Meadowood project.

Given that both community and library programs will operate from the kitchen, the project team set out to design a multipurpose—and therefore flexible—facility. Comprising 395 square feet, it will incorporate commercial-grade appliances and a pair of movable worktables that can shift from use to use, whether for food prep, serving, or cooking-class demos.

The proposed finishes will address functional as well as aesthetic needs. "We wanted to maintain the balance between a commercial kitchen and more of a traditional 'homelike' feel," explains Zuehlke. Stainless steel will be used in some areas, but warmer materials, such as solid surfacing, wood, and ceramic tile, will appear in the more public parts. Separating the kitchen from the adjacent community room will be a roll-down door

CONNECTING TO COMMUNITY At Meadowridge, a schematic (top) shows how the kitchen will fit into the branch, including a roll-down door to the adjacent community room. Center left, "homelike" fixtures will support patron participation, not just demos. Bottom, the kitchen will be host to a Good Snack Club to teach kids about healthy eating

that will open when programming, such as cooking classes, calls for it. And kitchen cameras broadcasting to wall-mounted video screens will come into play for larger gatherings.

Among some of the uses planned for the kitchen and community room, slated for a 2015 opening, is a new program called the Good Snack Club, which will invite kids during the school year to plan, make, and eat healthy afternoon snacks. Discussion is ongoing with a local community college's culinary program to provide cooking demonstrations. And community potlucks, which became popular but unsustainable, will find a new home at Meadowridge and Meadowood.

"The meals got moved around in the community depending on availability of an adequate space, so the addition of community space next to the kitchen will provide a reliable location for them," says Greg Mickells, director of Madison Public Library. "The gatherings have also become important for discussing community issues and sharing information."

Bringing everything full circle and reinforcing the connection to food, artist Victor Castro will compose a sculpture out of empty Tetra Pak boxes—cartons typically used for soup and shelf-stable milk, among other liquid foods—contributed by neighborhood residents, to stand on the walkway of the library.

NEW ORLEANS

Rosa F. Keller Library & Community Center

"Libraries are less about being places to study and read and more about providing for social and educational needs," says Kurt Hagstette, AIA, principal at Eskew+Dumez+Ripple (EDR), the architecture firm that reinvigorated this New Orleans library branch, devastated in 2005 by Hurricane Katrina.

The Rosa F. Keller Library & Community Center consists of two adjoined buildings: a 1917 bungalow that underwent restoration and extensive upgrades following the storm and a new building that replaced a 1990s addition that was deemed unsalvageable after the flooding. While the modern structure, completed in 2012, houses the library stacks, reading rooms, and research zones, the historic former residence—connected via a common entry vestibule and spine—is home to the community center, comprising a variety of meeting spaces and the kitchen.

The latter serves as a food-prep and pantry area for catered events at the library, as well as a classroom for healthy cooking programs. Within the existing kitchen's tight footprint of 260 square feet, EDR optimized the space with a cooking island and essential appliances, with enough room left over for adult and children attendees of classes, such as a recent five-week course for six- to 12-year-olds offered by the Tulane School of Culinary Medicine.

Custom neutral-toned millwork and a rectangular island, both composed of MDF core and laminate, replaced dark cabinetry and an awkward L-shaped counter, visually opening up and brightening the space.

BETTER THAN EVER After being damaged by Hurricane Katrina in 2005, the kitchen at New Orleans's Keller branch (inset, above) has been rebuilt and greatly improved

Outdated equipment was upgraded to stainless steel appliances, from a new Viking range hood above the island's Whirlpool gas cooktop to Crosley refrigerators. For finishing touches, the project team installed light-gray ceramic tiles on the floors, refurbished the original historic casement windows, and applied fresh coats of paint on the walls and window frames. Save for the exhaust hood above the range and a fire extinguishing system, the Keller kitchen came into existence with few logistical hurdles, as the rest of the library is equipped with sprinkler, fire detection, and alarm systems.

John Marc Sharpe, director of marketing and communications for the New Orleans Public Library, told *LJ*, "We love our food in New Orleans, and as the plans for the location were finalized, the idea of a food prep/catering kitchen evolved into an open kitchen that could be used for cooking classes and cooking demonstrations.... The next great New Orleans chef may be learning in that kitchen and that's fun to think about. The kitchen is in near continuous use."

COVELO, CA

Round Valley Public Library

In an underserved, rural California county comprising a small town, ranch land, and an Indian reservation, community members came together to create their own library—from fundraising to purchase a 7,200 square foot structure down to initiating the design details. The

Round Valley Public Library in Covelo opened its doors in 2010 to offer not only books but also the Commons, a community center with rentable Wi-Fi-enabled space, a retail coffee shop, and a covered patio. By 2012, the Commons gained a commercial-grade kitchen.

Although the building housing Round Valley was formerly a restaurant, its kitchen needed upgrades. "The layout of the kitchen went through a committee and community input meeting," says Diann Simmons, former vice president and grant writer for the Friends of the

Round Valley Public Library. "Final-ly, I sat down with everything and laid it out, and a volunteer contractor reviewed it all to make sure the lineup of the plumbing was as efficient as possible."

The equipment, situated along the perimeter of the 500 square foot room, includes multiple sinks and stainless steel prep areas along with refrigerators, a gas range, and a convection oven. Standard food-service Italian quarry tiles cover the floors as they are economical but also workhorses for high traffic and spills. And a worktable at the center is actually a butcher block–topped mobile cart that can be easily repositioned for catering needs, or clearing enough floor space to accommodate group classes common to the library.

HOMEGROWN
The Round Valley commercial kitchen (r.), like the rest of the library, was a grassroots effort. As well as hosting events and classes, the kitchen is used for canning. The Friends site lists available equipment

Yet the kitchen does far more than service the library's coffee shop, events taking place in the Commons, and classes—it helps sustain the county residents, from small businesses to low-income families.

"During the summer and fall, when local produce is abundant, there is usually someone canning here at least twice a week," says Isabelle Le-Mieux, the Commons manager. "Anyone can rent the space to can or cook whatever they want." Canners may take home their goods to feed their families, or sell them through the coffee shop. Citing two businesses that rent the space to make products to sell off-site, LeMieux adds, "In California, food that is prepared in a certified commercial kitchen can be sold elsewhere. Our facility allows local businesses to thrive because they can produce food here at low overhead cost."

Finally, lockable storage units allow the kitchen to function as a local distribution site for low-income families to collect from the state-run Food Pantry.

STOCKHOLM, SWEDEN

TioTretton

Tween-aged kids are the cooks in a library in Stockholm. "The kitchen fills the same purpose in our library as it does at home—it is a place to sit

down together, do homework, eat an afternoon snack, and share stories," says Amanda Stenberg, one of the librarians who staff the tweens-only TioTretton. (For more on the unusual institution, see "Stockholm's TioTretton Library Gives Tweens a Space of Their Own," p. XXX.) Stenberg continues, "Cooking is also a way to create stories through experimenting with flavors and ingredients." The ability to experiment without there being a single right answer is particularly important to this age group, according to Stenberg. The kitchen, which also houses the library's cooking-related collection, also helps fulfill architect Ricardo Ortiz's vision of a "library for all senses."

OPEN TO EXPERIMENTATION
TioTretton's open kitchen appeals to all the senses as cooking gives the tween patrons a chance to explore without worry

Carved from within the 1,200 square foot library, which was completed in 2011, the generously proportioned, 323 square foot open kitchen is tastefully finished with a white subway-tile backsplash, wood cabinetry, and stainless steel elements. At its center is a spacious wood-topped dining table, with stools tucked underneath.

Additionally functioning as a worktop, the table features open storage shelves in its base, while panels in its top open to reveal power outlets for plugging in portable electric burners. Tweens can also bake using ovens installed in a wall beside the cabinetry. Overhead, suspended pot racks hold various utensils such as whisks, graters, and spatulas. And when not in use for cooking or eating, the kitchen's multipurpose table hosts all manner of workshops, from music making to arts and crafts.

AUSTIN, TX

New Central Library

When asked about the connection between Austin's upcoming New Central Library and food, the library's facilities processing manager, John Gillum, explains, "Our director, Brenda Branch, said we're all becoming foodies, and she's right. One of the most popular things we get requests for is that our growing body of local, world-renowned chefs come to the library and talk about their new cookbooks." He adds, "And people would say 'it would be great for them to cook for us!'"

The six-story building, set to open in 2016, was designed collaboratively by local firm Lake | Flato Architects and Boston's Shepley Bulfinch Richardson and Abbott. An architecture and design practice already well versed in libraries, Shepley Bulfinch points out that it had previously worked on a public library in Eugene, OR, that included a café.

"As the role of the library is expanding to become a city's gathering and convening place, it's embracing nontraditional functions like kitchens, cafés, Maker spaces, and exhibit, gallery, and event spaces," comments Sid Bowen, AIA, managing principal of Shepley Bulfinch. "The kitchen element reinforces the library's important civic role."

Located off of one of the library's entrances, a six-story atrium overlooking Shoal Creek will hold a multipurpose event space that will incorporate the kitchen. Really a two-part feature, the kitchen will consist of both built-in and mobile units that tuck away when not in use, a solution devised by the project teams to keep the equipment from dominating the space's ambiance when noncooking programs are in play. This strategy was also a way to maximize space: when

KITCHEN TO GO The cooking elements of the multipurpose space at Austin's in-progress New Central Library roll away when not in use

Sliding barn doors will open to reveal the built-in elements, ranging from a sink and pot storage to double ovens and a refrigerator, with finishes including stainless and blackened steel. Meanwhile, the mobile island will house all the "extroverted" items—cutting board, cooler drawer, cooktop, and plating area—as the cart will face an audience seated in the space's bleachers. Because the design teams anticipate that some of the cooking events will be shown on-screen, they selected light-colored, solid surfaces for the cart's countertop for good color rendering on TV.

Sheila Kim is Products Editor for Architectural Record *magazine and Editor of* SNAP *(*Sweets News and Products*) magazine. She was previously managing editor of* Contract *magazine and a special projects editor for* Interior Design

fully opened and in use, the kitchen takes up a footprint of about 90 square feet; packed away, it encompasses only 48.

DATE LIBRARY BY DESIGN, SPRING 2011

A Learning Commons for Kids

Three New Hampshire elementary schools apply the learning commons concept, familiar to higher education, to younger students

By Laura Wernick

The hottest strand in the discussion about the design of public schools today is not about whether the library will remain as a repository for books in the future but rather how best to optimize the use of the space. The pressures on the school library are real. Technology is playing an ever-increasing role in teaching. The written word is finding its way into ever more convenient electronic modes that can contain ever larger quantities of information. Books, particularly for older children, will become less necessary. Meanwhile, the cost per square foot for school construction projects continues to rise as the dollars available for capital projects fall.

A design learning commons concept for three new elementary schools in progress in Concord, NH, may just provide a new model.

Shaped by three pressures Driven by the system's superintendent, Christine Rath, discussions during the initial planning probed the very nature of the future of K–12 learning. Rath pointed to several pressures that affect how we view the library in the 21st-century learning environment. First, learning is a collaborative process between students and educators, and spaces should support collaborative learning.

Second, these spaces and their materials should be immediately accessible to the educator both for ease of access and for ease of supervision. Literacy is and will continue to be a fully integrated component of all learning. Reading is a daily activity, and books that have traditionally been located in the library need to be dispersed so that they are readily accessible to students in the classroom and not limited to weekly visitations to the library.

Third, learning is dynamic and fluid, therefore educators and students need a variety of spaces to support the range of activities that take place when learning happens. These spaces will most likely need to change over time, so they should be designed with built-in flexibility. Students require small group meeting areas with Internet and multimedia access. They should have project spaces where hands-on activities might be ongoing over the course of days or even weeks. They need storytelling corners, presentation and performance spaces, as well as research areas and a place to learn how to conduct it properly. Access to technology must

be seamless and ubiquitous throughout. In other words, the most valuable traits of any library can be shared throughout the building.

A new model for traditional learning Active and ongoing discussion has shaped a plan for the library that addresses Rath's vision.

All three schools are under way and scheduled to open in September 2012. Each has a two-story classroom academic wing, which will be matched by a 30'-wide, two-story-high learning commons. Comprised of multiple project spaces, media/performance space that will seat two classrooms' worth of students, and a storytelling area, the learning commons will contain book shelves, display areas, and storage cabinets. There are also support spaces for special needs students. Wireless technology will be available throughout.

This commons houses a small, enclosed traditional library space that can seat one classroom's worth of students and holds several hundred books. The design keeps sight of the traditional purpose of the library but rebalances the roles.

Teachers will no longer be constrained by the four walls of their classrooms. The learning commons has enough space for multiple classes to partake in a special activity, a small group to undertake a research project, or a single student to find a quiet spot for reading. Because every classroom in the academic wing also has a window looking out onto the commons, supervision will be possible from the classroom even if students migrate from their desks.

Beyond the benefits for teachers, the learning commons also opens up new possibilities for parents and potential for after-school use. Parents will be encouraged to participate in or supervise activities taking place in the learning commons, while the after-school program will have access to the space without interfering with the day school teachers' classrooms.

This is an experiment. In Concord, leaders are confident that the elementary school learning commons will become a special resource for tudents, faculty, and the community and a model for libraries nationwide.

Laura Wernick, AIA, REFP, LEED AP, senior principal with HMFH Architects, Cambridge, MA

Tomorrow Visualized

NCSU's new Hunt Library is designed to inspire the researchers of the future, using large-scale visualization tools By Meredith Schwartz

As I got ready to tour the James B. Hunt Jr. Library at North Carolina State University (NCSU), Raleigh, last spring, as part of the Association of Research Libraries (ARL) meeting held nearby, the buzz about the newly unveiled building had reached such a level that I expected to find it, however cool, overhyped.

It wasn't. It was exactly the right amount of hyped.

"Every corner of the Hunt Library is designed to be memorable and stunning," the library's vision claims. Grandiose as that might sound, those corners deliver.

In an era in which many libraries even at great institutions are struggling to do enough with less, it's refreshing to see a university able and willing to invest in the library as both the symbolic and the operational core of the institution. The project was funded by $115.2 million in state appropriations, plus donor support.

Building an inspiration The vision for the Hunt Library is ambitious in the extreme: to "create spaces that encourage collaboration, reflection, creativity, and awe" and "to be a place not of the past but of the future." The university made such an investment because it feels the library will be a competitive advantage. "A signature library," Susan K. Nutter, vice provost and director of the NCSU Libraries and the 2005 *LJ* Librarian of the Year, explains "would help us recruit the very best students and the very best faculty and to serve the community as an inspiring place of excellence and passion and ideas and vision…. You cannot be in this building without realizing that something very important is happening at this university."

"This building was designed from the start to be an icon, a dramatic representation of how transformational technology and a commitment to the growth of our community will thrust [NCSU] even further into the foreground," said Chancellor W. Randolph Woodson when the library officially opened in April.

The library is indeed iconic and anchors the universities' new Centennial campus. One of the ways it does so is in the thoughtful integration of technology. For all that the Hunt features cutting-edge technology deeply baked into its design, it never gives the impression that any piece of tech is there only because it can be. Each piece has been thought through to serve a present user need, as well as to adapt to changing needs of the future.

"Much of the design strategy behind the [library] was to pour our resources into the sorts of spaces and technologies that support NC State's reputation for producing students and researchers who live easily and naturally with technology and learn through collaboration," explains David Hiscoe, director of communications strategy for the NCSU Libraries.

Since NCSU and the other research triangle academic institutions nearby—Duke University and the University of North Carolina (UNC) at Chapel Hill—are the hub of a thriving community of technology firms, part of the mission of the library is to support not only students and faculty but the corporate, government, and nonprofit partners that work with the students and scholars on Centennial's campus.

MACROVISION High-def MacroTiles make up a giant screen in the NCSU Hunt Library's iPearl Immersion Theater

Designing a process The Hunt Library wasn't built in a vacuum, or according to the vision of a single person. Snøhetta, the Hunt Library's lead designer, also helped refine the master plan for the Centennial campus as a whole to accommodate the 221,000 square foot library and "more forcefully integrate" the existing terrain. (The firm also designed the Library of Alexandria, Egypt, among many other high-profile projects, and has been honored with the Mies van der Rohe Prize for Contemporary Architecture and the European Award for Urban Public Space.)

North Carolina firm Pearce Brinkley Cease + Lee served as executive architects, and Meyer, Scherer & Rockcastle, Ltd., developed the NCSU Libraries' master plan in 2002. The program for the library was created in 2008 through an iterative series of interviews, briefings, discussions, visioning sessions, workshops, and meetings. It took an expansive view of stakeholders, meeting with many groups besides students and library staff. In addition to the architects, DEGW did the programming, while Buro Happold worked on sustainability and Davis Langdon on cost management.

Consulting with staff was particularly important, because the Hunt Library was designed to run with no new staff, though Hiscoe says they did get a few new positions when it opened.

Making an entrance From the first floor entrance of the Hunt Library there is not a single book in sight, and there's not a staff member, desk, or chair, either. Instead, the focal points are a staircase and a window, called Robot Alley, through which students and visitors can watch the on-site bookBot machinery in action. The 50' x 160' x 50' bot (actually four robots) is excavated 20 feet below the first floor and houses some two million volumes in one-ninth the space of conventional shelving, delivering the desired title within five minutes and at a substantial cost savings compared to traditional stacks. Nearby, a large touch screen displays Virtual Browse, which tries to replicate the experience of

serendipitous browsing in open stacks by showing the titles that would be located near the original book if it awere shelved by subject (in fact, the book bot stores books by height in more than 18,000 metal bins).

Once up the stairs, students pass through the Emerging Issues Commons, an airy, high-ceilinged space brought to human scale with curved display walls and an electronic ribbon-style sculpture, which features interactive exhibits created by the Institute for Emerging Issues, a think tank founded by Hunt himself, who served as North Carolina's governor from 1977 to 1985 and 1993 to 2001. (Not many libraries have their namesake actually working in the building, but Hunt does, chairing the institute.) From there, visitors pass into more familiar library spaces. They are greeted by a one-stop service center on the right and a glass-walled Apple Technology Showcase on the left, a gadget bar where students can try out the many devices and technologies available for loan.

Past the service point, the iPearl Immersion Theater is an open area encompassing a large, curved video display wall built of the Hunt's signature high-definition Christie MicroTiles. This is one of five such display walls in the building. The iPearl showcases current events, library and university initiatives, and the work of NCS faculty and students. During the ARL tour, it was packed with students watching a sporting event, but Hiscoe tells *LJ* it is also well known for displaying student-taken photos of the library itself via the My #HuntLibrary initiative.

REALLY BIG DATA Putting books in the robot makes room for high-tech data visualization and creativity spaces at the Hunt Library. The striking exterior (ctr., l.) illuminates the Centennial Campus. Innovative features inside include (clockwise, top l.) the Game Lab, the Rain Garden Reading Lounge, the 21'-wide Christie MicroTiles wall in the Game Lab and in the Creativity Studio. Putting such cutting-edge technology in the hands of undergraduates is virtually unheard of, but it gives students a huge leg up after graduation

"Students sent us over 1,700 Instagram photos of Hunt in the months after we did our soft opening," says Hiscoe. "We were quite frankly stunned at the response and how much it showed an appreciation for the new library."

As Hiscoe explains, the lower floors of the library are about community. As users climb higher, the functions get more rarified and the technology more intense.

The library as lab When people talk about doing research at the university library, they usually mean in books that have already been written or at least in archives. As a result, as Ithaka's fifth faculty survey found this spring, since the advent of remote digital resources, STEM researchers in particular have made less use of library buildings themselves, even as they

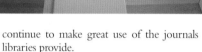

continue to make great use of the journals libraries provide.

The Hunt responds with a new library role. Since it is the primary library facility for faculty and students in engineering, textiles, and other science programs, NCSU reenvisioned the library as a physical site where STEM research is conducted: not chemistry, biology, or physics experiments but research so new it doesn't already have a home and requires equipment that crosses disciplines and departments, that occurs where big data and the tools to handle it intersect. "At the core of the vision for the Hunt Library is the ability of our students, faculty, and partners to immerse themselves in interactive computing, multimedia creation, and large-scale visualization—tools that are enabling revolutionary ways to see and use information," the library's vision statement says.

The library hosts a Maker space featuring two 3-D printers and a laser cutter, but physical objects are only a small portion of what students and faculty create at the Hunt.

Since NCSU is home to a top video game design program, NC State's Digital Games Research Center, incorporating a game design lab is a no-brainer. The flexible 20'x 5' Christie MicroTile display allows a single game to be played on a full screen that rivals an art house movie theater; or with multiple stations equipped with eight video gaming systems, several can be played at once. The room also exchanges data with laptops and mobile devices. Housed in a glass box, the lab creates visual interest for other students without the noise that could disturb their studies. For designers who want to make their mistakes in privacy, the glass can be turned opaque.

There's even a student-created video game based on the Hunt Library's book circulation patterns, a collaboration between the college of design and the department of computer engineering. It can be played by four people using Kinect systems, only in the game lab itself and is "an incredible amount of fun," says Hiscoe.

Yet Hunt's offerings of high-tech laboratories for creating and testing original work isn't limited to games or even to work in technological fields. The Teaching and Visualization Lab is just as useful for the digital humanities, if not more so. The "black box" theater design includes 270° immersive projection on three walls, with 3-D capability; a professional-zoned audio system, and cameras for real-time video capture, broadcast, and collaboration. An open ceiling, exposing the rails from which equipment is suspended, makes it easy to swap in even newer technology as it becomes available.

The space is used for everything from control room simulation to big data decision-making to game research, and it's designed with flexible infrastructure to grow with advancements in the field. Among the many uses of this space so far: a recreation in 3-D of the 17th-century cathedral where John Donne preached, earth science students experiencing the birdsong audible in a nearby wild environment, and a simulator to train naval ROTC midshipmen to operate the bridge of a modern warship.

Meanwhile, the counterpoint to the black box of the visualization lab is the "white box" Creativity Studio, which is arts-focused. It has movable and writable walls, a theater lighting kit, 3-D projectors, videoconferencing, and video, film, and animation production for green screen and motion capture.

The library itself does its own research—testing new tech for possible incorporation—in a technology sandbox out of the public eye. From that back-of-house area, adjacent to the server room, a single person can run the whole building's voice and video. In addition, cloud-based virtualization of servers and storage means most technical operations can be moved to another building in a pinch. The server room itself "pushed the envelope" on design, Hiscoe says, using a "hot aisle" in place of a raised floor, which he expects to pay for itself within two years by saving money that would otherwise be spent on cooling. It, too, was designed to grow to twice its current capacity, with extra racks and cabling.

As always, of course, cutting-edge technology is a fast-moving target. Hiscoe tells *LJ* that some of the original plans for the tech infrastructure had to be scrapped because the equipment was putting out too much heat in the visualization lab. The Hunt tech staff had to increase the number of racks in the server room instead.

Seen and heard AV technology is central to the Hunt Library's mission. In addition to the intensely technical lab spaces, a presentation practice room offers a place to rehearse and record live presentations in a seminar room setting: perfect for massive open online courses

CONTEMPLATION & COLLABORATION
(Clockwise from top l.): Dorothy and the Oz troops would appreciate the yellow staircase that leads down to the Quiet Reading Room; the Skyline Reading Room, plus terrace, offers unobstructed views of the Centennial Campus. No room for dry conversation in the stimulatingly hued Rain Garden Reading Lounge. Students in Robot Alley study the space-saving bookBot, which frees room for other uses. Whiteboards are as key to 100 group study areas as wireless

patron experience seamless, such as lockers that include outlets for students to store and recharge their laptops and other gear at the same time.

For solo work, or relaxation, the library offers the Rain Garden Reading Lounge, a popular subject of My #HuntLibrary photos. It includes colorful soft seating and low curved shelves that house current reference materials, new and classic works in engineering, computer science, and textiles; publications by NCS authors; and a circulating sf collection.

Photos are often taken from the balcony lounge, which overlooks the rain garden and features more colorful, contemporary furniture. As does the entire library, which has 75 different kinds of chairs in 115 colors, including one custom-built for the library by furniture crafters Thos. Moser (see sidebar). Why so many? "The spirit of this building is the spirit of discovery; we want that sense of play," Hiscoe says. Playful as they are, and as much fun as he says they were to pick out, the furnishings were also all designed to stand up to heavy use. All told, the Hunt holds about 1,750 seats, doubling NCSU's seating capacity to ten percent of its student body, though still short of the UNC's standard of providing library study seating for 20 percent of the student population.

An oval view reading lounge houses recent publications in computer science, textiles, and engineering, selected print journals from publishers such as the Institute for Electrical and Electronics Engineers (IEEE), and seminal titles such as *Science* and *Nature*. Meanwhile the Quiet Reading Room, while airy and sleek enough not to be out of place, is the most traditional-feeling library space in the building.

(MOOCs) or flipped classrooms. A video seminar room features a telepresence video collaboration suite for working with scholars who could be on the other side of the world. Two media production studios offer state-of-the-art tools for creating and editing digital media, including a green screen curtain system; four music rooms are equipped for audio recording, creating and mixing music, audio and video transfer, and digital media editing, including MIDI keyboards as well as and digital media workstations.

Meanwhile, in the "fishbowl," users are the visuals: the glass-walled seminar room is "uniquely designed to promote the open exchange of ideas," since passersby can watch those inside make use of a perceptive Pixel multitouch display. The room is popular with visiting recruiters, among others. In the Usability Lab, those inside are watched in another way: it is equipped with video-capture cameras and tools for assessing user interaction with software and interfaces.

All told, the school invested $9 million in technologies, which were pretested for two years by Maurice York, head of IT for Hunt and a 2013 *LJ* Mover & Shaker, and his 22-member team. York even converted an office in the old library into a "Mini Hunt"—a scale model of the technology infrastructure of the Hunt Library, with computing, digital imaging, and "digital media backbone" technology, funded by $300,000 in donations and equipment loans from tech companies Dell, Christie Digital, and Extron Electronics. Nothing was wasted. "The Mini Hunt was actually built from components of the 'real thing,' so its pieces are now part of the actual walls over in Hunt," Hiscoe tells *LJ*. Amazingly for a building that requires so much electricity, it still manages to be Leadership in Energy & Environmental Design (LEED) Silver certified, with ecofriendly touches like batting made from recycled blue jeans to help shape the acoustics of the space. Given how much of this library is about aural as well as visual experiences, it makes sense that the soundscape is as carefully designed as what meets the eye.

Making room for people While design, in the sense of intentional construction of spaces for use, is everywhere in evidence in the labs, their highly reconfigurable nature and changing displays tend to make the look of the physical components themselves fade into the background. Elsewhere at the Hunt, a distinctive visual aesthetic is more in evidence in glass walls both interior and exterior, open plans, wildly colorful seating, and more Christie MicroTiles configured into a variety of shapes.

The Hunt is engineered for everything from solo work to many kinds and sizes of collaborative projects up through mass events. Simply put, the library spaces are just plain fun. They are spacious but never cavernous, with plenty of intriguing nooks and little livable touches that make the

Uniquely Hunt Aaron Moser, director of the Moser Contract division of library furniture manufacturer Thomas Moser, designed a Bank of England–style chair specifically for the Hunt Library and named it the Hunt Chair. Some 125 of them, with accompanying tables, were installed in the Hunt Library's Quiet Reading Room.

The collaboration marks the third time Thos. Moser has partnered with NCSU. Moser presented the chair to its namesake, James B. Hunt, a former governor of North Carolina, at a dinner honoring the library.

Except for the staff-only bookbot section, it is the only spot in the library to have that old book smell. "There needs to be a library somewhere in this library," Hiscoe quips. The reading room is set off from the open plan with high shelves and features tables and the Moser seating. When the ARL tour came through, every seat was full.

The Lake Raleigh Learning Commons features computer workstations set up both for individual and collaborative work, with floor-to-ceiling windows on three sides and views of the lake (according to Attention Restoration Theory, viewing nature through windows helps students focus better). The NextGen Learning Commons includes interactive computing, gaming, and new technologies.

For collaborative work, apart from the specialized labs, almost 100 group study rooms include whiteboard walls; flat-panel displays; thin-client computers; web-based video conferencing; a table cubby with laptop, power, and auxiliary connections; speakers; and a touchpad controller. There are other, less traditional alternatives for group work as well, such as the "Idea Alcove," an open space with whiteboard walls and table seating. Also, free-range rolling whiteboards are available; a

surprising number were in use by students collaborating in the open areas. Graduate students and faculty have their own dedicated spaces for both individual and group work, which require ID to access, so they can work apart from undergraduates.

For the largest groups, an auditorium with a raised stage and seating for 390 doubles as a classroom and event venue. A multipurpose room serves as meeting and presentation space for the Institute for Emerging Issues. There's also an auditorium-style presentation room within the institute with fixed seating for 92. The Skyline Reading Room and terrace on the fifth floor, the highest point on the lush green NCSU campus, can be turned into an elegant event space for university functions.

It is a capacity that will likely be called on to house the library community, itself eager to be inspired, again and again. In addition to the ARL event this past spring, the Hunt will host on October 6–8 the second annual Designing Libraries for the 21st Century Conference. Rightly so.

Meredith Schwartz is Senior Editor, News & Features, LJ

DATE LIBRARY JOURNAL, OCTOBER 2013

Making Spaces

Creating and signaling zones in the library can avoid friction and the need for signage By Aaron Schmidt

With school back in session and students returning to the library—sometimes of their own free will, sometimes grudgingly—the library can seem quite full again after the late summer lull. This is a great time to think about the different demands that are placed on library spaces and how to manage these demands to ensure that everyone can use the library to do what they want to do.

Zones Libraries offer patrons two types of space-related experiences that they can't get on the web: space for quiet contemplation and space for in-person collaboration. Creating different zones within a library for these varying and incompatible behaviors is an effective way to guarantee user satisfaction.

To some extent, such zones develop organically in our buildings. Spaces for children and teens are often a bit more boisterous than other parts of the library, for example. Being more explicit about what sorts of activities can happen in dissimilar parts of the library

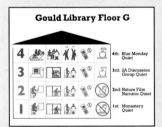

helps to make certain that there are indeed spaces for everything from quiet contemplation to rambunctious Wii tournaments. Yet making rules and creating zones can be an uphill battle if librarians disregard the way these zones develop inherently. Let patron behavior guide the design process.

Creating zones Environmental cues in your library affect how people behave. Spaces with big, comfortable chairs spaced widely apart invite individuals to sit and read. Tables with outlets attract people with devices. Computers at a boomerang-shaped desk with a few chairs will be a draw for kids. Walk through your library to assess the message that your spaces send. Is it clear what sort of behavior the space is meant to facilitate? Are the spaces logically

placed throughout the building? Do you have spaces for all the activities your library wants to support? Answers to these questions can help steer you to develop spaces for great experiences. If you find that the spaces in your library aren't being used as you intended, ask yourself why. Consider carrying out a "5 Whys" exercise to get to the root of the problem. If furniture is often moved from where it was designed to live, it might be an indication that the arrangement isn't meeting member needs. Consider rearranging.

Zoning signs Ideally, your spaces will be so masterfully imagined that they'll elicit proper behavior, everyone will have their space, and lions will coexist with lambs. But perhaps you'll need to augment the design of your spaces with some stronger cues: signage. Consider signs a last resort. Not only are they difficult to execute well, their efficacy isn't proven. To shape member behavior, libraries often slap up regulatory placards, attempting to tell people how to act. No one likes to be lectured to, and this punitive approach just creates painpoints in the library. Instead, create signs that are informative, directing people to where they can accomplish what they want to accomplish. These signs [left] from Minnesota's Carleton College's Gould Library are a great example. Not only do they let people know what sorts of activities disparate spaces are designed to accommodate, they do it in a light, humorous way.

Small spaces Adjusting to different types of behavior does not require a large building. Consider the rhythm of the day and shape accordingly. The morning and early afternoons might prioritize book groups and reading, while the late afternoon might give preference to students studying and having fun.

As always, taking the time to consider the needs of library members—and establishing the library suitably—will yield great results. Making the library useful and usable is a great start. Combine that with friendly library workers delivering excellent customer service, and, soon enough, your library will seem even more full!

Aaron Schmidt (librarian@gmail.com) is a principal at the library user experience consultancy Influx (influx.us). He is a 2005 LJ Mover & Shaker. He writes at walkingpaper.org

Bright Lights, Gig City

Chattanooga's fast connectivity drives flexible creative library space
By Sarah Bayliss

"When I came on board in March, I found myself in a gig city, but the library hadn't kept up," says Chattanooga Public Library (CPL) director Corinne Hill (a 2004 *LJ* Mover & Shaker). She approached Mark Kiehl, chief information officer for the City of Chattanooga, and said, " 'We need to be a gig library, because we're in a gig city.' He stepped up to the plate."

By "gig city," Hill is referring to an urban area with citywide gigabit-per-second Internet service. Chattanooga was one of the first in the nation to implement such a system, provided by the Electrical Power Board (EPB), a city agency, through a fiber-optic network.

For Chattanooga, having "the gig" means an opportunity to attract new business. The city is even sponsoring a competition in which entrepreneurs with winning ideas receive financial incentives to move to Chattanooga (see: www.thegigcity.com/gigtank). Similarly, Hill, along with CPL's new assistant director for technology and digital initiatives Nate Hill (no relation; he is a 2012 *LJ* Mover & Shaker), hopes to turn the library into a creative hub that will include a competitive art and technology residency program, drawing cutting-edge talent to the library and its community.

The main library building was brought up to gig speed without any rewiring, which opens up major redesign and programming opportunities for the future. For CPL, using the gig to upload books, videos, and periodicals in a fraction of the time it used to take is just the beginning.

The cost of setting up CPL's gig access, in the ballpark of $26,000, Corinne Hill says, was paid for by the city. The library, previously a city-county library with two IT staff, became a city department last year, and the city took sole responsibility for funding the library. "As a city department, we can receive Internet access through the city contract, which is half the monthly costs we were paying," she says. "We used those cost savings to pay for [updating] our computer equipment as we moved to the gig." She adds that the library's IT staffers moved to the city's IT department, further reducing costs.

In terms of future library redesign, transforming CPL into a completely "wireless, deskless" place is practically a given for Director Hill, who admits that "I've always had a problem with the reference and circulation desk." She would like to see a place where "you bring your own device and even the librarians are wireless and deskless," adding that she is drawn to the "Apple store concept," with librarians roving the floor with the tools to help. Along with plans to overhaul the children's area, she envisions an environment where patrons can author and publish material that would be uploaded directly to the library catalog, where library users could write and post reviews. Her strategy for bolstering equipment includes "emphasizing donations from vendors," she says, adding that the library is currently in a trial period with two vendors that she hopes will bear fruit.

Big dreams Dreaming bigger, intellectually and space-wise, Nate Hill has plans to take the concept of the maker space (ow.ly/d9Z7H) to an entirely new level. With Corinne Hill's full support, Nate Hill aims to turn the library's loftlike, 17,000 square foot fourth floor, which has been a storage area for 30 years, into "The 4th Floor," a multiuse creative space that would be a "public media lab, an information commons, a gallery, a theater,

a classroom, and a maker space," he says. While this concept is still in the early planning stages, the gig's wireless configuration allows Nate Hill to brainstorm possibilities for the space that would not have been feasible before.

He envisions the 4th Floor as a residency program similar to Eyebeam, a nonprofit art and technology center in New York (Eyebeam.org), or San Francisco's Gaffta (Gray Area Foundation for the Arts, Gaffta.org), a center for creative technology with a socially conscious element.

Referring to Eyebeam and Gaffta, he says, "I'm trying to find a way to do similar things to allow the community to come in and use the gig and then give something back." Like other forward-thinking libraries, "we want to provide access to tools and leverage this so people can create and author." He sees the 4th Floor as a "collaborative, cocreative space for entrepreneurs, artists, scholars, children, cooks, clowns, and characters." 4th Floor residents would have an allotment of funds to buy books and other information resources they need during their stay, after which the library would keep the materials and circulate them.

Ideally, residents would have access to the 4th Floor 24-7, adds Nate Hill. Opening their work up to the library community, they would also host public programs about their work and exhibit it in a 4th Floor gallery space at the conclusion of their stay.

And how would the 4th Floor pay for itself? Again, partnerships and sponsorships. In Nate Hill's plan, "We will break down content and media production into different types of activities, each of which we call a 'module.' Each module will be operated with a different community sponsor or partner," he says. "Examples of modules might be audio remix and record, video remix and record, collaboration space, scanning, digital design, and others."

As Director Hill sees it, the new "digital divide" is not between people who have access to technology and those who don't but between those who have access to the gig and everyone else. These plans are helping to close the new gap.

Kiehl takes a more broadly historic view, using the city's illustrious history of transportation as a metaphor. "The Chattanooga Railroad is where you moved stuff," he says. "Now we've invented the road that can go anywhere, and you don't have to follow the exits."

Sarah Bayliss has written for LJ, the New York Times, Boston Globe, and ARTnews magazine, among other publications

Customized User Design

Designing to fit your community's needs
By Marta Murvosh

The challenge of providing services to a changing community while operating more efficiently made the Denver Public Library's (DPL) leaders realize they couldn't afford to be all things to all people—at least not at every branch.

After zeroing in on each branch's demographics and user patterns, librarians ascertained three different user groups and developed different strategies, such as refining the service delivery, and put them into play in 2005 and 2006. "It really is borrowed from marketing from the business world," says Susan Kotarba, director of public services at DPL.

The 2007 passage of the citywide $550 million Better Denver Bond Program, with $52 million earmarked for DPL, offered the chance to go further. Library leaders then asked architects to develop

architectural and furnishing styles to serve each of the three specific user groups and the programs that target them.

DPL selected three Denver-based firms—studiotrope Design Collective, Humphries Poli Architects, and OZ Architecture—to develop its three architectural styles: Contemporary, Language and Learning, and Children and Family.

"Denver has done a bold thing and really stuck their neck out and

experimented," says Joseph Montalbano, architect and managing partner at studiotrope Design Collective.

Contemporary branch customers want the latest trends. Language and Learning branches offer multigenerational programming to allow adults to build new skills. Children and Family branches allow young children and their caregivers to experience the library together and engage in early literacy activities. DPL also has a few hybrid libraries, including its Central Library and the Blair-Caldwell African American Research Library (where research also is emphasized) and the recently opened Sam Gary Branch.

In addition to upgrades, including wireless technology, self-check, and automated handling at three existing and three new branches, renovations would make several branches more inviting, easier to use, and more adaptable to changing neighborhoods.

"You needed to come up with a set of concepts that could be applied to all branches and various budgets," says Ozi Friedrich, a Humphries Poli library design specialist who created the Language and Learning architectural style.

FAMILY INTERACTIONS
The Denver Public Library's Green Valley Ranch Branch focuses on children and their caregivers using the library together

Models of library service are nothing new. Neither is designing a building to suit its users. Both practices are recommended by professional library associations. Few libraries can afford to launch a systemwide renovation and building program. Those that can generally rush to build after funding is approved, says Friedrich, who was a librarian in New York City before joining Humphries Poli as an aspiring architect.

What makes DPL's approach unusual is that library leaders took the time to tie the building program to service delivery by creating architectural styles for each. "To be successful you have to embrace the fact that you don't know where libraries are going and you need to design spaces that are multifunctional, multigenerational, multicultural, and technical," studiotrope's Montalbano says.

Since passage of the bond, DPL's operating budget has tightened, resulting in reduced services including limiting many branches to only 32 hours each week, Kotarba says. The tight budget picture makes it even more imperative for DPL to move, reconfigure, and reuse furnishings and fixtures easily. Reduced construction costs have allowed DPL's money to build three new branches and to renovate the Central Library and 13 branches built between 1913 and 1996. "We originally were planning for 11 branches and were able to stretch it to 13," Kotarba says.

Construction continues. Once complete, Denver neighborhoods will have 26 libraries.

Contemporary

Contemporary branches' tech-savvy patrons live fast-paced lives and are attracted to the latest trends and immediate experiences—and they can help themselves, Kotarba says. This led to the development of the Beehive, a brightly colored glass-enclosed space for meetings, classes, events, and impromptu gatherings. Outside the Beehive, patrons will find high-demand items, staff picks, best sellers, and a staff person ready to discuss the latest releases. The branches are designed for patrons to get what they need very quickly, Kotarba says. Contemporary branch patrons desire to be empowered, stimulated, or surprised, studiotrope's Montalbano says. "This type of person expects to have one of these three things happen or they won't come back."

Ross–Cherry Creek Branch

After the Ross-Cherry Creek Branch reopened in 2010 following its $1.2 million renovation, the average daily door count jumped 38 percent, from 900 visitors to 1250, says senior librarian Brent Wagner. The new furniture, carpet, bright colors, and inviting lighting may have attracted more visitors from the surrounding upscale neighborhoods and nearby mall. Wagner and his staff have observed faster visits, likely encouraged by the bright yellow and orange paint, self-service holds, and four self-check machines.

"This is hard to explain; it does not seem as frenetic as it used to be," Wagner says.

While foot traffic rose, Cherry Creek's annual returns dropped from about 700,000 to 270,000 items. This dive may be caused by the low processing speed of the branch's automated sorter, possibly leading heavy library users to frequent other branches, Wagoner says.

To improve traffic flow and help patrons discover things for themselves, Montalbano says he divided the Cherry Creek vestibule to direct incoming traffic past the Beehive and away from the self-check devices. Montalbano wanted to ensure that patrons would naturally encounter librarians and other staff.

SPACE TO COLLABORATE The Ross-Cherry Creek Branch's (top, l. -r.) colorful Beehive is the hub of activity, flexible enough for both library and community uses. New furniture, carpeting, and lighting attract visitors from surrounding upscale neighborhoods. The 28,490 square foot Sam Gary Branch (below) lights up the Stapleton Town Center, while inside (at r.) laptop-friendly furniture cozies up to a warm fireplace where users can relax and enjoy the space

"If you do need to ask a question, you don't need to go far," Montalbano says. The reference desk moved from a corner to a more central location; librarians now felt like they were part of the building. "It's much easier to determine who needs help and who wants to be left alone," Wagner says.

Sam Gary Branch (hybrid)

To meet the needs of a few neighborhoods, DPL leaders realized hybrids of two or more service deliveries were needed. Opened in August, with 28,490 square feet, the $12 million Sam Gary Branch combines the Children and Family and Contemporary service deliveries and architectural styles.

The Beehive found in Contemporary branches was modified to include technology-enabled furniture, with four to six computers or smartphones connected to two monitors. Small parent or business groups are expected to use the area to collaborate, Kotarba says.

The interior is divided into three areas. Visitors will see popular materials found at a Contemporary branch and computers nearest to the entrance. Just past the computers, the adult fiction and the children's collection are collocated, similar to the Children and Family layout. The nonfiction area offers cozy laptop-friendly furniture near a fireplace. At night, illumination from the library's clerestory windows brightens the neighborhood.

"Everyone in this community has a front porch, and they wanted (the library) to be the front porch of the community," says Tracy Tafoya, a principal at OZ Architecture, who designed the Sam Gary Branch.

Language and Learning

The hallmarks of the Language and Learning service delivery include community learning spaces with digital whiteboards, laptops, and movable furniture, Kotarba says. These fixtures enhance programs aimed at building technology, job search, English speaking, and other skills. Books and other non-English-language items are prominently displayed.

"The other thing about Learning and Language libraries is that they are very welcoming," Kotarba says. "This is as much about finding staff who are fluent in Spanish or Vietnamese, who are multilingual, as it is about spaces where you feel welcome or comfortable."

Humphries Poli's Friedrich kept the user in mind to develop the architectural style.

"People come to the library in search of a better quality of life," Friedrich says. "That led us to start looking at what would be the needs of people in those particular situations."

Learning and Language branches offer adult and children's programs simultaneously to make it easier for parents and grandparents to participate while they are caring for children. At the Montbello Branch, rolling partitions were added to the community room to offer parents and grandparents a sight line of the adjacent children's area, says Emily Hackett, Montbello's senior librarian. "The wall can be all the way open or halfway shut. Children can be occupied with crafts while their parents are applying for jobs," Hackett says.

Woodbury Branch

When the Woodbury Branch reopened in 2010 following its $657,000 renovation, library users discovered the elegant wooden roof trusses in the 99-year-old Carnegie Library and much more. The renovation included much-needed improvements to plumbing, electrical systems, flooring, and furniture and the installation of self-check machines. The changes to the building's layout improved the traffic flow, brightened up the walls, and illuminated both ceilings and floors.

"What I've heard from customers is, 'Wow! You got more space,'" says Lisa Murillo, Woodbury's senior librarian. "It's still the same square footage. It's brighter, lighter, roomier."

The upgrade to the Renaissance Revival building garnered the 2010 Mountain States Construction Bronze Hard Hat Award for renovation of a historic structure. Humphries Poli's Friedrich decided to move the nonfiction collection to the second level of the library's 1966 addition to concentrate quieter activities in one area.

To connect the upper story with the atrium, Friedrich had sections of the solid-wood, curved railing replaced with glass etched with the word *library* in several languages. Now, many library patrons in this diverse older neighborhood head to the second level to study, read, or work. "It's more utilized now than it was before," Woodbury's Murillo says.

PATTERNS OF PROGRESS The Woodbury Branch's second level (top, l.) is exposed through cutouts in the etched glass rail system. Signage (top, r.) efficiently addresses the multicultural needs of the library users

West Denver Branch

Scheduled to open in fall 2013, the as-yet-unnamed $12 million, two-story branch in West Denver will have an interior courtyard on the second level to fulfill neighborhood residents' desire for a safe place to experience the outdoors, Kotarba says. "Colfax is a pretty rough neighborhood in places."

The neighborhoods served by the library range from those undergoing gentrification to trouble pockets and offer an incredible diversity of Hispanic, Anglo, Asian, and Jewish residents, Kotarba says.

Like other Language and Learning branches, the lower level will collocate space for programs near the children's area for simultane-

ous, multigenerational activities. An easily adaptable collaboration area is planned for the second floor; a glass "perch" over the northwestern entrance will offer views of Rocky Mountain National Park and stations to listen to music, Montalbano says.

Uniting each is a ground-to-roof translucent architectural feature called the Wonder Wall. It will house ducts for hot and cold air exchange and the automated book return. It will also draw natural light into the library, Montalbano says.

On the exterior, a pattern of colorful, textured stucco squares represents the diversity of the neighborhoods coming together. "We call them threads of the community. As they thread their way through the Wonder Wall, they become a quilt," Montalbano says.

Children and Family

The Children and Family architecture style focuses on young children and their caregivers experiencing the library together. To accomplish that goal, educational toys called Discovery Pods are spread throughout each of the renovated Children and Family branches, for example, having them mounted on shelving units in the adult collection. The kids and adult books are collocated. "It's really designed so adults can browse for popular things with their kids still around them and within hearing range and in sight," Kotarba says.

Computer terminals offer room for two or three people to share one workstation and pair a children's computer with an adult terminal, says Tafoya of OZ Architecture, which developed the architecture style. This "parallel play" approach allows parents and children to work side by side or together, she says.

"The biggest distinction is how you lay out the library," Tafoya says.

Changes in existing branches made a huge difference to patrons' experience. At the Virginia Village Branch, the $730,000 renovation included lowering shelving height, opening the floor plan, adding intimate seating areas, and upgrading lighting and upholstery, but the square footage remained constant. "At Virginia Village, people walked in and said, 'How much did you add onto the building?' " Kotarba says.

Green Valley Ranch Branch

To design the $12 million Green Valley Ranch Branch, Dennis Humphries, a principal at Humphries Poli Architects in Denver, focused on the Stapleton neighborhood residents' desire to see the library reflect the area's agricultural heritage and its ties to Denver International Airport. Humphries coined the terms *iPlains* and *ePlanes*. Wavy aerodynamic shapes hang from the library ceiling, and four sections of the library's overhanging roof tilt up at a slight angle like airline wings. Abstractions of aerial views of crops are found in the carpets and landscaping.

A Discovery Pod constructed from a 737 cockpit attracts the most attention.

"Everything within the building was really organized around the reference to the iPlains and the ePlanes," Humphries says. "It was quite amazing that it was generated by the community."

In the seven months following Green Valley's 2011 opening, 4,231 new library cards were issued, Kotarba says, indicating the new branch is reaching nonlibrary users in a neighborhood with one of the highest concentrations of children in the city. Picture books are checked out almost as fast as they are shelved, says Green Valley Ranch senior librarian Colleen Galvin. The Colorado Association of Libraries selected the Leadership in Energy & Environmental Design (LEED) Gold-certified branch as the 2011 Library of the Year.

For Galvin, success is measured by the interaction among families. One of her favorite anecdotes is of three toddlers and their caregivers getting to know one another. While the tots played with large foam letters at a Discovery Pod, three older men who were fathers or grandfathers exchanged tips about their Blackberry-style smartphones. "It's exactly what we want to see in the library," Galvin says. "It was working exactly as this library was designed—the community to get together and share information."

NATIVE ENVIRONMENT The Green Valley Ranch Branch's landscaping (l.) was sown from Denver's agricultural heritage

The future Denver Public Library has already begun to look to the future by mining the 2010 Census and data from its new integrated library system with a goal of looking even deeper at its community's needs, Kotarba says.

Architects involved in the process say that bold leaders, community support, and the willingness to spend the time and money to develop a data-driven vision would be needed for another library system to adopt DPL's approach of creating architectural styles to match service delivery and guide renovations.

"The future of libraries is just unknown. The number one response as an architect is to make them future proof," studiotrope's Montalbano says. "We need to design in a way that is culturally flexible."

Marta Murvosh, MLS, is a freelance writer/researcher and aspiring librarian living and working in Northwestern Washington. You can follow her via www.facebook.com/MartaMurvosh

8
keeping current

VISIONING THE FUTURE

How do we break new ground when thinking about library design? Sometimes, it's all about seeing new trends and reflecting back, and sometimes it's about shaking up how we think, as with a deck of cards called the Idea Kit. The projects in this chapter—shared from *LJ*'s design coverage since 2009 as originally published—tap trends, some quite literally identifying trends to watch and others illustrating big ideas influencing space design, such as the need to anticipate the impacts of climate change. Captured by LJ in one moment in time, some of these projects may look very different today, but the trends that shaped them remain influential for future library projects.

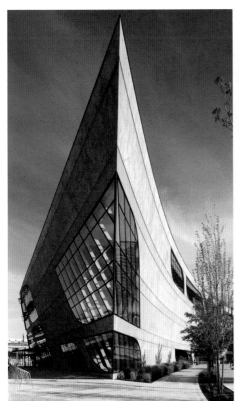

Designing 21st-Century Libraries

By Peter Gisolfi

Public libraries are busier and more popular with patrons than ever. Today's library is a place for social interaction as well as quiet reading. It is a community cultural center, not simply a repository for books. It is a welcoming building with a design focus on transparency, not a series of isolated spaces.

These changing operations directly affect the layout and organization of library buildings. When libraries construct a new building or transform an existing one, they have the opportunity to create a library that meets these needs.

These changes in the service model also influence how libraries are staffed and how patrons use them. Library patrons expect staff accessibility and opportunities for instruction and learning. So, libraries today must be designed to accommodate more simplified administrative operations and new staff functions.

OPENING UP The trend toward transparency among spaces is evident at the new Darien Library, CT

Eleven Emerging Trends

It is often difficult to recognize changing trends while they are still in flux. That said, consider the typical characteristics of today's 21st-century library. While the library remains an inspiring public building with an important civic presence, many other aspects are different:

1 An informal community cultural center

2 Transparency among spaces so patrons can be seen and more easily served

3 Reading spaces interspersed within the various collections

4 Larger and more varied spaces for children and teens

5 Community, meeting, and activity rooms of varied sizes

6 Daylight in all areas of the building

7 Connections to outdoor space

8 Spaces devoted to computer and Internet instruction and online research

9 Automated systems, and increased staff efficiency

10 Flexibility to accommodate future requirements

11 The library as a community model for sustainable practice

Eight Ways We Were

We are all familiar with the libraries of the latter part of the 20th century. The library of that period was and had:

1 A quiet place (no talking, food, or drink)

2 A repository for books, with large areas devoted to stacks and the collections

3 An imposing circulation desk for manual checkout and return

4 A modest community room

5 A guarding-the-books point of view from the staff

6 An extensive collection of encyclopedias and other print reference materials

7 An inspiring place, often the main reading room

8 A civic presence for the library in the fabric of the town

9 Oddly, in many settings, libraries like this werestill being built only five or ten years ago.

Nine New Ways We Use Libraries

Emerging trends in library building design dramatically affect how the library performs—and vice versa. Today's patrons and staff use the library differently:

1 Increased number of digital materials reduces space devoted to book collections

2 Automated self-checkout reduces or eliminates the circulation desk

3 Digital card catalog OPAC stations are scattered throughout the library rather than centralized

4 Wireless Internet access throughout the library lets patrons bring their own devices, decreasing the need for banks of stationary computers

5 Automated materials handling systems in larger libraries free up staff and shorten wait times

6 Staff are more accessible to patrons and less separated from them

7 More extensive programming for children and teens is offered

8 Cafés induce informal socializing and an enhanced sense of community

9 Community room, meeting rooms, and even art galleries have a wider agenda

HEIGHT AND LIGHT
Top: larger children's and teen spaces are the future, such as this expanded kids library at the Byram Shubert Library, Greenwich, CT. Left: connecting to outdoor space is an emerging trend, such as the double-height reading room at Longwood Public Library, Middle Island, NY, which is open to a new outdoor reading court

Whether you build a new library or transform an existing one, do not build the best library of the previous century. Create an environment that facilitates new patterns of interacting, learning, and accessing information and is sufficiently flexible to accommodate changes that inevitably will come.

Peter Gisolfi is a licensed architect and landscape architect and professor of architecture and landscape architecture at the Spitzer School of Architecture at the City College of New York. He is the author of Finding the Place of Architecture in the Landscape *and is senior partner at Peter Gisolfi Associates, Architects and Landscape Architects. He can be reached at pgisolfi@petergisolfiassociates.com*

DATE LIBRARY BY DESIGN, SPRING 2013

Giving the People What They Want

By Sarah Bayliss

"It's the largest investment in our 90-year history," says Sari Feldman about Ohio's Cuyahoga County Public Library (CCPL) plan to renovate or rebuild 18 of its 28 branches.

The $110 million spate of rebuilding, led by executive director Feldman and detailed in CCPL's Facilities Master Plan, will create new and updated library facilities that the library says will save CCPL $4 million a year.

Those savings are particularly meaningful, because since 2008 CCPL's revenues have dropped by $14.9 million owing to state budget cuts, and since 2009 property tax revenues declined by $7 million.

The library raised funds by selling $75 million in bonds, using $25 million from library capital funds, and raising an additional $10 million through a capital campaign, according to Feldman.

"Eight or nine years ago, we recognized that we had many branches that needed replacement or major renovation," says Feldman, who recently won the 2013 Charlie Robinson Award, given to public library directors deemed risk-takers and innovators over several years. "We could not expect cities or schools to put this on the ballot for us. They could barely pass their own issues. So we called together 40 representatives from across our system—government officials, clergy, school superintendents, and people connected to the library in some way. We met about five times over six months and analyzed our story and how we could move forward both to continue a high quality of service and do it out of better facilities."

In 2009, the library contracted Cleveland's Bostwick Design Partnership to create a comprehensive facilities assessment, which, after board

review and public comment, the board approved in June 2010. Things are in full swing now, with several branches under construction. "We have six ribbon-cuttings for replacement buildings in 2013," Feldman says.

The plan maintains that efficient renovations and sustainable, one-story structures with fewer service points and open floor plans will better serve CCPL's 47 communities in greater Cleveland. Along with perks like better technology, homework centers, recording studios, cafés, drive-through windows, easier browsing, and, in one of the larger facilities, a 400-seat auditorium, the branches are conceived to be vibrant community gathering places.

Gathering Input As such, community involvement has been key to every step in the planning process, with advanced feedback about what people want from their neighborhood libraries, both in service and style, defining each new design.

This influence shows, for example, in two very different new facilities: the modern, geometric Warrensville Heights Branch, which opened on April 21, 2012, and the Olmsted Falls Branch, with a dark red exterior and classic peaked roofs, which opened on February 23 of this year.

Planning the Warrensville Heights facility, the first of the new buildings to be completed, CCPL held larger meetings and then eight smaller community focus groups to gather ideas, says Feldman. The old branch was a cement block. "The number one thing people wanted was natural light," Feldman says, and "a great community meeting space, traditional quiet space, and lots of room for youth to interact."

Stylistically, the community favored "a very contemporary style—glass and steel," says CCPL marketing and communications director Hallie Rich. The library was conceived as part of an economic development program for Warrensville Heights, and the city bought and gave the library 4.25 acres to develop, says Feldman. The resulting $9.75 million, 25,000 square foot structure, conceived by Cleveland's Holzheimer Bolek Meehan Architects, is collocated with a new YMCA.

HANDS ON New at the Warrensville Heights Branch is a multiworkstation computer area and a cool recording studio for public use

Olmsted Falls patrons, by contrast, were "looking for a building design that would fit in with the reserved architectural style of the community," says Rich. Hence, the traditional profile of the $1.75 million, 6,000 square foot new Olmsted Falls branch, designed by the Cleveland-based Van Dyke Architects LLC. As with these two buildings, "all of our architects and construction managers are local," says Feldman.

While Warrensville Heights is a success by any standards—circulation is up over 100 percent and visits by 125 percent, says Feldman—she realized, moving forward, that "there might be a better way to gather information than focus groups." CCPL adopted what she calls a "world café" model of community engagement. First, it took the meetings "out of the library" and into "a community center or a YMCA or a school," places that are "easy for people to get to, with lots of parking."

The world café element comes into play inside, where CCPL sets up six tables displaying photographs of sample library spaces—unidentified—for the public to browse through. "Each table is dedicated to one element of the design: exterior, children's spaces, adult spaces," and more, says Rich.

"We number the photographs and have library staff stationed at each table so that residents could say, 'I love number 12, but I hate number six,'" she says. "We say, 'What is it about number 12 that you like?' We try to zero in on the elements they're looking at."

Feldman observes, "Having these images there is powerful, because it sparks people to think in a way that they didn't expect. They are seeing unique and progressive kinds of spaces and that shapes and changes the feedback. They think of things they never imagined."

"We have these community meetings outside the library, multiple times, and send communications to the residences," Feldman adds. "If people can't make the meetings, they find a way to give feedback."

Some results? Envisioning a new Mayfield Branch, scheduled to open in April, "They asked for a lot of natural materials," says Rich. The building is located in the midst of a park and wetlands district, so "they wanted something that integrated with that natural environment." The library has been designed so that the entire back wall overlooks trails and wetlands.

Planning a replacement Orange Branch, "We went in expecting the feedback to be asking for a more traditional, stately design," says Rich. Instead, "the feedback has gravitated toward more contemporary than we expected." Community members also like the idea of natural materials—wood, stone, and glass.

The new South Euclid/Lyndhurst Branch will replace one currently located in the Telling Mansion, a historic structure that the library plans to sell. Not everyone is happy about this, and a petition has been launched protesting the plan.

"There is a lot of affection and nostalgia for the historic building," says Rich. Nonetheless, as the process moves forward with construction set to begin this summer, "what we're hearing from focus groups is that they want cozy, comfortable space," as in the historic setting, as well as "more openness with lots of natural light, which is not a feature" currently. A larger meeting room space and a more browser-friendly floor plan are also part of the scheme. The new $12.6 million, 30,000 square foot facility is scheduled to open in fall 2014.

The most financially ambitious project is the new Parma Branch, a $15.6 million, 43,000 square foot facility that will open its doors this fall. Since "we don't have a main library" in the CCPL system, "the investment is all back into the community," says Feldman. "The community involvement is one of the best pieces of our story."

Sarah Bayliss (shbayliss@gmail.com) has written for LJ's Movers & Shakers feature and Library by Design *supplements*

How Social Media Built a Library

Surrey City Centre Library, British Columbia, Canada By Sarah Bayliss

In fall 2009, Bing Thom Architects (BTA) won a stimulus grant from the Canadian government to build the new $36 million (Canadian), 77,000 square foot Surrey City Centre Library, envisioned as a centerpiece of this fast-growing community outside Vancouver, BC. The caveat: use it or lose it. In exchange for the funding, construction had to be finished in 18 months—half the usual time allowed for such a project. "We got the grant in November and started working in December," says Michael Heeney, principal at the Vancouver-based BTA. "By February, we were under construction."

The accelerated schedule meant there was no time to conduct essential public meetings and focus groups to find out what the community wanted from their new library. BTA's solution: use social media.

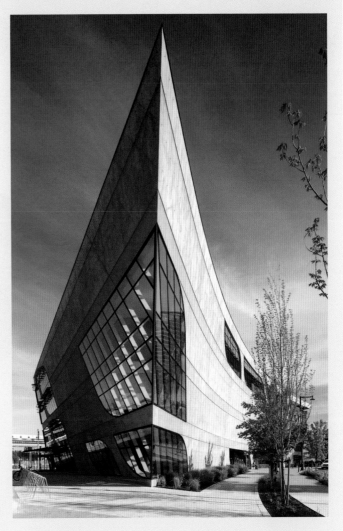

The birth of the Ideabook Collaborating with the Surrey librarians, BTA set up an "Ideabook," using Facebook, Twitter, Flickr, and a library blog to display design concepts and ask for public input. Right away, "People started chiming in," says Heeney, in an undertaking that would have significant impact on both design and service.

At the height of the process, the sites were getting 6,000 hits per month. By contrast, about 30 people typically attend one community meeting, says Heeney. And while focus groups tend to draw an older crowd, the largest percentage of the new library's online "fans" were under 25. Also, in Heeney's view, the second largest group, women between 35 and 44, reflected a segment of Surrey's working family population that would not usually take time to attend evening and weekend forums.

Some requests were predictable, says Surrey chief librarian Melanie Houlden: more computer training, more books and DVDs, and more programming in general. Others were less anticipated but just as important. The Muslim population asked for a prayer room, Heeney says. The rising number of people who work at home wanted small rooms they could use for meetings. Kids requested a clock in the spacious children's area, a place to draw pictures, and couches where their parents could relax while waiting for them.

On Flickr, people posted images of architecture they liked, much of it in keeping with the soaring, open environments they were seeing in BTA's plans. Pictures of China's ultramodern Shenzhen Library showed that structure's dramatic, grand staircases, which double as informal seating. Images of the Central Library in Amsterdam revealed biomorphic chairs and airy white spaces. Other pictures ranged from the open-plan Seattle Central Library to colorful murals in an airport in Moncton, NB.

People-centered design All of this feedback informed BTA's existing commitment to creating an uplifting community destination, with central areas that could double as performance spaces. The architects also saw a need for smaller, "living room"-type places where people could read or work.

"We spent a lot of time making sure there were opportunities for people-watching," says Heeney. "There is a sort of natural, voyeuristic desire for people to know what's going on around them." A request for a quiet workplace resulted in a glassed-in study area.

Two enormous staircases ringing the central atrium are key to the Surrey library's final design, a sleek four-story building, which, owing to the tapered shape of the site, also conjures associations with a ship. As Houlden says, "These beautiful staircases work in two ways—either you sit and enjoy the view outside, or settle in with laptops and books." In addition, the stairs serve as bleacher-type seating for events and performances.

On opening day last September, 10,000 people filed through the building. Now that the community has opined on the library, Houlden and staff are soliciting more online input "about where to go from here," service-wise, she says.

The new facility replaces a 10,000 square foot, "sad little building" that was built in 1974 and used to be a plumbing supply store, Houlden notes. The library staff went from providing eight public computers to 80; from running a suburban-type, "drive-by" facility to a city library envisioned as a community hub. There is "so much opportunity," she says.

Opportunity knocks for BTA, too. "We got into this process by necessity," says Heeney of the Ideabook approach. "But it's now become a standard part of our practice."

Sarah Bayliss has written for LJ, *the* New York Times, Boston Globe, *and* ARTnews *magazine, among other publications*

Slaying a Sacred Cow with a Deck of Cards

A 52-card Idea Kit spurs brainstorming about library design By Sarah Bayliss

When architecture firm GouldEvans participated in *LJ*'s Design Institute (DI) last year in Phoenix for the first time and took on the task of suggesting design ideas to Clark College's Cannell Library in Vancouver, WA, Tony Rohr, principal at GouldEvans, asked himself, "How do we handle this?" The answer took the shape of a deck of cards referred to as the Idea Kit.

The job of Rohr and the GouldEvans's team was to think about Cannell Library's needs and, during two group sessions, to present their ideas to Michelle Bagley, Clark College dean of libraries, e-learning, tutoring, and faculty development, along with the other librarians attending the meetings. Bagley had outlined Cannell's design issues and goals to Rohr and his group through conference calls prior to DI. The student body at this commuter college has exploded from 7,000 when the library opened in 1990 to 17,000 today. As a result, Cannell Library had too little space to accommodate everyone using it. It also had a poor layout for patron needs and noise issues, among other concerns. But expanding was not an option at that time.

Bagley had previously gone through a programming meeting with an architect "that didn't go anywhere," says Rohr. So he wanted to make sure the GouldEvans–led session was fruitful, though it would be up to Bagley whether to follow up or not on the ideas it generated.

"Our firm has a long history of doing interactive workshops with clients," says Rohr, who steered the DI discussions with fellow GouldEvans principal Steve Clark. "I thought, 'If we go in there and just put up our drawings, they're going to fall asleep.'"

He was also mindful that the session participants, all seasoned librarians, would have valuable ideas about Cannell, particularly with regard to staffing and services, that he might not have considered. While he and Clark prepared boards and sketches outlining their recommendations, they decided that they wanted Bagley to hear ideas from the group first. What GouldEvans was really striving for, Rohr realized, was a brainstorming session. "We said, 'Let's figure out an exercise where the participants engage in dialog. Then we'll unveil what we brought with us.'"

The 52-card solution Rohr and his team went "round and round" during a DI planning meeting trying to figure out how to make the experience dynamic. Five days before the meeting, they landed on a solution: a riff on "architecture playing cards" used for brainstorming with clients in the past, tailored to libraries and dubbed an Idea Kit. This custom-designed deck of 52 themed cards, slightly larger than a standard deck, was created to catalyze discussion between Bagley and the attending librarians.

"We had six people on the phone talking about this—five architects and a graphic designer—and the ideas started flowing," says Rohr. With that momentum, GouldEvans designed and printed the decks, with 52 unique cards, within three days.

What's on the cards Each card has a single image on one side and on the other side library-related words or phrases intended to

see and be seen

casual seating can be positioned in high traffic areas for social study, as well as more contemplative areas for serious study.

gouldevans

slay a dragon

where does risk hold you back?

what dragons can you slay?

PLAY YOUR CARDS RIGHT Top left, GouldEvans architects Tony Rohr (l.) and Steve Clark educated attendees at *LJ*'s Design Institute Phoenix in fall 2011 on their Idea Kit concept, working up space planning ideas on the spot (left). Top right, University of Ottowa Law Library director Margo Jeske (l.) and Scottsdale Public Library director Rita Hamilton (r.) work with the Idea Kit and attendees to rethink the Cannell Library space

trigger ideas. Some sample images are a large pink fingerprint; colorful LEGO-type blocks; a single hand or eye; bookshelves; and two interlocking gears. In Rohr's experience, such pictures are worth a thousand words because they inspire open thinking and let the mind roam. "Certain presentations work better with one image rather than seven PowerPoint bullet [items]," he observes.

The words and phrases on the cards' flip side are divided into three thematic, color-coded categories. Blue letters relate to design and spacial concerns, with concepts like "concierge model," "dual-use rooms," "off-site collection," and "roving reference." Pink letters cue librarians to patron needs and their libraries' assets with terms such as *ethnography*, *times are a-changin'*, *partners*, *unique resources*, and *Heart: The library is the heart of the community* (a quote from Nancy Pearl, *LJ*'s 2011 Librarian of the Year). Yellow words deliver big-picture wake-up calls such as "slay a sacred cow," "see the obvious," "slay a dragon," and "listen to that hunch."

These yellow "freedom cards," as Rohr calls them, "are intended to help people figure out, 'What is keeping you from making real progress?' It gives them the opportunity to think much bigger."

Slaying a sacred cow, for instance, might mean reconsidering open hours or rethinking a librarian's vow to "never put books behind enclosed stacks." But Rohr's team also "wanted to make sure the cards captured the little things in daily practice as well as the big things that go way to the top of the administration." Hence, the nitty-gritty "boilerplate" library issues at one end of the spectrum and mandates like "be engaged now" at the other.

Playing the game At each of two DI breakout sessions, Rohr and Clark posted the library floor plans and then created teams of five or six participants, giving each group a deck of cards. They assigned Bagley to a team during each meeting and told the groups to take 20 minutes to debate how they would solve their challenge and select the five key cards that would help suggest solutions. The groups then posted their chosen cards on the mounted floor plans and talked about their interpretations of and solutions for the design challenge. In the concluding minutes, Rohr and Clark presented their own ideas.

"There were two incredible outcomes" from using the Idea Kits, says Rohr. "One was that the participants didn't sit there and look at one another." The cards give everyone in the room a "tool" with which to participate. At any typical brainstorming session, Rohr adds, there's no need to worry about getting the extroverts involved. "There are others who are introverts," he notes. "They need some help. They are not going to say something on their own, but they can play that card. They say to themselves, 'I am emboldened to say this thing.'"

For Bagley, the cards provided a kind of brainstorming lingua franca. "Everyone comes to the table with their own language," she says. The cards offered a "shared vocabulary. We were saying, 'Let's look at this card and think about what that means.'"

The freedom cards, she says, brilliantly offer a neutral way to address potentially emotionally loaded issues. "Slay a sacred cow," for instance, is another way of asking, "What are we trying to protect?"

"It is easier to play that card than to have someone say, 'We need to figure out why we're holding on so tightly to this policy,'" Bagley says. The different combinations of cards, she adds, lead to unexpected ideas from everyone in the group.

Some ideas, however, don't fit the cards. "We just kicked ourselves for not having blanks," says Rohr. No worries: DI participants used paper to create their own "wild cards" and put them up alongside the others. One of Bagley's sessions, upping the idea of roving reference, created a card commanding, "Everything on feet or wheels."

Winners all As Rohr and his team had hoped, Bagley "was getting commentary from her peers rather than directly from the architects. Everyone present is a librarian and essentially a knowledgeable client. They are all leaders of their organizations. We had a polished person telling her, 'You have to move these stacks out. This is prime real estate.' By the end of the session, the client was saying, 'I think you're right.'"

After getting home, Rohr incorporated photographs of the card-covered floor plans into a scrapbook-like PDF report. Back at Cannell Library, the report made it much easier for Bagley to debrief her staff about the DI meetings. Looking at the photographs of the cards in play, Bagley says, "The folks in my library were able to get a much more real sense of the floor plans and process-oriented suggestions than they would have if they had to rely on me taking notes" during the sessions.

Would she use the cards again? Without hesitation. "I brought a deck of cards back to the library," Bagley says. She plans to break it out during an upcoming renovation planning meeting.

Sarah Bayliss has written for LJ, *the* New York Times, Boston Globe, *and* ARTnews *magazine, among other publications*

DATE LIBRARY BY DESIGN, FALL 2012

Transforming Tech

Cleveland Public Library looks to Apple for lab inspiration

By Sarah Bayliss

Challenge: How to turn an ornately designed, inconveniently shaped basement into a sleek, technology-driven community space? This was the question that Bostwick Design Partnership faced when taking on the task of creating TechCentral, Cleveland Public Library's new technology center on the lower level of the library's downtown Louis Stokes Wing.

The roughly $1 million renovation involved transforming the area, which had housed the library's AV collection in tightly spaced stacks, into a state-of-the-art tech center with the open-plan appeal of an Apple store. Operational since June, the 7,000 square foot TechCentral's main elements include 90 desktop workstations, the "Feature Wall," which is a 70 square inch interactive screen, a "TechToybox" displaying new wireless loanable devices, MyCloud personal computing services, and a 3-D printer. Employees in orange coats roam the area, offering help as needed or scheduling one-on-one training. As TechCentral manager C.J. Lynce says, "The focus is not, 'We have 90 computers.' It is, 'This is a place to learn.' We want to be not just a provider but an inspiration."

Jumping hurdles The architects had to clear hurdles in their quest to create a "calm, welcoming space" from what existed before. First, the layout: the area in question was "an awkward, L-shaped space that you enter on the thin line of the L," says Richard Ortmeyer, a principal at Bostwick Design. Before, the first thing patrons were confronted with when entering was a "highly textured, stainless-steel reference desk" designed in the 1990s. Located under an arch with marquee-like spot lighting, the enormous jagged desk emphasized the "us and them" divide between patron and employee, says Ortmeyer. However, those at the library who remembered how much the desk cost at the time were reluctant to let it go.

Other design impediments included "gigantic, overscale blue columns" that are signature elements elsewhere in the library and a mural-sized, orange-and-green tile wall flanking the desk on both sides. There was also a problem with wayfinding: walking into the building, patrons weren't always aware that the downstairs space existed.

Ortmeyer and his colleagues would have loved to have started with a clean slate, scuttling the desk, columns, and tile wall. While the library board agreed that the desk could go, it would not dispense with the columns or the intricate mural.

THE COLORS OF TECHNOLOGY Cleveland PL's TechCentral uses as much white as possible to focus on the multimedia. A mural-sized orange-and-green tile wall was grandfathered into the space, and lighting on its back edge makes the colors pop. Orange-coated employees assist users, who will sit in orange chairs in front of computer stations displaying "curvy, custom craftsmanship" that allows the work spaces to work together

With those parameters, the architects got to work. Their overall scheme: make as many things white as possible, abolish any sort of us/them dynamic, use elegant flowing forms to complement the arch, and employ strategic lighting to direct patrons toward the services at hand.

No whitewash Deciding to paint everything white, including the previously mauve ceiling, was the easy part. "Of all colors, white allows the library to focus on its multimedia," says Ortmeyer. Next, with the desk out of the way, the architects opened up the area behind the arch so that it was accessible to patrons. Within this expansive space, in place of the desk, the first thing visitors spy is the interactive screen feature wall and the TechToybox. On either side of these, patrons find an understated white help desk area on the left and a checkin area on the right.

As another key element, Ortmeyer and colleagues created two sleek white "laptop bars" running along the tiled walls and curving gracefully under the open archway into the reception and checkin areas. Elsewhere, two additional laptop areas and rows of computer stations also feature the "curvy, custom craftsmanship" that makes the various work spaces "all one thing rather than visually separate."

Lighting is key "Lighting was also key," Ortmeyer notes. While his colleagues would have loved to replace all the lighting, the budget would not allow for that. Still, convinced that strategic lighting "guides you to where you want to look," they added indirect illumination at key points. Before, it looked like the librarian behind the desk and under the marquee lights, was on center stage. Now, cool underlighting beneath the reception, checkin, and work surfaces, accomplished with concealed LED panels behind translucent resin, draw people to those areas.

Since the tile wall was there to stay, Ortmeyer and colleagues added lighting on the wall's back edge, making the colors more vibrant. Then, to punctuate the rest of the all-white space, "we picked one of the colors in the mural to allow it to pop," says Ortmeyer—resulting in orange chairs, which complement the employees' bright orange coats.

In addition to the surface design considerations, technological flexibility was also critical—"wire management and durability," Ortmeyer says. "A raised floor system"—a $60,000 access floor—"allowed us to make the space as flexible as possible." Other budget line items included $535,000 for overall construction; $200,000 for furniture, fixtures, and equipment; and $42,400 for multimedia.

Another $33,600 went toward an innovative wayfinding scheme, branding, and media walls, undertaken by Karen Skunta and Co. This included visual branding, signage across the library's main buildings, inside and out, highlighting the changes underway. Skunta also designed the interactive media on the feature wall.

The architects' attention to craftsmanship resulted in occasional time spent laying on the floor looking up at the chairs and tables, along with "many debates about the widths of the workstations," says Ortmeyer. After he and colleagues "carefully calibrated" measurements, "we customized them to be larger at the ends so that people can work together."

When Ortmeyer came into TechCentral not long ago to show it off to his parents, he was immediately approached by a staff member in an orange coat. "A young tech guy whom I hadn't met started to speak," he recalls. "He started telling me about the cool elements in the library. It was [an] exciting experience."

Sarah Bayliss recently wrote about Canada's New Surrey City Library for LJ *and was an editor for* School library Journal's Top 100 Children's Novels and Picture Books

DATE LIBRARY BY DESIGN, FALL 2011

The Heart of the Campus

Commitment to building a highly engineered university library tuned in to its users' needs By Lynn Blumentstein

When Lee Van Orsdel interviewed for the position of dean of Grand Valley State University Libraries, Allendale, MI, in 2005, one of the job's top stated priorities was overseeing the construction of a new main library. Van Orsdel got the job, and, judging from her enthusiastic description of the project to *LJ*, her passion "to do more" was likely a determining factor.

While there is no confirmed schedule for construction (the project is still in the early planning stages), Van Orsdel's vision, inspired by a visit to the Saltire Centre at Glasgow Caledonian University in Scotland and by ideas the architecture firm SHW Group presented in March 2008, is clear. (For a summary of that presentation, visit tinyurl.com/VisioningWorkshop.)

The library as academic mall The new library, to be called the Mary Idema Pew Library Learning and Information Commons, will "challenge all traditional assumptions about library design," taking cues from retail, museum, and other nonlibrary environments, Van Orsdel told *LJ*. It will be flexible enough to serve the needs of the current student body as well as those of future generations of users.

Though Van Orsdel and her staff find inspiration in watching students work, she feels their skills in the areas of presentation, writing, research, and technology can be improved and envisions the new library environment as being specially engineered to help develop those skills further.

Van Orsdel sees the library as part of an "information knowledge market," the equivalent of an "academic mall."

To that end, the library will partner with other student service entities, like the writing center and the speech communication department, so that "students can shop for the services they need." Though there is already a writing center elsewhere on campus, Van Orsdel wants to put a satellite "in the path of the student."

Other major presences to cohabit the building include the Center for Scholarly and Creative Excellence and the Student Summer Scholars Program. The IT department will run the equivalent of an Apple Store Genius Bar, with IT troubleshooters on hand or available by appointment.

Funding and design Funding is not yet secured for the $70 million project, whose cost includes renovating the current 59,000 square foot library to serve as classroom and office space. But the capital campaign is already under way, with $20 million of a $30 million target for private donations raised to date, and Van Orsdel hopes to secure other funding sources by 2010. (For information on giving opportunities, visit tinyurl.com/GrandValleyCampaign.)

The design team at SHW Group is shooting for Platinum LEED (Leadership in Energy and Environmental Design) status. The campus of 24,000 students has no predominant architectural style, so the library won't be constrained design-wise. The building will be 145,000 square feet and four stories high, "with the ability to see up and through," Van Orsdel said, as the design principle guiding the project.

The Grand Rapids, MI–based company Steelcase will work with the library to develop prototypes of furniture that optimally supports collaborative learning. Other projected features include an automated retrieval system and, perhaps, a rooftop garden.

Staff issues and more Additional staff will be needed in the larger library, but the number won't be determined by the building's size, said Van Orsdel. Efficiencies such as single-service points will be implemented, and wayfinding will be simplified.

How will these decisions and others be made? An existing Library Council, comprised of five division heads and one representative from each of the three personnel levels, will join faculty and student reps to form a new university library planning committee. Focus groups will add valuable insight.

The library as the academic heart "We want to create a context in which we are a strong partner in serving the university's educational mission," said Van Orsdel. "We are positioned to become the academic heart."

The building will have a lot of glass, so that it will light up at night, symbolically serving as a beacon—transparent to users—and as a statement: "This is where the academy lives."

Lynn Blumenstein is Contributing Editor, LJ

The Comeback Kids

Recovering from a natural disaster can be long, hard, and expensive, but some libraries are seizing the chance to rebuild better than ever By Marta Murvosh

When the Cedar River breached its banks in 2008 to flood downtown Cedar Rapids, IA, the entire first floor of the two-story Cedar Rapids Public Library (CRPL) Downtown Branch drowned in the deluge.

The natural disaster occurred at the start of the recession, causing the library's Board of Trustees to question whether it could find the funds to relocate and replace the building, says Susan Corrigan, a library board member. "You kind of forget what the dark days looked like, but we had some really dark days," says Corrigan. However, ultimately the board was successful. Corrigan headed up the Building Committee and served as board president while the new facility was constructed.

The new $45 million, 94,000 square foot Downtown Branch opened in August 2013, sitting 28 inches above the record-breaking high-water mark. The replacement building includes expanded space for children and teens and offers flexible meeting and gathering space, a café, a green roof, and an auditorium, along with views of the nearby park and cityscape. It's certified U.S. Green Building Council Leadership in Energy & Environmental Design (LEED) Platinum and has won at least five architecture awards, according to designers OPN Architects.

What kept the board and library leaders moving forward was a dream of changing how library service was delivered to patrons. "We didn't lose sight of that vision," Corrigan says.

Vision and determination are two of the qualities that various library leaders and architects around the country used to rebuild libraries demolished in a variety of natural disasters. A number of these libraries have emerged better connected to their communities and stronger than before.

More than seven years after Hurricane Katrina devastated the Southeastern United States in 2005, the New Orleans Regional Library reopened five buildings after operating out of trailers for years.

In New York City, Brooklyn Public Library's Coney Island Library and Queens Library (QL) at Peninsula were flooded in 2012 when Superstorm Sandy battered the East Coast. The Peninsula and Coney Island libraries each used the rebuilding efforts to find opportunities to improve the facilities' ability to act as a gathering place and technology hub.

To the south, a tornado tore through Birmingham, AL, in April 2011, peeling the roof off the Birmingham Public Library's (BPL) Pratt City Branch. The library reopened this past February and renewed its place as a community core. It has attracted 100 new cardholders each month from February to July, says Deborah Drake Blackmon, BPL's Pratt City Branch manager. "There's been a significant transformation since the tornado. It has really increased what the library means to Pratt City and to the city of Birmingham," she says.

STANDING STRONGER Birmingham's Pratt City Branch came back from a 2011 tornado (inset) with an aerodynamic roofline built to channel winds and safeguard against future damage

Raising resistance When natural disasters occur, the Federal Emergency Management Agency (FEMA) provides funding to help government agencies restore or replace buildings. However, that money doesn't cover all costs, and it comes with requirements to improve a structure's ability to withstand future disasters. In some cases, libraries like Cedar Rapid's Downtown Branch relocate to higher ground, including adding fill to slope the site higher. "We built the library up as far as we could but still have it be walkable and wheelchair accessible," Corrigan says.

To make the Queens Library at Peninsula more storm- and flood-resilient, a knee-high wall was added, says Queens Library VP over capital and facilities management Frank Genese. The wall should allow a couple of feet of water to surround the library without breaking the windows, which smashed during the recent storm, letting in the floodwaters, he says.

Both the Peninsula Library and the Coney Island Library will use durable flooring and furnishings that can be cleaned easily after a flood.

As with many libraries in flood-prone areas, the Peninsula, Cedar Rapids, and Coney Island buildings moved expensive mechanical equipment to the roof. "We did take the opportunity to rethink this space and what we could do if we ever had a catastrophe like this again," says Brett Robinson, Brooklyn PL's executive VP of finance and administration.

At Birmingham's Pratt City branch, the $1.8 million reconstruction project included a new aerodynamic roof that channels a tornado's swirling winds, says Director Renee Blalock, who retires this September.

A RISING TIDE The new downtown branch of the Cedar Rapids Public Library (above) reopened in August 2013 in a new location after the record-breaking 2008 flood that swamped the city's downtown (inset).

A sophisticated drainage system on the roof, which feeds runoff into a sculpture on the side of the building, will prevent sagging under the weight of torrential rains. Tornado-resistant glass fills the windows. The staff room and the women's restroom can serve as a tornado shelter for up to 30 people. "The storm shelter is just in case. Our hope is that we would always close early," Blalock says. The library did exactly that during the 2011 tornado, closing five hours before it struck.

Making room for community During reconstruction after a natural disaster, library leaders tend to focus on relocating irreplaceable items to safer locations and/or expanding the library's function as a community gathering space, says Beth Joy Patin, a doctoral candidate at University of Washington's (UW) Information School (iSchool) who studies the role of librarians and libraries during disasters. "We're seeing more collaborative spaces, seeing more technology hubs, more computers and places where people can bring their own (computers)," Patin says. That makes sense, given that these evolving roles for the public library may have been less of a priority when legacy spaces were originally designed. In addition, disasters that don't directly impact the library building may bring community members out in force to use library resources in their own recovery.

Expanding public space when restoring a building may mean giving up something. To add more computers in the Coney Island branch, where a third of residents lack high-speed access at home, the space for the collection dropped by 20 percent, says George Joseph, Brooklyn PL deputy head of capital planning. "We also changed to a much more open layout and offer more public meeting space than there had been previously," Joseph says.

Other libraries automated some circulation functions and reduced staff work areas to gain room for meeting rooms, technology centers, and teen zones or just to gather. Some libraries tore down walls or reduced the circulation footprint.

Coney Island Library and Peninsula Library were not the only structures to need rebuilding after Sandy. Of the six Brooklyn branch-es damaged by Sandy, the Coney Island Library was among the worst hit, inundated with five feet of water. Peninsula was the only one of the four Queens Libraries to undergo transformation, rather than being restored to its prestorm state. (The others had been recently upgraded before Sandy hit.)

For Peninsula, which is scheduled to open in early 2015, library leaders decided the estimated $2.4 million renovation should include adding an automated book return and materials sorter, as well as moving two walls to add a classroom dedicated to adult learning. Teens at Peninsula will discover a big-screen television, a green screen, and equipment for computer gaming all in a spacious 1,000 square foot area devoted to them. An open layout combined with a bright palette of blues, oranges, and yellows, along with wood, will provide patrons seeking escape from cramped apartments the space to sprawl, says Andrew Gale of IDG Architects, the firm that redesigned Peninsula. "We want it to be a neighborhood beacon," QL's Genese says.

In Cedar Rapids Downtown Branch, natural light immerses the building, offering welcoming, formal, and impromptu meeting spots. "We have a lot of places in the library where you can go and have your space, a book club, or a little nook to hang out in and read, places that Bob [Pasicznyuk, former director] says that they can celebrate life in," Corrigan says.

Celebrating their roots Both Brooklyn's Coney Island Library and Birmingham's Pratt City Branch tapped into the history of their respective communities for the rebuilds.

When the Pratt City Branch reopened in February, patrons discovered many of their suggestions had been implemented, including additional meeting rooms with presentation equipment, a business center, and increased wireless and technology capacity, as well as expanded space for children and teens, Blackmon says. The community's coal mining history is showcased throughout the branch in cabinets and walls and even underfoot. A terrazzo floor marks major landmarks on the city's walking tour and provides spontaneous local history and geography lessons. "The children think it's like hopscotch when they see these numbers and different shapes," Blackmon says. "We have to explain [that] these are where these places are in Pratt City, and this is where you are."

As part of the post-Sandy restoration effort, architects and library staff working on the $2.7 million Coney Island Library reconstruction salvaged pieces of the hurricane-destroyed historic boardwalk, Steeplechase Pier, and incorporated the wooden planks into the building's ceiling, says Salvatore Coco, a partner at Beatty Harvey Coco Architects, which did the renovation. Architects also delved into Brooklyn PL's archives to find historic images of the boardwalk and its attractions, including the iconic parachute jump. These images became a wraparound mural-sized collage covering the interior walls. Walking into the library resembles a stroll into the boardwalk's history. "What we were looking for was more of a retail aesthetic for the library, to make it more appealing to stop in and browse, to make it a place that you really felt invited to come into, to know it was a public space and to know it was open to everyone in the community," Coco says.

Landing on the fast track
As with the Queens Library at Peninsula, which needed upgrading before Sandy hit, a natural disaster can also accelerate priorities already in place. Such is the case at California State University–Fullerton's Paulina June & George Pollak Library, where a magnitude 5.1 quake this past March destroyed the ceiling on four floors in the library's south tower. Repairs are estimated at around $7 million, and the university has applied for both state and federal disaster aid, as well as exploring other funding options such as a revenue bond, says Fullerton's provost and vice president for academic affairs José L. Cruz.

The damage accelerated the university's efforts in the Cal State systemwide initiative called the Libraries of the Future, Cruz says. As part of the initiative, librarians must consider the use of tangible and electronic collections in future and determine where to house collections both physically and virtually before repairs are planned. A consultant specializing in library safety will help evaluate the situation. Any decisions must be coordinated with the libraries as the five other Cal State campuses in

STORMY WEATHER Furnishings, books, DVDs, CDs, and equipment at the Queens Library at Peninsula in Rockaway, NY, drowned in the 2012 deluge that was Superstorm Sandy. The architect's rendering (inset) of the future restored adult reading area features more computers and places for patrons to gather

corporating those improvements into the new building went smoothly, Corrigan says. For their efforts, members of CRPL's management team were named *LJ*'s Librarian of the Year in 2009.

Pasicznyuk also wanted the bulk of the meeting spaces on the second floor, forcing visitors to walk through the library to attend events in the auditorium or on the roof, hopefully enticing them to return, says Bradd Brown, a principal at OPN Architects. In the first ten months since the building opened, the green roof hosted 19 events and eight weddings. As well, the library staff have kept a keen eye on how people use the space and made suggestions, such as moving furnishings and adding electrical outlets, Corrigan says. "Flexibility in our space was very important. As the world changes, we really wanted to," Corrigan says.

BUILDING IN HISTORY Mural-sized historic photos of iconic boardwalk amusements and salvaged wooden decking (left) tie Brooklyn PL's Coney Island Library to its famous beachfront attractions, a mere two blocks away. The texture of the vinyl floor reflects the grain in the ceiling

the Los Angeles basin because the six institutions share their collections, as well as with the Fullerton Faculty Senate. Meanwhile, the library has moved programs and services to its northern tower, and upon request staff fetch items from the damaged sections, which are barred to the public. "The main problem we have right now is safety," Cruz says.

Temporary testing
Leadership at CRPL decided the flooding provided an opportunity to transform library service. First, the board hired Bob Pasicznyuk as director, who envisioned the library having a flexible design that can respond quickly to patron needs. (He has since accepted the directorship at Douglas County Libraries, CO.)

To put his vision into place, Pasicznyuk and the CRPL staff used the temporary library as a testing ground for his ideas, says Mindy Sorg, lead interior designer at OPN Architects, the firm that designed the new downtown branch. There, staff perfected the radio-frequency identification (RFID) tags and automated check-in and replaced the large circulation desk with smaller self-check kiosks. Pasicznyuk wanted library staff on the floor working side by side with the public. Once tested, in-

Lessons to share
The leaders of Queens, Brooklyn, Birmingham, and Cedar Rapids libraries say partnerships with other government agencies, libraries, area businesses, and the community proved invaluable in rebuilding and offering service to patrons during and following the disaster. Municipal and state governments helped with paperwork and with preparing for the disaster before it occurred. Public-private partnerships resulted in grants and donations.

When CRPL's Downtown Branch flooded, its Iowa sister library systems in Hiawatha and Marion offered service to patrons until a temporary library opened. OPN Architects was already under contract to upgrade the flooded branch, and interior designer Sorg worked the phones asking vendors to donate flooring and furnishings for the temporary facility.

Libraries can apply for federal grants to create disaster response plans because FEMA in 2011 designated libraries as critical infrastructure, says UW iSchool's Patin. This sort of preparation can makes a difference in how quickly libraries respond. After Katrina, librarians in Texas brought laptops to the Houston Astrodome to help people who lost their homes with FEMA paperwork and contacting loved ones, Patin says.

In New York City, libraries coordinate with the New York City Office of Emergency Management. Following Sandy, the Queens Library rolled into action, sending book buses to take the place of the closed facilities. They provided printouts of information on emergency services, FEMA, and the upcoming election. "We're the first there, and people were so excited to see the library there," says QL's Genese.

"Be ready to mobilize if you're a library," Genese says. "People will be looking to you for help, and if you're not prepared to do that, it's going to be a problem."

Marta Murvosh, MLS, works as a library associate for a regional library system in northwestern Washington. You can follow her at www.facebook.com/MartaMurvosh

9
the next generation

NEW LANDMARK LIBRARIES

Look no further than *LJ*'s New Landmark Libraries for living examples of excellent library design at work in settings large and small. We'll always be drawn to the such iconic libraries as Boston Public Library and, more recently, Seattle Public Library, but there is a whole roster of new icons being built as we take library service and design into the future. Named in two rounds, public library and then academic library, the New Landmarks project identified recent efforts to tap for design that will resonate long into the future. In total, 15 buildings were designated as New Landmarks, and another 12 were noted as Honorable Mentions. Add to these a new round focused again on public libraries that will be published in September of 2015 in *Library Journal*. Together, the New Landmark Libraries point to a vibrant design future for projects of all sizes.

The New Icons

As prototypes or think tanks, these 20 exciting libraries will inspire the next generation of library buildings By Louise Schaper

Across the country, new library buildings illustrate how to serve patrons best in spaces that anchor communities, inspire learning, and model what public buildings can be. But where should a librarian look when setting out to build or redesign space for a community—a rare and often singular opportunity in a librarian's career?

At *LJ*, after years of tracking new library buildings and renovations and exploring innovations in design, it became apparent that there was no master list of the best libraries to tap, in person or virtually, for inspiration and insight into coming trends. There were, of course, the big-news libraries that anyone diving into library design will discover right away—New York's historic main, reinventions in Seattle and Minneapolis by Rem Koolhaas and Cesar Pelli, respectively, as well as smaller highly touted projects such as Darien Library, CT, and so many more. *LJ* wanted to get beyond those to the relatively unknown gems, large and small, that raise the bar, responding to trends in green design and shifts in service models. To do so, *LJ* decided to select the New Landmark Libraries that will shape the next generation of library buildings.

Treat them as prototypes or use them as think tanks for your next library construction or renovation project—these ten New Landmark Libraries, and ten Honorable Mentions, deliver what you need to know to plan your library of the future.

That puts 20 libraries—spread across the country—on an itinerary for a virtual or real trek that will fill any notebook with great ideas to adapt.

What's in a New Landmark The eye-popping concepts in these New Landmark Libraries—like newsrooms, living rooms, kitchens, built-in branding, mica-encrusted siding, and re-dos of mid- to late 20th-century architecture—prove there is a new generation of smart, sustainable, and stunning buildings out there. Designed with the latest service concepts in mind, they put a whole new spin on the relationship between form and function.

A panel of 16 judges, most librarians, a few architects, were brought together to develop criteria and select the first group of ten New Landmark Libraries, focusing on public libraries opened in the last six years.

One judge astutely questioned whether a building could be a landmark without first standing the test of time. Yes, to be a New Landmark Library, it can.

That's because we define a new landmark as a professional exemplar for someone setting out on a new building project—a library to mine that isn't as well known as the biggies. There's plenty to learn from those, of course, but the New Landmark Libraries project is a quest to find and highlight less-well-known library buildings that offer exciting and sometimes paradigm-breaking design in response to community needs and changing times.

To find them, the judges developed six criteria (see sidebar) ranging from quality design and construction to sustainability but also encompassing innovation, functionality, beauty and delight, and response to community context and constraints.

The future of library buildings Library buildings, which some have predicted would have already gone the way of coliseums, show every sign that they are even more essential. Our winning libraries are regarded as community living rooms for self-learning, experiencing culture, connecting, communicating, and tapping into information and entertainment. And, it seems, no matter the struggles to design and pay for them, after they are built they garner widespread community support, see rapid growth in use, and often transform the neighborhood or community.

Perhaps a counterpoint to the increasingly virtual experience of life, these library centers offer what we all yearn for most—to share a common yet uplifting space in pursuit of core needs.

Libraries are the new economic engines. Where many an enlightened community leader understands that placement of a library spurs economic development, revitalizes decaying areas of town, and stimulates neighborhood growth, very few understand that the design of the library itself has the potential to lift the spirits of the people. That is what makes the difference between good and iconic libraries.

Trends snapshot The first half of the past decade saw the emergence of many now common library building ideas, such as flexibility, self-service, automated materials handling, wireless, cafés, and sustainability. The second half solidified those innovations and brought forward some new ones. The New Landmark Libraries demonstrate a refinement in the trends of the past decade and showcase newly emergent ideas.

Get greener While over half of our New Landmark Libraries are Leadership in Energy & Environmental Design (LEED) certified or awaiting certification, all of them bring a plethora of green building strategies.

Sustainably is how libraries are built now. That's because building green saves a lot of operating money and provides a far more comfortable and healthy space in which to work and visit. Imagine a new building without the unhealthy effects of outgassing. Green buildings mean more money for direct services, because, with the right siting, building envelope, roof material, and windows, along with efficient lighting, plumbing, and HVAC equipment, energy and water costs can be reduced by a minimum of 25 percent a year—if not twice that.

Flex for an unfolding future Flexibility, or the relative ease of future changes in how libraries deliver services, is another key trend. While it began to emerge in the 1990s, it is fully embraced by our New Landmark Libraries. Key components are an open floor plan, expansive sight lines, lower shelving and freestanding and adjustable service desks, and, instead of walls, demarcation of zones via shelving units and strategic placement of furniture. Open floor plans are easier to control and, for the Poplar Creek Public Library, IL, that means less vandalism.

Use fewer and smaller service points The single point of service represents the greatest shift in service delivery of all the new ideas. Partly reflecting tough economic times that have taken a toll on staffing, a single point of service usually means a combined reference, children's, teen, and circulation desk that oversees a single-story library, usually under 50,000 square feet. It's often located in the middle of the action, with all services in view of the desk. As the first in the Phoenix Public Library to adopt a single service point, Agave Library found that an elliptical shape with two access points works best because it eliminates the "back of desk" security issues and maximizes egress. Plus, its location in the library is so visible it needs no signage.

Win with self-service While this trend has been growing throughout the past decade, self-checkout is standard in our New Landmark Libraries. Technologies like RFID and automated materials handling systems along with self-checkout can eliminate the need for additional employees even with vastly increased space, as at the Durango Public Library, CO. At Poplar Creek Public Library, self-service and a slew of automation technologies allowed its circulation staff to get out on the floor to greet people and help them get what they need. Anythink Wright Farms, CO, delights in its decision to put self-check kiosks at the logical place, near the exit, rather than the trendier scatter approach. The result is a whopping 95 percent self-check rate.

Think collaboration Libraries increasingly acknowledge the collaborative nature of users through the design of group study rooms, but some put together spaces designed especially for collaboration, such as the "newsrooms" at Appaloosa Branch Library, AZ, "Anythink" rooms at Anythink Wright Farms, and collaborative workstations and booths at Hamilton Mill Branch Library, GA.

Borrow from museums Enough about being like a bookstore. We

2011 Winners

1 Poplar Creek Public Library
Streamwood, Illinois

2 Palo Verde Library/Maryvale Community Center Phoenix Public Library, Arizona

3 Cesar Chavez Branch Library*
Phoenix Public Library, Laveen, Arizona

4 Hamilton Mill Branch Library* Gwinnett County Library System, Dacula, Georgia

5 Durango Public Library*
Colorado

6 Sammamish Library King County Library System, Sammamish, Washington

7 Appaloosa Branch Library
Scottsdale Public Library, Arizona

8 Agave Library Phoenix Public Library, Glendale, Arizona

9 Roseville Library Ramsey County Public Library, Roseville, Minnesota

10 Anythink Wright Farms Rangeview Library District, Thornton, Colorado

*A three-way tie was broken by scores on Overall Design and Construction Excellence

Honorable Mentions

Anacostia Library District of Columbia Public Library, Washington, DC.

Eastern Avenue Branch Library Davenport Public Library, Iowa

Kilton Public Library West Lebanon, New Hampshire

Library! at Cole & Ustick Boise, Idaho

Maple Grove Library Hennepin County Library, Maple Grove, Minnesota

Mission Bay Branch Library San Francisco Public Library, California

Plainsboro Public Library New Jersey

Richmond/Senator Milton Marks Branch Library San Francisco Public Library, California

Westhampton Free Library Westhampton Beach, New York

White Tank Branch Library and Nature Center Maricopa County Library District, Waddell, Arizona

can see what's happening to them. Let's borrow the best ideas from wherever they exist. Really good museums offer a mix of awe, time-resilience, sacredness, and marketing know-how that is ripe for mining. Roseville Library's (MN) interactive wall within the children's section and terrazzo maze as the children enter evoke those special kid places in museums. The globe lighting at Poplar Creek Public Library, along with its iconic furniture and "far out" experience, also is a nod to museum-quality spaces.

Be more retail-like Thinking "retail" has begun permeating library design. Sadly, it often doesn't go beyond poor imitations of bookstore display tables or mall façades. With so much to learn about how to market materials and serve customer needs, we'll likely see more from this trend. Our New Landmark Libraries demonstrate a profusion of refreshingly simple design and service ideas that draw inspiration from retailing principles. They make the inside transparent to the outside, link the library to the rest of the community with pathways and more, cut jargon, and foster browsability—and that's just for starters. It will be innovation, not replication, that will generate an entirely authentic and uniquely "library" experience.

Apply a minimalist ethic If there is anything that is a given in design it's change. A decidedly fresh, geometric, and minimalist aesthetic has emerged in many of our New Landmark Libraries. Warm-toned walls and Craftsman style of the late 1990s and early 2000s look decidedly dated against these new, more transparent libraries. Natural materials like stone and wood continue to be popular, but they are given a cleaner approach. Some of our winners, like Agave Library, use self-finishing materials and polished concrete floors, while others like Roseville Library and Poplar Creek Public Library rely on white to form a stark background punctuated by master-planned pops of color to denote portals and differentiate spaces. Anacostia Library in Washington, DC, an Honorable Mention, presents a fresh approach to the same site on which the old library stood. With a big green roof canopy uniting a series of "pavilions," Anacostia is a modern, bright, and glassy surprise in a neighborhood where very little development has occurred in recent years. Sammamish Library, WA, another glass-walled pavilion with a smart minimalist ethic, relies on nature and an

inherent sense of whimsy to infuse warmth and awe. And while some new buildings evoke the past, the best avoid imitating it.

Save the neighborhood We have shopping centers, town centers, and civic centers, so why not "library centers"? Differing from libraries of the past, several New Landmark Libraries offer unique services that meet local needs and expand the library's reach. Such initiatives can truly transform neighborhoods. A library is an economic development tool, so wherever you put a library you have constant activity during open hours. Nearby shops get more foot traffic. A marginalized area becomes hopeful, safer, and more desirable. Whether you call it "smart growth," "new urbanism," or "healthy communities," libraries are tools for community revitalization and sustainability.

The Criteria
The New Landmark Libraries criteria, developed jointly by the judges and *LJ* editors, cover everything from quality to sustainability to innovation. Applicants shared how their building project measured up to each of the following and submitted supporting photographs. When planning a building project, consider using these criteria as a checklist.

1 Overall design and construction excellence New Landmark Libraries demonstrate overall design and construction excellence with consideration of the (1) appropriateness and quality of materials; (2) connection between interior and exterior spaces; (3) durability of building finishes and furnishings; (4) appropriateness of materials used given local circumstances; and (5) response by the community including recognition, additional funding, and/or symbolic significance.

2 Response to community context and constraints New Landmark Libraries respond to their community context and constraints with consideration to (1) how public and staff input shaped the design; (2) any neighborhood improvements such as pedestrian access; (3) any incorporation of multifunctional uses; (4) any creative solutions to local constraints; and (5) an appropriate physical setting.

3 Sustainability New Landmark Libraries must be sustainable, particularly with regard to (1) site selection and development; (2) water efficiency; (3) energy use; (4) materials and resources used; (5) indoor environmental quality; and (6) ongoing education, outreach, and operations.

4 Functionality New Landmark Libraries maximize functionality in the delivery of library services. What design elements improve service delivery, experience, and accessibility for the public and staff?

5 Innovation New Landmark Libraries respond to current and anticipated demographic, cultural, and technological changes in innovative ways. Does the building test and prove the viability of new knowledge and assumptions?

6 Beauty and Delight New Landmark Libraries give the visitor an initial impression of beauty and delight. Judges looked for evidence of a "wow" factor that delights visitors—and any local, state, or national recognition—and considered how it relates to the design, if it is long-lasting, and why.

---

1 ## Poplar Creek Public Library | Streamwood, Illinois
Architect: Frye Gillan Molinaro

From Eyesore to Eye-Catcher

Poplar Creek, one in an emerging club of "pop" libraries, packs punch by merging 1960s style with present-day prognostication. Bold thinking, driven by a desire for sustainability and reinforced by community input, led to the project's success.

It all started with a challenge: how to renovate and expand a 44,000 square foot brutalist style building into a modern-day cultural center for residents to adopt as their own.

Regarded as a district library, the underused 1966 formed-concrete structure is located in a residential neighborhood but was uninviting and austere. Library leadership wanted to give it a new image as a vibrant, flexible, and functional gathering place that would have a fresh green ethic and a focus on technology. The design team was faced with how to expand without creating an imposing structure that fit even less well in the neighborhood.

Several rounds of public meetings and lots of staff comments unearthed other issues, like the need for more meeting and study rooms, concerns about pedestrian safety when crossing the street to a remote parking lot, and discomfort from noise pollution created by mechanical equipment.

Reinvention by intervention The new Poplar Creek is a perfect solution, as well as a genuine response to residents' needs. According to one of the judges, it represents a "superb intervention with spectacular spaces." Another commented, "This is one I would travel out of my way to see. [It is a] great example of how to work with an existing building." Another said it was "an impressive reworking of a brutalist nightmare."

The community agrees, now embracing it as a valuable part of their lives.

That elevated status followed a series of decisions. First, linking the site to city hall and the police department with a new bicycle and pedestrian path resulted in a 400 percent increase in bike and pedestrian access. Second, a glass beacon tower at the west entrance signals that there are important services inside. Third, the "kick-ass" design entices users of all ages to spend time in the unique environment. And, perhaps, most significant, community involvement resuscitated library support and built ownership early on.

To avoid overwhelming the adjacent homes, the addition matches the original's height wherever possible. This was done by burrowing 40 percent of the new structure into the earth to minimize the size impact and to fit with the existing building, which was partially recessed.

Nonetheless, this library packs a wallop. The new façade includes expanses of glass that communicate transparency. Large splashes of color, recycled rubber flooring, unexpected forms, and surprising use of technology all go into the huge wow factor present here.

More, including style, for less Poplar Creek more than doubled in size yet pays $17,000 less in annual utility costs—compare that to the estimated $70,000 more it would have faced had it been built conventionally. The plethora of green technologies includes a gigantic planted green roof that serves as extra insulation, LED light fixtures, occupancy sensors, a lighting control system, dual-flush toilets, sun "scoops" to capture heat in the winter and release it in the summer, and high-efficiency boilers, water heaters, and chillers.

Smart planning led to even more savings and benefits. The open floor plan and focus on self-service meant no additional staff were needed and allowed the library to reduce the security detail by one guard. Installing a traffic light at that problematic intersection took full advantage of the remote parking lot, dropping the number of new spaces needed. Increased efficiencies in the workroom enabled circulation staff to serve as floating customer service specialists and greeters at entrances.

These choices complement similarly strong and stylish architecture signatures. The main area, the Amoeba, is a curved platform floating in the middle of the floor plan that allows for views and connectivity to the lower level. A 100' LED panel lightwall sets the mood for the space. Easily programmable, it has a daily opening and closing "ceremony," much like human-brokered ones in Japanese stores, that serves to greet patrons at opening and alert them to the approaching closing time.

The Green Zone, the most courageous spot in the library, is a tech area that links the adults and children's spaces, and, given its bright green color, it has caused quite a stir. Children, of course, love it!

Together, these bold moves mean the Poplar Creek renovation and expansion raises the bar on library design.

Vitals

OPENED 2009

Major expansion

Main Library

SIZE 96,846 square feet

COST $23.7 million

POP SERVED 66,639

---

2 | Palo Verde Library/Maryvale Community Center | Phoenix Public Library

Arizona | Architect: Gould Evans Associates + Wendell Burnette Architects

Reinvigorating a Community

Look no further if you've ever wondered just how much a shared-use project can bring to an inner-city neighborhood. To get the answer in Palo Verde, they took a somewhat disheveled park with a big pool, added an interconnected community center and a library, then mixed in pedestrian walkways that link up to public transit and are cooled by native shade trees. Now a beloved but dilapidated park that was a liability is an asset, and the community is invigorated and involved. In short, Palo Verde Library/Maryvale Community Center is a living demonstration of how cross-pollination creates stronger services and neighborhoods.

This shared-use facility brings the Parks Department and the library together on the same campus to emphasize the connection between the mind and the body. In the process, it has created a safe place in which to learn, grow, and play. It's a great example of "whole community" or "rejuvenation" design—where strategic public investment improves the quality of life, and the inherent value, of a part of town.

Perhaps the best news is that now there is a mixing and sharing of visitors across the services, new types of cardholders for each, and a built-in teen volunteer force that increased over 600 percent in the first year. Already some homes on the park perimeter have been improved.

Open design breeds engagement Early input from residents and staff has had a lasting effect. Many residents feel a sense of ownership to keep the building safe and vandal free. Cooperation between Parks and the library resulted in extra program spaces such as a shared auditorium that seats 250, a private staff lounge, a weight room, a walking track, a health advice office, and senior and teen lounges that were not in the original budget. Plus, acoustical treatment for the gym means it can be used as a secondary multifunctional space for either organization.

Large expanses of glass make the activities in each space visible to the other across a central shaded promenade. What better way to "connect the dots" between these mind-body services. Plus, the transparency helps prevent inappropriate behavior and makes everyone feel safer.

"Streets" inside the shared complex, as well as those to the pool and into the park and beyond, serve as pedestrian links to park amenities, parking, public transit, and the surrounding neighborhoods.

Vitals

OPENED 2006

New construction

Branch Library and Community Center

SIZE library:
16,000 square feet
community center:
27,000 square feet

COST $10 million

POP SERVED 148,719

In the library, flexibility, the byword of today's modern library, was achieved through column-free spaces and a type of raised flooring called low-profile access floors that accommodate easy changes. The open plan allows for staffing at two prominent service points to survey the action across the space.

Standard sizes, uniquely used The tight budget of $137 per square foot was met through the use of standard-size, maintenance-free materials. Plus, the owners wanted materials that could stand up to the vandalism and abuse that comes with a high-use facility.

Green principles led design choices but without pursuing LEED. The successful effort to reduce required parking by more than half saved money and was green, indeed, but it took a citywide parking study of like settings to get a variance. Xeriscaping and native plants help to reduce the urban heat island effect. High-efficiency water-cooled heat pumps offer a five-year payback. In staff areas, recycled rubber tile flooring, ubiquitous in New Landmark Libraries, is low maintenance and sustainable. Daylighting strategies include a series of spectacular daylight tubes that punctuate the high ceiling and flow light into the big box–like central space.

By ditching the cellblock look of the past to create an architectural presence so transparent and unified in design, Phoenix has successfully woven the mind-body spirit of this inventive collaboration into the fabric of the neighborhood community. Need more proof? The community center has the highest foot traffic in the Phoenix Parks Recreation System, and the library has the second highest for Phoenix Public Library branches. Stealing words from one judge, the project is an "an absolute marvel" and a must-see for any community even casually considering a multiuse facility.

3 Cesar Chavez Branch Library | Phoenix Public Library | Laveen, Arizona
Architect: Line and Space, LLC

A Living Room on the Lake

Cesar Chavez Branch Library, one of Phoenix Public Library's gems, is designed to provide a living room to a community without a civic center. Its site, on the urban edge of a popular 40-acre park and perched on the bank of a humanmade lake, is both accessible and attractive to surrounding neighborhoods. Its decidedly green design honors the desert environment with innovative solutions to living in an arid landscape.

Twice the size of the system's other branches, it aims to meet the needs of a rapidly growing community with many young families. How? The library offers 24,000 items and interactive displays for children five and younger. Teens call their area "R3" for read, relax, and rejuvenate.

An open design plan, another New Landmark Libraries signature, gives this library long-term flexibility—an advantage when facing changing needs and service models. But unique space is not compromised. The teen niche offers computers, MP3 listening stations, and a plasma TV for DVD viewing in a semi-enclosed environment. The children's area is defined by indoor and outdoor reading spaces, a sculptural security fence made from recycled materials that turns into a mobile, a ceiling-suspended kite sculpture, and a brightly colored sculptural wall and ceiling in the story room.

Vitals
OPENED 2007
New construction
Branch Library
SIZE 25,234 square feet
COST $5 million
LEED-NC Silver certification
POP SERVED 62,866

Staffers get a nod in this smart design, too. They can enjoy their own open-air patio and plenty of natural light in their work spaces. Some of the heavy lifting is done by strategically placed walk-up and drive-up book drops that empty directly into the circulation workroom where sorting occurs.

Respect for the Sonoran sun The library uses an innovative but commonsense approach to sustainability. The building was given proper solar orientation to minimize energy and maximize daylighting. Then by partially building into preexisting earth mounds, the library is better insulated. Another strategy that is common to green buildings is the use of insulated low-E glazing that helps reduce heat gain through window glass.

With large cantilevered overhangs that create shade and shield the interior from the sun, this modern desert library is clad in low-maintenance concrete masonry, steel, and aluminum, much of it locally sourced and some of it left exposed to highlight its natural beauty.

The "green" rooftop does overtime. Made of a highly reflective insulated foam system that is coated with a UV treatment to protect it from degradation, it decreases the building's heat-island effect while also functioning as a vast water catchment surface. Funneling rainwater into the lake for later use for park irrigation turns the lake, which the submitters call a "contradiction in the desert," into an asset as a massive storage tank.

Water is also salvaged by harvesting condensation from mechanical units and distributing it to landscaping via an underground perforated pipe.

Creature comforts that pack "wow!" In another innovation, customers using the library's reading patio can tune their own outdoor microclimates to feel up to 20 degrees cooler. That's achieved by pushing interior exhaust air, typically vented through a roof, through adjustable spot diffusers in the outdoor patio. This reuse of air conditioning makes the patio habitable even in the warmest months.

The Cesar Chavez Branch gets a strong "wow" response. Sitting on the edge of a park next to a busy street, it offers passersby exposure to what a modern library and responsibly designed desert building are all about. This branch, said one judge, has an "incredible connection between building and landscape." It is downright earthy yet exceedingly up-to-the-minute and, well, futuristic.

4 Hamilton Mill Branch Library | Gwinnett County Library System
Dacula, Georgia | Architect: Precision Planning, Inc.

Blessed by Location, Elevated by Art

Skateboarders, often the scourge of library staff for their sidewalk capers, are encouraged to visit the Hamilton Mill Branch of Georgia's Gwinnett County Public Library by the sheer nature of its location.

Set in a five-acre corner of an 88-acre park with a skate complex and numerous sports venues, this library is a lure. It offers both skateboarders and drivers of hybrid and high-efficiency vehicles priority parking but also facilitates access by pedestrians with walking paths connecting all the park amenities.

What one percent can do That clarity of vision extends to the building, which Executive Director Nancy Stanbery-Kellam envisioned as an artistic space that honors the boundless pursuit of knowledge. The design is driven by a desire to create a nature-language experience.

The "integration of arts in the building is notable," said one New Landmark Libraries judge. That's the result of a brainstorming session between Stanbery-Kellam and the county's facilities director. Inspired by the federal General Services Administration (GSA) "Art in Architecture" program, they required architects, as part of the RFP process, to set aside and incorporate one percent of the construction costs for art.

A single artist, Maria Artemis, created the remarkable exterior Rain Stone sculpture and the 67 inspiring art glass panels that feature paintings and literature, located throughout the library. Those pieces and other materials loudly call out water, earth, and sun themes, as do the green building choices deployed.

Eamon Shelton, capital projects manager and LEED AP, expects water consumption to be reduced by 80 percent off baseline because plants and trees were chosen wisely—there is no grass—and water-efficient drip irrigation does the job where needed. The building is clad in what looks like traditional brick but is actually made entirely of materials that would otherwise end up in the waste stream (via www.greenleafbrick.com). Flooring from recycled rubber tires anchors staff areas and the story time nook, while rapidly renewable bamboo highlights a number of locations and surfaces—like the periodicals flooring, screen panels in the storytelling tower, and veneer at the help desk. Sunlight is harnessed through judicious window placement, and light sensors control human-made lighting in accordance with the amount of available natural light. Careful building alignment along with diffusion panels eliminates direct sunlight spots.

A tight budget and cramped site—common constraints—led to creative solutions. Solar photovoltaic panels weren't in the budget, but library leaders had the fortitude to install the electrical system and roof

structure to support them later. And while fitting the building program into a tight corner space might have meant giving up a loading dock and recycling center, this innovative design put those facilities at the front of the building but set back and masked by a beautiful gate made of recycled plastics.

From good to better An open floor plan with a single staff desk along with properly oriented 60" shelving keep sight lines open and ensure everyone has expansive views of the park beyond the glassed north wall. Several booths and workstations with large monitors and lightweight configurable seats and tables are designed to enhance group work. A mix of movable and stationary seating can be easily reconfigured. The help desk sign is visible from virtually all angles, while the children's area sign is visible from the entry.

Noise, a problem at other branches, was brought under control by ceiling-hung sound baffles, acoustic materials, lined ductwork, and fabric treatments on furniture and walls, as well as a quiet HVAC system.

This LEED-NC Gold-certified building is expected to reduce energy use by 25 percent. A chunk of that savings is the result of using Energy Star–rated computers that drop computer-related energy use by 45 percent annually. Sustainability is incorporated into daily operations through recycling in all public and staff areas, green pest management, and green cleaning services and guidelines for cleaning staff to follow.

The words "*Bonus intra. Melior exi. Come in good. Go out better.*"—inscribed at the entry—speak to the library as a gateway to a better future and aptly tag this library's innovative design as a model for others.

Vitals

OPENED 2010

New construction

Branch Library

SIZE 20,805 square feet

COST $4.62 million

LEED-NC Gold certification

POP SERVED 44,594

---

5 Durango Public Library | Colorado

Architect: Barker Rinker Seacat

Setting a New Gold Standard

Durango, CO, has garnered many "best" awards for retirement, skiing, and education. Now it's the library's turn to make this scenic resort and college town shine. And it does, inside and out—embracing the town from its site on the edge of the Animas River and offering those inside, according to the submission, "the most magnificent views available...through its many windows." Users can gaze at mountain peaks, watch the train run past the library along the Silverton Narrow Gauge Railroad, or ponder nearby historic church steeples.

At three times the size of the previous library building and with land to expand, the new Durango Public Library is a proactive response to the city's projected growth. Not surprising for a town in such a locale,

this community of 16,000 holds preserving the environment near and dear, a value reiterated throughout the building's design and construction.

A passion for place During initial planning, achieving LEED Gold certification didn't seem feasible. When community members insisted, however, the city and library wholeheartedly plunged into creating Colorado's first LEED Gold library. Projected over its first 20 years to use 40 percent less energy than conventional buildings, Durango Public Library has set the standard for the city's municipal buildings and gained the attention of the Governor's Energy Council.

While the site, on the grounds of a relocated hospital, brought significant challenges, it was, with its scenic setting and proximity to public transportation and extensive pedestrian and bicycle trails, a perfect place for a library. But to make it work, architects needed to fit a 42,000 square foot building onto a narrow parcel without distracting from the views, or impacting the river, causing environmental harm.

To protect the Animas River, the landscape plan incorporates a retention pond, water catchment in parking lots, low-water-use plants, and green space—all to filter runoff and reduce water consumption.

Another challenge was to ensure that no particles from the attractive but dirty steam locomotive that runs alongside the library end up degrading the library's air quality. The solution: special filters to keep them outside.

Visitors can't help but notice the aluminum sunshades jutting out from the windows. These are ubiquitous in green buildings because they are a low-cost and permanent solution to sun mitigation. In the morning, light is let in. But in the afternoon, the shades block the strong light of the hot sun. Inside, self-adjusting shades and the automatic lighting system that dims and brightens in response to the amount of daylight complete the library's approach to daylight harvesting and management.

Pursuing LEED certification has helped to advance green construction in the area. Some contractors got so enthused that they became LEED-certified builders.

"Homey" by community consensus Inside, the building was programmed to require no additional staff beyond three custodians. RFID, self-service, and an automated materials handling system reduce staff load despite increased use. Staff desks were minimized and a focus on getting out on the floor to assist users was implemented.

Flexibility was also a core principle. Like other new breed libraries, Durango is designed with a raised floor above the electricals and ventilation to facilitate future changes. One immediate benefit is that heat and cooling comes from the floor rather than blowing down on visitors from upper walls or ceilings. Most lights are attached to stacks instead of the ceiling.

While the library gives off a decidedly "homey" feel, with its two fireplaces and lots of wood, it comes equipped with numerous computers, a teen space that feels like a café, many different areas to read, Wi-Fi inside and out, and program rooms designed to flex for a variety of uses. This came right from the community's wish list: most of the ideas from focus groups and staff were put into effect—except for the bowling alley.

While Durango Public Library's architectural statement is more understated than some other New Landmark Libraries, it is a model of quality, functionality, response to community context and constraints, sustainability, and siting. Listening to residents and building a first-class, ecofocused facility pays off big.

Vitals

OPENED 2008	
New construction	
Main Library	
SIZE 42,000 square feet	
COST $12 million	
LEED-NC Gold certification	
POP SERVED 51,600	

---

6 Sammamish Library | King County Library System
Sammamish, Washington | Architect: Perkins + Will

The Heart of a New Downtown

It's rare to be able to design a downtown from the ground up. Sammamish, WA, a growing suburban community outside Seattle, did just that with its Civic Plaza. The library, a key part of the town's vision, has been built as a "bookend" to this outdoor plaza. It's right near city hall, a network of bike and pedestrian paths, a wetlands preserve, several schools and religious facilities, and venues for major happenings like the farmer's market and outdoor concerts. As a result, the library is place making, a building block of community vitality.

What makes Sammamish Library so distinctive is its strong connection to its stunning natural surroundings. Walls of glass frame mountain or wetland views, while ample daylighting strategies gather sunlight, a treasured Northwest resource.

Soaking up the sun Just walking into the warm and wood-clad entry, visitors know they are somewhere special. A distinctive slot window lets kids follow returned books on their conveyor belt journey back into the library. Cleverly designed displays for books and other materials offer welcome pause. Then the main room delivers the big "wow" with its open plan and long views beyond. It's a space soaked in daylight through a series of skylights and a surround of clerestory windows.

Sammamish helps define the new class of "flexible" libraries. Maximized spans and fewer columns ensure easy changes for the future. Sporting scaled-down and adjustable circulation and reference points, it's not, however, one of the new one-desk libraries, though reliance on RFID, self-checkout, and an automated materials handling system relieves staff workload.

Wayfinding is enabled by large brightly colored signs, as well as a color-coding system that links color, font, and material type. Polished concrete floors form pathways to the functional areas.

From the whimsical arrangement of LED lights in the children's area that resemble a constellation of stars to the views of the Olympic Peninsula to cyberbars perched along the library's full-height glass walls overlooking the plaza, delight comes from the variety of spaces that offer different materials, scale, finishes, and light source.

Here the meeting room was placed in the heart of the library rather than on the periphery near the front door. This erased the problem of a dark and uninviting entry. Also, integrated in this way, the space can be used for activities like quiet study and story times when meetings are not scheduled.

Green choices, big and small The site presented serious runoff issues, but storm water was effectively reduced by a three-pronged solution: an elaborate rain garden system rings the building and site, a green roof is planted with sedums, and permeable concrete paving allows the water to seep in rather than flow away. Another key was to locate the parking under the building, reducing the total footprint.

Other green features include a geothermal HVAC system that saves a lot of energy; radiant heating for warmth and temperature stability; durable and long-lasting materials; an exposed steel structure; and the use of reclaimed native elm, ash, and maple for countertops and rapidly renewable bamboo for stack tops and end panels. Like other recent green libraries, operable windows make for happy occupants.

These choices, big and small, ensure that Sammamish Library is a "very fine structure [and has] incredible presence," as one of the judges noted. Residents will, no doubt, reap long-term benefits like improved livability and sustainability from the city's decision to make the library the centerpiece for the town's core.

Vitals
OPENED 2010
New construction
Branch Library
SIZE 20,000 square feet
COST $8.8 million
POP SERVED 45,780

---

7 Appaloosa Branch Library | Scottsdale Public Library | Arizona
Architect: DWL Architects and Planners Inc.

A Shimmer of Green in the Desert

Rising up to take in the mountain views, the Appaloosa Branch Library embodies its "desert mirage" theme. Exterior walls are covered in iridescent mica that shifts color throughout the day and helps repel the desert heat. The dynamic structure—perched at one end in a mound, surrounded by drainage arroyos, and anchored by a seemingly suspended 275'-long wall and steel-clad segments—appears to float in its landscape.

But the Appaloosa Branch is no mirage. It delivers a very real 31 percent energy savings off conventionally built facilities and generates a huge amount of pride in staff and area residents.

The right kind of transparency The library's position within a curve in a road allows drivers to spot activity as they pass—this transparency is an important visual signature of many New Landmark Libraries.

Customers can pick up or return items through a drive-up window, park energy-efficient vehicles in special spaces, enter restrooms without touching doors, and see real-time energy use as they walk through the entry corridor. They'll find librarians walking around looking for customers to help or at information stations. If the library gets too noisy, patrons seeking silence can hole up in the quiet study room.

This library is designed around social spaces. In the "newsroom" adults can chat, read newspapers and magazines, and watch TV. A club space for teens includes its own meeting room. Interactive children's displays encourage even crawling infants to learn, hands on.

Vitals
OPENED 2009
New construction
Branch Library
SIZE 21,242 square feet
COST $6.47 million
LEED-NC Gold certification
POP SERVED 72,000

Beautiful and sustainable The new building reclaimed a dirt parking lot used by tourists visiting this cowboy town, offering instead a watering hole of sorts for locals and visitors alike.

Careful siting, 20° off the north-south alignment, maximizes the ability to deal with the sun. A small, expandable solar photovoltaic system helps lower energy costs, as does daylighting that keeps electric lights mostly off during the day. The skin of the building helps keep it cool because it is separated from the rain screen by an inch to form airspace. Heat in this space causes the air to rise through a vent so energy is carried away by convection.

Ecominded staff and customers will appreciate that 60 percent of the countertops are made of recycled paper and 94 percent of the cabinetry is recycled sorghum. They might also appreciate that the contractors were so effective at recycling construction waste that there was no garbage removal for the first six months of construction. Another environment saver is the library's parking lot surface: permeable decomposed granite pavers that minimize water runoff.

It's no wonder that Appaloosa won the Western Mountain Region AIA Honor Award and the Most Sustainable Building of 2010 honor from *Real Estate Development* magazine. Its vision of libraries and eco-conscious construction will likely inform many libraries to come.

8 Agave Library | Phoenix Public Library | Glendale, Arizona
Architect: will bruder PARTNERS

How the West Was Won

The Agave branch of Phoenix Public Library might have been called the "Leftover Library" had the designers and stakeholders failed to rise to the challenges the project confronted. First, the site was a cheap, blighted, and virtually invisible spot between a strip mall and a residential area. Then, worse still, the budget got shorted when the library system had to borrow from the shared bond monies to complete earlier projects.

The designers drew on both the area's history and typical retail construction methods for solutions. A soaring "cowboy" false front, riffing on those used in frontier towns, gives the library scale, presence, and distinction on par with its position in the community—at a very low cost. Self-finishing materials like exposed gang nail trusses decreased cost and added design power. Tucked behind the soaring façade is the same basic inexpensive masonry shell seen on the library's retail neighbors.

Less is best Several public input sessions yielded a common desire for the reading room to feel like a "public living room." Arranging the three service areas—children's, periodicals and fiction, and teens—along a wall next to a reading garden provided each with its own view and direct access to a discrete section of the garden. Unique rugs and colors that coordinate with the adjacent garden blooms give each its own identity.

That Agave Library has garnered many awards including an Honor Award, AIA Arizona 2010, might have something to do with the project's "less is best" philosophy, which translated into fewer walls, carpets, paints, and finishes. It also led to more self-finishing materials, concrete floors,

Vitals
OPENED 2009
New construction
Branch Library
SIZE 25,410 square feet
COST $6.65 million
POP SERVED 40,000

and block masonry walls because no-VOC use (volatile organic compounds) is better than low-VOC use. Native, low-water-use plants and trees planted on the 3.8-acre site save water.

It also has less in terms of service desks, as it is the first Phoenix branch to be designed with a single service point. The result is a boatlike 18' x 12' elliptical form with two access points for security. One side, facing the entry and self-check, is counter height, and the other, facing the computers and collections, is desk height. This centerpiece, partially lit by skylights and topped by the stunning large-scale sculpture overhead, is so visible that it needs no signage.

User-centric solutions throughout Clever ideas are seen everywhere. Custom self-check counters include spaces for rubber bands, paper, and slots for quick cases for media. An etched bar on the Corian counter pinpoints the sweet spot in the 3M RFID system; the RFID reader pad is mounted under the counter to keep the surface simple to understand and clutter free.

A flexible public "electronic island" that can be closed off for computer training resolves the quandary of how to put public access computers to dual use.

The teen space feels private from within, yet it is visible from the single service point. Located as far as possible from the children's area, it is also clearly visible from the street—so that teens inside can be seen by other teens outside.

Despite budget constraints, Agave staff were a high priority in the design. Every staff station has a window and view, and the staff lounge is equal in quality to the public spaces.

Visionary as the Agave Library is, Richard Jensen of will bruder PARTNERS says it wasn't designed "for a future we don't know." Nonetheless, he adds, "it is equally foolish to not design for the ease and opportunity for change to happen."

9 Roseville Library | Ramsey County Public Library | Roseville, Minnesota
Architect: Meyer, Scherer & Rockcastle Ltd.

Pop Goes the Library!

In writing about the newly expanded and renovated Roseville Library prior to its opening, Holly Wenzel, managing editor of RosevilleReview.com, cautioned that those used to the earth-toned and wood-hued former library "are in for a multi-colored, day lit shock."

The jolt hits on the main floor, an active "marketplace" of most-used services like new materials, holds, computers, media, and the café. It's a

retail-inspired space organized for easy browsing, but it's also the entrance to a veritable domain of exciting design ideas applied well.

Zoned for discovery, coded for pleasure The ideas include color-coded areas, solid surface–topped study tables for ease in removing scratches, beaucoup feet of recycled rubber floor tiles to take the constant

traffic, and frameless windows that create views while bringing in light. The white walls and bright colors signal a new trend in interior design and invite community members to view this expansion as a clean slate.

From the marketplace, customers are drawn to the three main zones of the library—teens, children, and adults—by portals and colors inspired by Minnesota springtime. For teens, it's poppy and orange. Magenta and lime green excite the children's room, as do low browsing bins. Deeper greens and tans anchor adult areas and focus on seating.

The design seeks the holy grail of flexibility, aka insurance against future changes in library use. At Roseville that means movable display fixtures on stack ends; service desks that can be easily moved or scaled to the desired size; furniture that can change in use to fit the media format of the day; technology "benching"—few legs and long work surfaces allow for easy resizing of workstations; adjustable displays on casters; and a lighting design that eliminates costly future reworking of the ceiling and lighting fixtures.

Transforming a worn-out, dark, and confusing 1980s single-story space into an open and light-filled two-story hub with a decidedly green ethic wasn't easy. A site that backs up to residential yards meant many community meetings, even during construction, to work through issues of scale and location of lighting, windows, and landscaping. One solution: tall windows capture light and allow views of the mature tree canopy but block views into the adjacent backyards with an elegant translucent film.

Vitals

OPENED 2010

Major expansion

Branch Library

SIZE 74,175 square feet

COST $12 million

PENDING LEED-NC Gold certification

POP SERVED 48,860

The greenest building already exists Green decisions ripple through the building form, furnishings, finishes, and fixtures. Some are common to green buildings and others stand out. Working with the existing library, despite its status as a community eyesore, was inherently green. That reuse extends to the "old" furniture and shelving, which are complemented by well-made and green new furnishings.

The new furniture includes children's chairs made from recycled yogurt containers and study tables made locally from local materials. Recycled glass is found in the two terrazzo floor murals—the maze

at the entrance to the children's area and in the main entry lobby.

Durability and low maintenance were also considered, with fabrics treated with nanotechnologies to resist moisture and staining and carpet tiles that sport stain-hiding patterns.

Another green decision was to build up, not out. "Adding on vertically is not always structurally possible, but this was at least one case where it was the best solution," commented one judge. Results of this decision were multiple. They include outdoor reading areas, more green space, improved storm water management, and water-saving features such as a rain-collecting cistern outfitted with a tap so that children can water the garden. Plus, it allows the building to harvest daylight efficiently through expansive clerestories.

This eco ethic inspired a zero-waste opening, dissemination of public information about the green features, including outdoor signage on groundwater management themes, and partnerships with a local energy provider to offer energy meters for checkout and with the county for public programs on sustainable issues.

There's no doubt that Roseville is, in the words of the judges, "an amazing transformation" and a "dynamic improvement to an old-fashioned civic building." The designers broke through the design template of the 21st-century's first decade—and it is popular. Visitors pour in from all across the Twin Cities, the number of cardholders is nearly triple the population served, and circulation has soared since opening, tracking at about 5,000 checkouts a day.

10 Anythink Wright Farms | Rangeview Library District

Thornton, Colorado | Architect: Humphries Poli Architects

The Cure for Any Identity Crisis

It's hard these days not to hear about Anythink, the refreshingly unorthodox take on library services created by the Rangeview Library District (RLD) located outside Denver in Adams County, CO. It is proving to be the cure for any identity crisis that this county's library might have had.

As a result of a mill levy increase in 2006, RLD has been building, expanding, or renovating branches, all branded with Anythink and integrating design choices that start with how people use the space, not how to store books.

Anythink Wright Farms (AWF), the largest of the buildings and home of RLD headquarters, is an oasis-like environment—as per public input. Situated on nine acres, it nestles between two main arterials across from an elementary school and backing up to a residential area. The sense of an oasis was supported by blurring the lines between inside and outside with features like a back-to-back/inside-outside fireplace, a children's garden, and outdoor reading nooks. A city park developed next to the library also helps, as do interior materials and finishes like maple, natural colors, and reed-and-twig-embedded resin glass accents.

Working with the elements Raised flooring satisfies RLD's thirst for flexibility along with its quest for energy efficiency and comfort. Made of removable concrete plates affixed to steel pedestals, the floor system houses electrical and IT wiring, as well as ventilation and air distribution conduits. When changes are needed, they can be performed without disrupting walls or ceilings. Plus, air is circulated from below, thereby increasing the frequency and quality of internal air exchange, driving down heating and cooling costs and raising patron comfort.

Carefully planned from an energy use perspective, this building includes a highly efficient geothermal heating and cooling system, an automated lighting system, solar tubes, and light shelves to bring light deep inside. Harvesting daylight is a cost-effective way to optimize light and reduce energy use. Also, employing space adjacencies—grouping high-traffic areas and, separately, lower-use areas—allows heating and cooling for each to be tailored accordingly.

Designing in flexibility A hallmark of New Landmark Libraries is the open floor plan. Anythink Wright Farms employs a strategic placement of shelving, color, and wayfinding elements. The front of the library, replete with concierges to greet and assist, is for new book displays, self-service holds, and the Anythink café. Next, there are zones of books and other media on shelving. The goal was to design for self-discovery

by eliminating service barriers and creating a bookstore environment. "Anythink rooms" are traditional study rooms in disguise. Self-service kiosks, at the exit, absorb 95 percent of check outs.

Anythink Wright Farms is a counterbalance to those who would question the relevancy of libraries in the Internet age. Challenging hallowed library principles, its altered service model results in buildings that feel and operate much better than a bookstore. No Dewey Decimal System for RLD; cookbooks are in the "cookbook" section. No "sssh-ing"; this is a "homey" place to gather, interact with information, or catch up with friends and neighbors.

Rangeview fulfilled its mission—"We open doors for curious minds"—by opening Anythink Wright Farms, and it has also gone beyond to showcase its award-winning philosophy for librarians around the globe.

Ten More That Will Inspire

These New Landmark Library Honorable Mentions range from 7,500 to 74,000 square feet and offer plenty of ideas for your next library project

Anacostia Library

District of Columbia Public Library
Washington, DC | 2010
Architect: The Freelon Group Architects

A vibrant, futuristic beacon among brick duplexes, the Anacostia branch replaces the old library but with a whole new attitude. An open floor plan, with few full walls, ensures flexibility and easy visual control of public space. One of a series of new DC branches, this library is green inside and out. It features solar hot water, raised floors, a rain garden, and a bioretention area to minimize runoff. Most of all, though, it brings a revitalizing, transparent, and forward-leaning vision to the neighborhood.

Eastern Avenue Branch Library

Davenport Public Library | Iowa | 2010
Architect: Engberg Anderson

Davenport's Eastern Avenue Branch, anticipating at least Silver certification, is the only LEED public library in the area— and takes that status seriously. Carefully sited to maximize sunlight, the stone

and glass building also has special parking for low-emission vehicles, connectivity to neighborhoods through new bike and walking trails and city bus service. A 140-well geothermal HVAC system keeps energy costs down. Kiosks and educational walls share the sustainability message.

Kilton Public Library

West Lebanon, New Hampshire | 2010
Architect: Tappé Associates

A candidate for LEED Gold, the Kilton Public Library is also poised to be an economic driver given its Main Street location on an abandoned used car lot and its flexible, stunning interiors that blend New England sensibility and warmth with a clean, modern ethic. The radiant floor slab is sure to please story hour patrons while a front door/ back door approach highlights the best of small-town living. This library, paid for with private donations, also sports a biomass

boiler that takes advantage of a waste product such as wood pellets to generate heat.

Library! at Cole & Ustick

Boise, Idaho | 2009
Architect: Fletcher Farr Ayotte, Inc.

Boise's Library! at Cole & Ustick is a revitalizing force in a downtrodden retail center, now named "Library Plaza." The LEED Gold building, with 50 percent of its space devoted to youth, is a testament to the power of libraries to transform lives and businesses—and not just because it uses old blue jeans as insulation. It has transformed its location into an oasis in more than once sense—including a natural one, with landscaping that turned a parking lot into a terrain with fine views from inside and out.

Maple Grove Library

Hennepin County Library
Maple Grove, Minnesota | 2010
Architect: Meyer, Scherer & Rockcastle, Ltd.

The long winter must feel a lot shorter in the dynamic and surprising spaces in this branch built for one of the fastest growing Minnesota communities—with over one million checkouts in 2009. Hennepin County's Maple Grove branch packs in a 350-space parking ramp, a green roof with plantings, a gravel pit–based geothermal heating and cooling system, the flexibility of raised flooring for shifting service needs, mobile display units and interactive panels for children, and a hip computer bar for teens. More wow comes from invigorating colors against stark white walls softened by warm wood tones from rift-cut oak furnishings and millwork that echo the region's early pioneer spirit.

Mission Bay Branch Library

San Francisco Public Library | California | 2006
Architect: Santos Prescott and Associates

San Francisco's first new branch in 40 years, Mission Bay Branch Library is an exemplar for how mixed-use facilities can be an integral part of the urban redevelopment efforts that are revitalizing America's cities. The branch shares the building with affordable senior housing, retail establishments, an adult day health center, and a joint community space. More affordable to operate and readily accessible to residents, this library holds its own in the larger building but capitalizes on the synergies from such features as the shared 30kw photovoltaic solar system on the roof. Custom window displays for books draw in passers-by, as does dynamic public art enabled by the city's two percent for art program.

Plainsboro Public Library

New Jersey | 2010
Architect: BKSK Architects

Plainsboro Public Library benefited from the New Urbanism thinking of community leaders who used the library to anchor its new "Town Green" and add new functions such as classrooms, a health education center, an arts resource center, and the first children's science lab to be located in a U.S. public library. A number of interior design choices—hand-woven seating by a Thai artisan, fabrics by a Dutch industrial designer, and a text-based graphics element created from the first lines of an international group of famous novels, submitted by library patrons—reflect the ethnically diverse community.

Richmond/Senator Milton Marks Branch Library

San Francisco Public Library | California | 2009
Architect: San Francisco Department of Public Works Bureau of Architecture

A major renovation and expansion to San Francisco's Richmond/Senator Milton Marks Branch Library protects the historic integrity of this Carnegie library originally built in 1914, while bringing it decidedly up-to-date. Contemporary glass enclosures add a cool 4,000 square feet of usable space. Other fresh features are induction lamps that have a 100,000-hour life span, operable windows, raised flooring, jargon-free signage, the conveniences of a modern library such as a teen area and study rooms, and seismic protection—all of which celebrate the classic design.

Westhampton Free Library

Westhampton Beach, New York | 2010
Architect: Ward Associates, PC

Westhampton Free Library built a decidedly green building on the pedestrian-friendly site of the former library—proving with its 71 photovoltaic panels that harvest 16 kilowatts of solar power that an ecobuilding can look as historic as its setting. This LEED Gold library blends in with its quaint coastal location yet offers RFID, flexible interior spaces, raised access floors, an outdoor reading garden, large windows to enhance daylighting, and more, along with its huge energy savings and carbon reduction. Plus, since opening, it has implemented a green cleaning program and only buys Green Seal consumables.

White Tank Branch Library and Nature Center

Maricopa County Library District
Waddell, Arizona | 2010
Architect: DWL Architects and Planners, Inc.

Certified LEED Platinum, the White Tank Branch of Maricopa County Library District is located smack dab in a regional park, a beautiful locale, though at two miles from the nearest neighbor, it requires vehicular, or horseback, transport to get there. The vast interior, with one central service point, connects to the desert, with continuous views of the desert landscape through walls of windows that block the hottest light of the sun. The building generates 30 percent of its power from solar energy and houses the park's Nature Center, further multiplying its value to visitors.

Louise Schaper (lschaper@me.com), retired Executive Director of Fayetteville Public Library, AR, is a Library Consultant and Distinguished Visiting Librarian, New Orleans Public Library

DATE LIBRARY JOURNAL, JULY 2012

Standing Tall on Campus

These academic libraries will serve as design icons for the future

By Louise Schaper

After a successful launch of the inaugural New Landmark Libraries (NLL) in 2011 (*LJ* and *Library by Design* 5/15/11) focusing on public libraries, *LJ* is proud to present its second list of iconic NLL buildings. This time the spotlight is on academic libraries. Our five NLLs, plus two honorable mentions, will inspire and inform any building project. Don't hesitate to borrow the ideas and trends highlighted here for your library of the future, or use them to help change perceptions about what your library can do for your campus. Public and school librarians will also find inspiration and insight as the options are highly adaptable.

To find this year's winners, we solicited submissions for U.S. academic library projects completed between 2007 and 2011, including new construction, expansions, and major renovations. Using a set of six criteria, our panel of judges—a mix of library, architecture, and design professionals—winnowed the list down to the distinguished group.

Each of these libraries is profiled in greater depth in the pages that follow, but there's no doubt that this year's winners are all advancing the concept of an academic library. In each, the early planning focused on the needs of the student. Project leaders worked to identify the tools, resources, support, and experiences that aid learning and incorporated them, even when doing so meant breaking the mold.

Each project faced major constraints, like small sites, beloved or challenging existing buildings, or dual service communities, but each successfully overcame those limitations through stakeholder input, meticulous design, new partnerships, and a willingness to step beyond the norms of the past. By reinterpreting the concept of a library, these campuses strengthened their academic image and brought a new level of learning support, interaction, and study and research experience to their students and faculty. This is why they are the New Landmarks.

Trends like information commons, collaboration, flexibility, and sustainability have been informing the design of academic libraries over the past decade. The New Landmarks carefully hatch these concepts, yet go beyond to deliver the unexpected in functionality, innovation, and beauty. *LJ* has identified ten trends in these seven NLL projects.

Library as forum Goucher College Athenaeum exemplifies this trend. What makes this rendition of the commons so compelling and transformative, beyond its modernist visual delights, is the wrapping of this 24-7 library and other student support services around a central core of an amphitheater-like space whose use can rapidly shift depending on need. At Goucher, going to the library will never be the same.

Partner like never before There's no question that academic libraries are moving rapidly into the brave new world of partnerships. Witness the Maricopa County Community College District that partnered with Phoenix Public Library to create a joint library that sits at the edge of the South Mountain Community College campus. This isn't two libraries in one building; this is one library serving two different audiences.

Connect the campus Take Ohio State's William Oxley Thompson Memorial Library, which is sited on the campus's historic "oval." Its position between the original campus and expansion areas made it a connector building, but over time renovations removed access and the library blocked the way to different sections of the campus. By removing some of those earlier renovations and creating a clear path through the building, the library became a "public street" to all areas of campus. The result? Ohio State has a wildly successful new destination library.

Light the box The days of dark and dingy staff offices and stacks are gone. Architects have been mastering the art of daylighting, which, judging by our NLLs, is possible given even the most difficult constraints. Striving to be pedestrian-friendly, the University of California (UC)–Berkeley School of Law Library appears, at ground level, as a transparent pavilion. That's because most of the addition is below ground. By using an innovative system of natural and artificial light, like skylights, glass walls, and glass walkways, those underground floors are filled with daylight.

Be pedestrian conscious The new landmarks strive to welcome pedestrians. They acknowledge that passersby want to feel comfortable. Plus, because students and faculty like to walk, sit, and socialize outside, these libraries came up with enticing spaces that draw people inside. What better way to be welcoming than to have a friendly scaled building with inviting outdoor spaces? The addition to the UC–Berkeley Law Library steps down to street level with its transparent pavilion, gradually stepping down the mass of its addition across sloping terrain, creating a natural amphitheater. Goucher College designed its new Athenaeum to enable pedestrian access by rerouting traffic from the campus core.

The Criteria

Overall design and construction excellence.

Response to community context and constraints.

Sustainability.

Functionality.

Innovation.

Beauty and delight.

Support the whole student Start by asking how your library can support the whole student, and you might get responses that make your library a landmark. First, talk to students, faculty, campus professionals, and community members. That's what most of our NLLs did. Seattle University's Lemieux Library deployed large, representative committees, as well as focus groups, to solicit the thoughts and aspirations of students and other stakeholders. That input resulted in a central "iDesk," various help desks in major traffic paths, roaming librarians easily summoned on their iPhones, and many other features.

Repurpose collection space With many collections shrinking and the need for other types of spaces growing, some libraries are turning the square footage previously used for collections into seating. Ohio State is the prime example. It's $79 million library renovation included new construction, but square footage remained about the same. So, by shifting 40 percent of its collections and some staff functions off-site, Ohio State gained 1,800 new seats, related learning support services, and flexible study and collaboration spaces needed by students.

Flex for uncertainty Like our public NLLs, flexibility for an unknown future still rules the roost when it comes to design priorities. Goucher's Athenaeum installed the rails for compact shelving, but the shelves won't be set up until needed. Quick reconfiguration of the Athenaeum's varied spaces means just-in-time classrooms and the wheeled furnishings mean on-the-spot collaborations. Ohio State's entry-level floor space can be easily reconfigured to allow for informal gatherings, speakers, and performance spots.

2012 Winners

1 Goucher Athenaeum
Goucher College, Baltimore

2 Berkeley Law Library University of California

3 William Oxley Thompson Memorial Library Ohio State University, Columbus

4 South Mountain Community Library Phoenix

5 Lemieux Library and McGoldrick Learning Commons Seattle University

Honorable Mentions

Science and Engineering Library
Columbia University, New York

University of Arizona Poetry Center Tucson

Integrate IT While there are plenty of librarians to be found in our NLLs, some house IT staff and, like Goucher's Athenaeum, can provide in-depth technical support. The administration of Ohio State's William Oxley Thompson Memorial Library shares its offices with the campus chief information officer. The CIO operates the "Buckeye Bar" for laptop support and assists thousands of students with technical problems.

Gain by going Gold Three of the five NLLs, plus one honorable mention, are certified or pending Leadership in Energy & Environmental Design (LEED) Gold status. But all the NLLs and honorable mentions are decidedly green. The NLLs deploy the latest building system efficiencies, minimize their building footprint's impact on the surroundings, and improve the health of the internal environment through improved ventilation, advanced filtration, and the use of low-emitting materials and finishes.

---

1 Goucher Athenaeum | Goucher College
Baltimore | Architect: RMJM/Hillier

Crafted for a New Worldview

Our number one NLL facility, Goucher Athenaeum, crosses service boundaries, mixes library metaphors, and harmonizes a campus already known for its modernist aesthetic. Wholly new to this 1940s campus, the Athenaeum exemplifies the library as the intellectual, cultural, and social crossroads of campus. Library as "crossroads" or "forum" is a transformative notion unequivocally realized through this building's design, functionality, and siting.

Not only is the Athenaeum Leadership in Energy & Environmental Design (LEED) Gold certified, its design leadership is also reflected in the stakeholder input process, integration with the site, prominence of the book collection, and the inclusion of campus functions previously outside the library's scope.

A great glass ship Smack dab in the center of the library is the "Forum," a theater-like wide-open space for speakers, transmission of world events, performers, and lectures. Wrapped around this central organizing element is the library, replete with the familiar and the new. In fact, Nancy Magnuson, college librarian, describes the building's purpose as a student forum "anchored by a state-of-the-art library." Her description is representative of a project that stands as an exemplar to help others expand their thinking about strategic campus partnerships and the library's contributions to creating and sustaining the campus experience.

"A very fine project that will be even more successful as other buildings are erected near to it such that its exterior spaces are better defined," one of the judges commented.

A dramatic building, the Athenaeum is like a "great glass ship floating on a rolling sea of meadow greenery," according to Magnuson. It anchors the library to the campus and offers a "wow" view of the contents inside. The stacks, bounded by colorful ends, appear like brightly hued cornrows in a distant field—a signature view that will surely be symbolic of this project.

The design process started with input gathered via a plethora of channels like surveys, focus groups, and the obligatory task forces. A task force composed of all campus areas reviewed all input and made final recommendations to the president and architect. With a short list of principles underlying their efforts, the group pointed to the library being the key element of the project and all other components working to "complement or expand the reach of the library."

Durable material choices of glass, stone, wood, and copper on the exterior along with terrazzo, white oak, redwood, carpet, and glass on the interior respect the college's long view on educating future generations, a decidedly modern and sustainable concept. Recyclable carpet, durable furniture choices like solid oak carrels and tables, cleanable finishes, and fabrics like synthetic leather on soft seating are examples of that long-term thinking.

Its aggressive sustainability in design includes solar-heated water and an HVAC system that uses radiant heat, energy-recovery wheels, and displacement ventilation to maximize system efficiency. Occupancy sensors not only control lighting but also reduce heating and cooling when a space is unoccupied. A rain garden, along with two roof gardens, reduces storm water runoff.

Holistic thinking It's the incorporation of nonlinear thinking about the student that makes the Athenaeum a standout. The student is seen holistically with service delivery 24-7 that is geared to providing a place for study, collaboration, teaching, performing, reading, sleeping, exercising, and dining. Flexible spaces that can serve a range of needs from meeting place to parties to town hall are everywhere.

Rethinking how the library operates is what makes the building so successful. Many processes, once deemed effective and efficient, were replaced with new ways, like interfiling reference materials and bound periodicals into the main collection. Because those materials are weeded frequently, major collection moves are avoided.

Another punch for the Athenaeum is its connection to the broader community. It offers a curriculum resource center that serves not only students but also public and private educational institutions. For example, local school librarians, teachers, and administrators are invited to lectures. A community service center provides a tutoring program for children on Saturday mornings, mentoring services, and additional programming space to engage the community beyond the campus. Finally, the college's first art gallery, located next to a performance space, showcases the college's collection, as well as students' and known artists' works.

The list of nontraditional services offered is staggering. An information commons, jointly operated by the IT department, provides service from a dedicated IT help desk and separate, but nearby, librarian service desk. There are special rooms for research librarians to consult with students.

For the 24-hour student, an espresso station would not do. Instead, Alice's Restaurant, centrally located next to the Forum, serves sandwiches, salads, and other light fare. A radio station, called the Sound of the Gopher, can be seen by passersby and is wired into the Athenaeum's AV system, allowing for programs to be heard throughout the facility.

Exercise equipment is sprinkled throughout, and some spaces have no predetermined purpose whatsoever.

Plenty of classrooms, including one for the digital arts, join many small and large group study rooms and a "readers' loft" to provide formal and informal learning experiences.

Vitals

OPENED 2011

New construction

Main library

SIZE 103,000 square feet

COST $40 million

LEED-NC Gold certification

STUDENT POP 1,827

What's most compelling is that the Athenaeum responds to deeply held Goucher College values, yet openly departs from the 20th-century view of what a library should be. More than at any time in its history, it respects the needs of students and creates a far richer experience. With the 47 percent increase in use of the library since it's opening, the Athenaeum is a vibrant centerfold for student life and campus sustainability.

 Berkeley Law Library | **University of California, Berkeley**

Architect: Ratcliff Architects

An Airy Light Box for Legal Minds

The 55,000 square foot addition to the UC-Berkeley Law Library appears like an open and transparent one-story pavilion from the street, but it has a huge impact on the law library as well as the law school. That's because 44,000 square feet of library and connections to other parts of the law school are below ground. The 11,000 square feet above ground provide the perfect segue to the pedestrian scale of the streetscape.

Wedged between two courtyards, the pavilion-like structure is home to a café, student lounge, and lecture hall. Above it is a rooftop garden complete with dining areas, teaching and study spaces, and special-event capabilities. Indoor-outdoor social and academic activities are found elsewhere in the building, like the student lounge, whose movable glass walls open to a courtyard.

A clear set of project objectives—flexibility, shared spaces, appealing street presence, improved circulation, beauty, and materials that match the stature of the school—led to the stunning results.

A site challenge Conquering constraints may be why this project is so successful. It was no easy task to fit the addition into a former courtyard surrounded by the law school. The creative solution—to put two floors under ground—led to extraordinary results. It resolved the pedestrian traffic jams in the former overly packed library stacks by moving the collection into automated compact shelving in the new addition's two underground levels.

Surprisingly, these underground floors are filled with daylight. An expanse of glass connects the addition to the original structure and, in the process, allows daylight into the lower levels. Glass paving in the courtyards and skylights in the planter beds serve as daylighting conduits to a very pleasant and open experience on the lower levels. That's ingenious.

A wonderland Dark-stained cork flooring is a dramatic stage on which light and the neutral tones of the elegant materials and finishes perform. Along with the cork flooring, variegated cedar clads the ceilings above the reference desk to buffer sound and create the quiet needed for legal study. A monumental staircase of glass and granite is another conduit for light into the lower levels as well as a suggestive link between indoor and outdoor spaces. The backdrop of Indiana white limestone walls as well as figured eucalyptus walls makes this library a wonderland of beauty.

The building is on track for LEED Gold certification, and its sustainable strategies include an important symbolic gesture—restoration and reuse of the 100-year-old mahogany study carrels from the original building.

The addition becomes more open, airy, and public as it rises from floor to floor. At the lowest level is the least natural light, the most stacks, and some reader seats. The next level up has skylights, and it is used for staff offices, the service desk, reading rooms, conference space, and a student center. The third level up is dedicated to the café, lecture hall, lounge, and classrooms. Finally, the fourth level contains the main reading room, dean's conference room, classrooms, and a bridge. Visitors crossing over the bridge find a comfortable rooftop garden designed for outdoor learning and relaxation.

This addition, thoughtfully detailed to take advantage of the vista, including views of the Golden Gate Bridge, ties elegantly to the existing buildings and courtyard spaces. Who wouldn't want to walk by this building and, perhaps, stop and rest on its steps or in its café? A simple open and transparent box, it makes the most of the space to meet programmatic needs while creating a meditative experience for students and faculty.

"This is a wonderful diminutive project that ties to some real hulks of buildings in a delicate and beautiful way. It makes the existing buildings much richer, better," one of the judges wrote.

If buildings could talk, the ones surrounding this gem would sing its praises.

Vitals

OPENED 2011

Major expansion

Special library

SIZE 55,000 square feet

COST $50 million

PENDING LEED-NC Gold certification

STUDENT POP 1,050

---

3 William Oxley Thompson Memorial Library | Ohio State University

Columbus | Architect: Acock Associates Architects

For the Buckeyes, Less Is More

Ohio State's decision not to increase the size of it's 306,000 square foot library, originally built in 1913 and expanded in the 1950s and 1970s, might seem counterintuitive for this behemoth campus. But planners and stakeholders agreed that the best way to be student centered was aggressively to improve and refocus their library's space.

That strategy, coupled with restoring a historic east-west connection through the building to reignite the library's central position in the campus's historic "oval," resulted in a library with more usable space, tripling use to 12,000 daily visitors and rekindling a love of the library by faculty, students, and administrators that had long faded.

The exhaustive planning, careful consideration of the library as a symbolic and transformative place, and attention to every detail that could make or break a great student experience resulted in a watershed project for this campus. Not only is the result a new landmark for the profession, the process is ripe for gleaning and redeploying by other institutions. Gund Partnership was the associate architect.

Involving stakeholders A highly structured input process, involving layers of stakeholders, zeroed in on what parts of the existing library meant the most, what didn't work, and what would be meaningful. From there, a series of painstaking decisions of what to keep, restore, change, and remove took place. Five years of planning included a web-based suggestion box, systematic electronic surveys, and many meetings with alumni groups, staff, librarians, and faculty.

One of those difficult decisions involved the closed stacks developed in the 1950s. The stacks themselves were negatively perceived, but the tower in which they were housed was much loved. Retaining the campus landmark won out after considerable debate, but below the roofline its skin was removed and replaced with glass, creating a glass stack tower of books. The tower's top floor, once a mechanical room, became a reading and event space with stunning views of the campus and the community beyond.

Vitals

OPENED 2009

Renovation and new construction

Main library

SIZE 306,000 square feet

COST $78.7 million

LEED-NC No

STUDENT POP 56,000

Externally, the change was equally dramatic. Green space and a pedestrian connection to a lake replaced a parking lot. Pathways with reused flagstones, the preservation of trees, and the addition of 106 bike racks improved pedestrian access. An east-west thoroughfare through the building reintroduced a library-centric campus and eased pedestrian flow.

"It's a spectacular makeover of a facility overdue for refurbishment, creating a legible plan with open flexible space while celebrating the legacy stack tower and its collections as a central core element," a judge commented.

From dark to light From claustrophobic and dark, the library took on a light and airy presence. Historic and almost forgotten spaces that had been chopped and covered up were restored, including a 30'-tall ceiling in the 1913 "grand reference hall" that became symbolic of the entire effort. The demolition of the 1950 and 1977 additions and construction of a new west façade better balanced the scale of the original Beaux Arts building, delighting both students and visitors.

While the library wasn't a study hot spot before renovation, it certainly became one after. Even with reader seats increased by more than 100 percent, the 1,800 new seats are often not enough to satisfy demand at peak hours.

The space for increased seating wasn't free. It was captured from other functions. Forty percent of the collection is now housed off-site, with 1.25 million volumes remaining, largely in the tower. This includes 250,000 special collections volumes readily accessible via a central service point on the first floor. Additionally, some library operations were relocated to other facilities.

Strategic partnerships with dedicated space abound. Campus IT leadership and its laptop support service are located in the library. Dining services provides the café, and the Columbus Metropolitan Library System operates a leisure reading collection available to students.

Designed prior to Ohio State's Leadership in Energy & Environmental Design (LEED) certification requirement, the project, nevertheless, has a strong grounding in sustainability principles and energy-efficiency strategies. Decisions not to increase space but reuse the original and 1951 buildings, add green space, recycle existing furnishings, source locally, and deploy high-performance building systems,

materials, and finishes confirm that this project demonstrates an ecoethic.

How did a project of this size get funded? The Athletics Department rose to the problematic challenge with a $9 million kickoff gift. With that and a truckload of credibility stemming from extensive stakeholder input that led to a compelling vision of a library for the future, another $30 million was raised privately. The state and the university provided the remaining funding.

From a large but dark and claustrophobic facility, the planning leadership unearthed the essence of the building's 1913 roots and, with a well-orchestrated set of moves like celebrating the legacy stack tower, planted a thoroughly modern and spectacular library for the future.

---

4. South Mountain Community Library
Maricopa County Community College District and Phoenix Public Library

Architect: richärd+bauer architecture

Dual Purpose Defies Expectations

Phoenix is on a roll with its dual-purpose libraries. Last year, its Palo Verde Library | Maryvale Community Center was named a New Landmark Library. This year, the partnership between Maricopa County Community College District and Phoenix Public Library yields another winner. Street-side, the South Mountain Community Library wears a public library face, but its back side is all about the campus. Inside, the functions are seamlessly blended and appropriately distributed with a public focus on the entry level and an academic one on the upper level.

The building's strong rectilinear form, clad in copper planks broken by glass rooftop monitors, elevates the library's presence as a center of knowledge. These farm field–shaped forms along with abstracted patterns of cotton, sorghum, asters, and citrus on the interiors reference the site's agricultural heritage.

A treat to inhabit Leaders of both institutions—college and public library—were determined to give students and community members a special place to call their library. It's a "jewel [that] ties beautifully to the context from inside out...[and] seems to resonate with the environment it serves," commented one of the judges.

Whether visitors are camped out for a daylong research project or attending a story hour, this building, with its intense relationship with the outdoors, is a treat to inhabit. A no-nonsense layout makes way-finding a breeze so that new visitors feel right at home. That's largely because an initial goal for the project was to promote, not discourage, interaction and connection between students and community members.

Functionality, siting, and copper siding aside, this library is just plain gorgeous inside. Not your typical academic library, it features brightly colored furnishings, like purple Keilhauer upholstered seating and red Herman Miller Eames molded plywood chairs that sit like massed tulips in a garden. Acrylic panels lit by LED fixtures corral "the edge," an area of public computers on the upper level. A mural "printed" on a DaisyCake chain features young adults in various poses and serves to give the teen area privacy.

Light from the ordinary Materials and finishes engender a sense of lightness and fun. Playful, inventive, and, sometimes, surprising, the

Vitals

OPENED 2011

New construction

Main campus library and a branch community library

SIZE 51,600 square feet

COST $16.3 million

LEED-NC No

STUDENT POP 6,354

COMMUNITY 62,000

designs turned straightforward materials, like copper, wood, glass, steel, aluminum, and acrylic, into anything but ordinary. Digitally printed skylight liners, laser-cut guardrails, and water jet–cut aluminum panels provide endless interest.

Areas that might have been simple exposed drywall are clad in Forest Stewardship Council red cedar planks backed by an acoustical material specially designed by the architect to be quickly installed.

The windows with their integrated circuit pattern complement the copper planks. They are thin, vertical black frames broken by random horizontal rails—referencing the agricultural fields once occupying the site.

Comanagement of the facility happens from adjacent offices on the upper level. That positioning sets the tone for the rest of the services. The joint service desk at the entry is bidirectional: one half faces the campus entrance and the other half faces the public entrance.

A reason to revel The main level feels more like a public library with its meeting rooms, multipurpose room, children's area, cybercafé, Friends display, new item displays, writers center, express computers, teen area and lounge, and stacks. The upper level has a decidedly more academic feel, with group study rooms, nonfiction collections, special collections, presentation practice room, studio, quiet study spaces, classrooms, and staff areas. Power and data are easily accessed in the raised flooring, making future changes easy to accomplish.

A neutral palette of greys, browns, and whites forms a calming backdrop for head-turning material uses, iconic furnishings, and color pops that create an enlivening experience for the visitor. Warmth is delivered through the narrow cedar strips on some walls and ceilings, like the conference room, along with splashes of color like a red wall and red chairs in a group study room anchored by a neutral table topped by a securely fastened Flos Spun Light.

On the sustainability side, natural light enters through triple-layered insulated clerestories and light shafts, so even the entry-level floor benefits. That daylight harvesting plus occupancy sensors and a computer-controlled lighting system provide energy savings and a comfortable environment. Furnishings, like the Herman Miller Eames and Caper chairs, and finishes were selected for their low emission of volatile organic compounds.

On the exterior, the landscape is treated as cherished space. A sculp-ture-like mass of stone encased in wire, called a Gabion wall, contrasts with the weathering copper siding. Post lamps by Architectural Area Lighting are kindly directed downward to do their job without light pollution, and beds of low-water-use cacti, still in their infancy, stand at attention next along the entry route.

White Kartel Bubble sofas and kid-sized red Vitra Panton chairs carry the interior color palette outdoors and create a stylish children's courtyard that respects, without pandering to, adult expectations for youth spaces.

Inside and out, this dual-purpose academic library, with its civic status and academic approach, gives anyone—student or member of the public—a reason to revel in the innovative but graceful spaces that celebrate the desert environment and its agricultural heritage.

---

5 Lemieux Library and McGoldrick Learning Commons

Seattle University | Architect: Pfeiffer Partners Architects, Inc.

Library and Learning Transformed

When Seattle University leadership took on its largest single capital project—expanding the campus library to encompass a learning commons and create a campus hub—it created a landmark knowledge resource for the future that engages and inspires students today.

The goal was to create a Leadership in Energy & Environmental Design (LEED) Gold environment that provided a collaborative, stimulating experience for users. Inside, students would find quiet and active spaces; an array of artwork (including works by Henry Matisse); computer labs; book, journal, media, and special collections; the university's first media production center; smart classrooms; and academic support services like the writing center, research consultation, math lab, and tutoring and study assistance. Outside, students would be drawn to equally compelling spaces for socializing, studying, and exploring.

One judge had this to say: "This project is replete with superb spaces. While the details are well conceived, they are not overwrought. The conflation of architecture, landscape, and art makes for a beautifully sinuous project." Mithun was associate architect for the project.

A complicated task Still, it wasn't easy to accomplish. A complicated ten-year project grew the original 1966 library by 33,000 square feet without losing what stakeholders loved the most—the original veined white marble façade and double helix staircase that integrated a plethora of services into one facility and created linkages to nearby buildings while retaining habitual pathways.

The white marble façade was retained as an interior wall and made visible by glass curtain walls on the exterior. The staircase facelift is an ode to midcentury design. Dropped was the ideal notion of a single entrance/exit in favor of five entrances with door controls and monitoring for maximum convenience. Gained was a "learning commons partnership" to coordinate services in the multifunctional facility. The result is a stunningly transparent and airy library and learning commons at the crossroads of the campus.

Green expectations Students and all stakeholders were united in their expectation that the building be built and operated green. Going for LEED Gold certification was an easy choice and meant the reuse of the existing building and some furnishings; operation of energy-efficient systems and

Vitals

OPENED 2010

Major expansion

Main library

SIZE 125,640 square feet

COST $55 million

LEED-NC Gold

STUDENT POP 7,755

lighting; strategic harvesting of daylight; glass curtainwalls with special frit and UV coatings; low-emitting materials and furnishings; and the capture of 100 percent of the building's storm water runoff for use in water features and the landscape.

The site's slope dictated a step-down approach to a three-story addition. That strategy resulted in an addition that is appropriately scaled for pedestrian movement through the campus core. But now people stop to rest, read, or socialize in the new plaza, terraced amphitheater, meditation lawn, rain garden, and bioswale. Like a town square, these exterior spaces are a campus destination.

Creating gathering and contemplative spaces both indoors and out came as no surprise. From the get-go, planners stepped beyond standard programmatic needs and sought new opportunities. Many conversations with stakeholders shaped the direction, including two summer retreats by campus leadership. Soliciting input was taken seriously at all levels. The whole campus was invited to test seating options; students were queried via focus groups on size, layout, and furnishings; and the deans were invited to explore their need for a technology-rich classroom, which became the now-sought-after Boeing Room.

Educating the whole person Flexibility is a key organizing principle of this project. Staff work areas are outfitted with reconfigurable desk systems. All furnishings were selected to be durable, mobile, cleanable, and easily maintained. Raised floors throughout the addition contain data, electricals, and HVAC vents enabling future reconfigurations. Around-the-clock services are provided in an expandable zone that extends across most of two floors of the addition. Containment is handled by drop-down security gates and security via ID card access.

Internally, placement of services through the six-floor building is maximized for easy access. The Boeing Room is on the lowest level to accommodate events that occur outside of regular hours. The second floor contains the aforementioned partnership services and private cubicles for client meetings; an "iDesk" staffed during regular building hours; a café; and several classrooms with laptop and charging stations. Traditional book and journal stacks are on the upper floors, with special collections on the top floor. Help desks are located in major traffic areas, computer labs that support individual and group work are on two floors, and roaming reference librarians are available via iPhone. Over 950 seats and 200 computers are available for visitors.

By deciding to ponder deeply and question what a library is, Seattle University artfully crafted a library experience that matches its 21st-century focus on educating the "whole person…for a just and humane world."

Two More To Explore

These New Landmark Library Honorable Mentions span east and west, respond to special interests, and offer plenty of trends to tap for any library design brainstorm

Science and Engineering Library

Columbia University | New York
Architect: Rafael Moneo Vallés Arquitecto

Columbia University's new Science and Engineering Library (SEL) is the latest take on how libraries support science research and learning. Housed in a new state-of-the-art high-rise interdisciplinary laboratory building built over an existing ground-level gymnasium, this project required no additional footprint to accomplish its space goals.

One of the many reasons why this LEED Gold–certified project is unique and noteworthy is the building's location, which serves as a portal to the university's expansion into West Harlem, as well as access to a popular café. But it's the SEL itself—Pritzker Prize–winning architect José Rafael Moneo's bridge-like steel structure—that is the

magnet for students. The space, occupying two double-height floors and a half-floor mezzanine complete with great views of the campus and city, has become so popular that some campus blog posts by science and engineering undergrads request that only science and engineering students use this library. Davis Brody Bond Aedas was the associate architect.

Carefully conceived to foster innovation when it comes to advanced technologies, the Digital Science Center, contained within the SEL, is Columbia University Libraries' fulfillment of its vision to redefine library space for the 21st century. It offers over 50 high-end workstations, an array of advanced peripherals like 3-D mice, over six-dozen specialized applications for scientific analysis, plus live in-person and virtual research support and consulting for emerging technologies.

The SEL boasts over 345 seats, plenty of collaborative spaces like booths and study rooms, presentation practice spaces, and traditional print materials.

The end result is that the SEL, by creating energizing, smart, and collaborative spaces, has lured researchers out of their offices and into the library, created "library envy" in the nonscience population, and is a case study in the shift of libraries as suppliers of print to providers and facilitators of tools and expertise designed to accomplish research and learning.

University of Arizona Poetry Center

University of Arizona | Tucson
Architect: Line and Space, LLC

The University of Arizona Poetry Center has a long past. Dating back to the 1960s and its humble beginnings in a small cottage, it made history in 2007 when the university opened it as the first building on an academic campus devoted solely to advancing and promoting poetry and literature. Over 18,000 square feet houses a 70,000-plus item noncirculating collection plus myriad spaces and places for experiencing poetry.

Sited on the edge of a campus that sits proudly in the Sonoran Desert, the Poetry Center is designed to be water-wise, energy thrifty, and solar shading. A poet-in-residence apartment can be naturally ventilated and offers living, writing, and research space within steps of the center's collection of contemporary poetry.

Like many "centers of," this one has diverse stakeholders including university students and faculty, researchers, poets, community members, and poetry lovers everywhere. Many helped in planning the building through a series of programming workshops during which a dissonance of active and quiet space needs emerged. The architect carefully crafted a solution that made everyone happy by creating a building that "progressed toward solitude."

A munificent but delightfully spare building, the Poetry Center offers a distinguished reading series open to the public, academic support, community workshops, in-residence experiences for visiting writers, and special exhibits and cultural events. Comprehensive collection management, developed by Poetry Center staff and librarians along with the architect, was designed to control carefully the growth of the center's distinguished collection with annual review of items reaching the midpoint in their life expectancy.

The Poetry Center's architecture, with its modernist self shining through the angled glass wall and metal-sheathed roof lines at the entrance, is a major departure from the campus norm yet unflinchingly harmonizes with poetry's innate equilibrium of opposites. Never has there been so much needed attention brought to bear on verse.

Louise Schaper is a Library Consultant; Distinguished Visiting Librarian, New Orleans Public Library; and LJ's New Landmark Libraries project lead

Photo Credits

CHAPTER 1

Introduction
p. 11 Clockwise from top: photo courtesy of DCPL; photo by Smitty Miller; photo courtesy of Mesa County Libraries; photo by Kevin Henegan

In the Interims
p. 12 photo courtesy of DCPL. p 13 photos courtesy of DCPL. p. 14-15 top left box photo ©Mark Herboth Photography; top right box photo by Kevin Henegan; other box photos by Rebecca Miller; bottom photo courtesey of DCPL

Meet the Bookless Mobile
p. 16 top photo by Smitty Miller; center left photo by Chris Tuininga; center right photo by Smitty Miller

Repurposing Retail
p. 17 photo courtesy of Mesa County Libraries; p. 18 photo by Grouop 4 Architecture Research + Planning, Inc.; p. 19 top photo courtesy of Cedar Rapids Public Library

Inflato Dumpsters
p. 19 photo ©John Locke

Looking Through the Labrary Lens
p. 20 photo courtesy of Madison Public Library

Storefront Solution
p. 21 photo by Kevin Henegan; p. 22 portrait photo ©Sam Davol 2010; p. 22-23 photos by Rebecca Miller and Kevin Henegan

The Off-Site Librarian
p. 24 photos courtesy of Sam Wallin, Fort Vancouver Regional Library District

CHAPTER 2

Introduction
p. 27 clockwise from top: photo by Mark Boisclair; photo by Eric Hanson, Hanson Photographic; photo by Kevin Henegan

Powerful Partnerships
p. 28 photo by Mark Boisclair; p. 29 top left photo by Michael Shopenn/courtesy of Barker Rinker Seacat Architecture; top right rendering courtesy of The Library Design Collaborative, AJV-Tipton Associate, Cockfield Jackson, and Dewberry Architects; bottom rendering by Leddy Maytum Stacy Architects; p. 30-31 clockwise from left: photo by Coester Architectural Photography; photo by Gina Perille; photo by Eric Hanson, Hanson Photographic; photo by Geoffrey Baker; p. 32 clockwise from top left: photo by Sharon Risedorph; photo by William Wright; photo by Daniel Kabara; p. 33 rendering by RRMM Architects, Carrier Johnson, and Anderson Brulé Architects

Novel Library, Novel Design
p. 34 photos by Kathy Hellman

Capitol Designs
p. 35 photos by Kevin Henegan; p. 36 clockwise from top left: renderings courtesy of Philip G. Freelon, Perkins + Will; photo ©2011 Gordon Beall; photo by Kevin Henegan

Serving Two Masters
p. 37 photos ©Jeff Goldberg/Esto; p. 38 top photo ©Jeff Goldberg/Esto; bottom photo ©Anderson Brulé architects p. 39 photo ©Jeff Goldberg/Esto

CHAPTER 3

Introduction
p. 41 clockwise from top left: photo ©Robert Benson Photography; photo ©Lara Swimmer; photo ©Timothy Hursley; photo by J. Stewart Roberts

Growing Room
p. 42-43 inset postcard courtesy of St. Louis Public Library; all other photos ©Timothy Hursley; p. 44-45 all photos ©Timothy Hursley

History Updated
p. 46 photos by Teresa L. Jacobsen

A Cutting-Edge Undertaking
p. 47 photo ©Robert Benson Photography

Lighting Quality, Not Quantity
p. 48 photo ©Lara Swimmer; p. 49 photos ©Lara Swimmer; p. 50 photos ©Lara Swimmer

Is Your Library Accessible?
p. 51 postcard courtesey of North Brookfield Historical Society; photo by J. Stewart Roberts; p. 52 photo by J. Stewart Roberts; floor plan and drawing by Philip O'Brien

CHAPTER 4

Introduction
p. 55 clockwise from top left: photo courtesy of the B. Thomas Golisano Library, Roberts Wesleyan College, Rochester, NY; photo by Robert Mintzes, Peter Gisolfi Associates; photo by Dean J. Birinyi Photography

Light Done Right
p. 56 photo by William Taylor Photographics; p. 57 photo ©Lara Swimmer; p. 59 photo by Assassi Productions

San José's Green Art
p. 61 photos by Dean J. Birinyi Photography

State of the Art in Darien
p. 62 photo by Robert Mintzes, Peter Gisolfi Associates; p. 63 photos by Robert Mintzes, Peter Gisolfi Associates; p. 64 photo by Robert Mintzes, Peter Gisolfi Associates; p. 65 left photo by Alan Gray, right photo by Robert Mintzes, Peter Gisolfi Associates; p. 66 photos by by Robert Mintzes, Peter Gisolfi Associates

A Whole Systems Approach
p. 67 photo by Keelan Kaiser

Embracing Austin, Inside and Out
p. 70 photos ©MOKA studio 2013, courtesy of Lake|Flato + Shepley Bulfinch Joint Venture

A Zen-Inspired Approach
p. 72 photos by Rebecca Miller

Nova Scotia Sustainability Center
p. 73 photo by Heather Holm

Living Up to LEED Silver
p. 74 photos courtesy of the B. Thomas Golisano Library, Roberts Wesleyan College, Rochester, NY

CHAPTER 5

Introduction
p. 77 clockwise from top left: photo courtesy of Niños Conarte; photo by Rebecca Miller; photo by Charles Davis Smith

With Kids in Mind
p. 78 top photo by Charles Davis Smith; middle and bottom photo ©Lara Swimmer; p. 79 top left photo by Hedrich Blessing Photo; top right photo by Brandon Stengel; bottom left and right photos ©Lara Swimmer

Inspired To Climb Higher
p. 80 top left and right photos by Marcus Farr; bottom photo courtesy of Humphries Poli Architects

The Theatrical Library
p. 81 photo courtesy of Janice Davis Design LLC

Look, a Nook!
p. 82 top photo by Linda Spillman Bruns; middle photo courtesy of Madison Children's Museum; bottom photo courtesey of Janice Davis Design LLC; p. 83 top row left photo courtesy of Iowa City Public Library; top row right photo courtesy of Janice Davis Design LLC; middle left and right photos courtesy of The Classroom Creative; bottom photo ©Lara Swimmer; p. 84 top and middle row photos by Cecilia Kugler; bottom photo by Robert Walsh p. 85 top and middle row photos by Carlos Carbonero; bottom left photo by the Burgeon Group; bottom middle and right photo courtesy of Janice Davis Design LLC; p. 86 photos by Chuck Choi

Mural Magic
p. 87 top photo by Sam O'Keefe/Missouri S & T; middle and bottom photos by Walt Fulps

Over 13 Not Admitted
p. 88 top photo by Andreas Burmester; bottom photo by Ricardo Ortiz

Climbing the Shelves
p. 90 photo by Niños Conarte

CHAPTER 6

Introduction
p. 93 clockwise from top: photo ©Lara Swimmer; photo by Kevin Henegan; photo courtesy of Demco Interiors

Expert Makeovers
p. 94 photos courtesy of Kathy Schalk-Greene; p. 95 "before" photos courtesy of Kathy Schalk-Greene; all other Caldwell photos by Kevin Henegan; bottom left and right photos courtesy of Kathy Schalk-Greene; p. 96 "before" photos courtesy of Kathy Schalk-Greene; all other photos by Kevin Henegan

Library Inside Out
p. 97 photos ©Mark Herboth Photography

Let "Green" Creep
p. 98 photos courtesy of Fayetteville Public Library; p. 99 photos courtesy of Fayetteville Public Library; p. 100 photos courtesy of Fayetteville Public Library; p. 101 photos courtesy of Fayetteville Public Library;

Keep Excitement High, Costs Low
p. 102 images courtesy of HMA2 Architects; p. 103 images courtesy of HMA2 Architects

Same Budget, New Branches
p. 104 photo by Group 4 Architecture, Research + Planning, Inc; rendering ©SFS Architecture; p. 105 left photo by Group 4 Architecture, Research + Planning, Inc; rendering ©SFS Architecture; right photo courtesy of the City of Olathe, KS; p. 106 map courtesy of the City of Olathe, KS; rendering by by Group 4 Architecture, Research + Planning, Inc

Kickstart a School Library
p. 107 photos courtesy of Studio H

10 Steps to a Better Library Interior
p. 108 top photo by Brandon Stengel; middle and bottom left photos by MSR; rendering by MSR; p. 109 top left photo ©Lara Swimmer; top right photo by MSR; middle left photo by MSR; middle right photo by Assassi Productions; bottom photo ©Lara Swimmer; p. 110 top left photo by Assassi Productions; top right photo by David Patterson; middle and bottom photos ©Lara Swimmer

One Step at a Time, Turning to the Future
p. 111 photos courtesy of Demco Library Interiors

CHAPTER 7

Introduction
p. 113 clockwise from top: photo by Ricardo Ortiz; photo courtesy of NCSU Libraries; photo by Drake Busch

...And the Kitchen Sink
p. 114 renderings courtesy of Engberg Anderson; p. 115 top left and right photos courtesy of Rosa F. Keller Library & Community Center; bottom photo by Timothy Hursley; p. 116 top photo courtesy of Round Valley Public Library; bottom photo by Ricardo Ortiz; p. 117 photo ©Lake|Flato + Shepley Bulfinch Joint Venture

Tomorrow Visualized
p. 118 photo by Marc Hall/NCSU; p. 119 top left photo courtesy of NC State University; top right photo by Chuck Samuels/NCSU Libraries; middle photo by Marc Hall/NCSU; bottom left photo courtesy of NC State University; bottom right photo by Marc Hall/NCSU; p. 120 top left and right photos by Chuck Samuels/NCSU Libraries; bottom left photo by Brent Brafford/NCSU Libraries; bottom right photo by Chuck Samuels/NCSU Libraries; p. 121 left photo by Chuck Samuels/NCSU Libraries; top right photo by Marc Hall/NCSU; bottom photo by Chuck Samuels/NCSU Libraries

Bright Lights, Gig City
p. 123 photo courtesey of Chattanooga Public Library

Customized User Design
p. 124 photo by Paul Brokering; p. 125 top left and right photos by The Public Works; middle photo by Drake Busch; bottom photo by Brian Sendler p. 126 photos by Paul Brokering; p. 127 rendering by Studiotrope Design Collective

CHAPTER 8

Introduction
p. 129 clockwise from top right: photo by Roger Mastroianni; photo by Wayne Johnson; photo by Ema Peter, courtesy of Bing Thom Architects

Designing 21st-Century Libraries
p. 130 photo by Robert Mintzes, Peter Gisolfi Associates; p. 131 photo by Robert Mintzes, Peter Gisolfi Associates; rendering by John Evans, Peter Gisolfi Associates

Giving the People What They Want
p. 132 photos Roger Mastroianni

How Social Media Built a Library
p. 133 photo by Ema Peter, courtesy of Bing Thom Architects

Slaying a Sacred Cow with a Deck of Cards
p. 134 images courtesy of GouldEvans; p. 135 photos by Kevin Henegan

Transforming Tech
p. 136 photos courtesy of Cleveland Public Library

The Comeback Kids
p. 138 top photo by Larry O. Gay/Birmingham Public Library; bottom photo by Melinda Shelton/Birmingham Public Library; p. 139 top photo by Wayne Johnson; bottom photo by Perry and Jan Walton/Marion Airport; p. 140 top photo courtesy of Queens Library; rendering courtesy of Queens Library; bottom photo by Emily Andrews

CHAPTER 9

Introduction
p. 143 clockwise from top left: photo by Eric Staudenmaier; photo © Brad Feinknoff; photo by Michael Shopenn, courtesy of Barker Rinker Seacat Architecture

The New Icons
p. 144 clockwise from top left: photo ©2011 Steve Whittaker/www.whittpho.com; photo by Timmerman Photography, courtesy of Wendell Burnette Architects; photo by Bill Timmerman; photo by Brian Robbins, Robbins Photography, Inc.; photo by Michael Shopenn/courtesy of Barker Rinker Seacat Architecture; photo by Paul Brokering; photo ©Lara Swimmer; photo by Bill Timmerman; photo by Bill Timmerman; photo ©2011 Patrick Bennett; p. 146 ©2011 Steve Whittaker/www.whittpho.com; p. 147 photo by Timmerman Photography, courtesy of Wendell Burnette Architects; p. 148 photo by Bill Timmerman; p. 149 top photo by Brian Robbins, Robbins Photography, Inc.; bottom photo by Michael Shopenn/courtesy of Barker Rinker Seacat Architecture; p. 150 photo by William Wright Photography; p. 151 photo by Bill Timmerman; p. 152 photo by Bill Timmerman; p. 153 top photo ©Lara Swimmer; bottom photo by Paul Brokering; p. 154 left photo by Nairn Olker, Ally Photography; right photo by Seth Gathright Photography; p. 155 top photo courtesy of San Francisco Public Library; middle photo by Sharon Risedorph; bottom left photo by Jeffrey Totaro; bottom right photo by Bill Timmerman; p. 157 photo by Jeff Tryon; p. 158 photo ©2011 Steve Whittaker/www.whittpho.com; p. 159 photo ©Brad Feinknoff; p. 160 photo by Bill Timmerman; p. 161 photo by Eric Staudenmaier; p. 162 left photo by Michael DeVito; right photo by Robert Reck Photography

Institutional Index

Architect & Designer Index

DISCARDED